Newsgames

Newsgames

Journalism at Play

Ian Bogost, Simon Ferrari, and Bobby Schweizer

The MIT Press
Cambridge, Massachusetts
London, England

For information about special quantity discounts, please email special_sales@ mitpress.mit.edu

This book was set in Stone Sans and Stone Serif by Toppan Best-set Premedia Limited. Printed and bound in the United States of America.

Library of Congress Cataloging-in-Publication Data

Bogost, Ian.
Newsgames : journalism at play / Ian Bogost, Simon Ferrari, and Bobby Schweizer.
    p. cm.
Includes bibliographical references and index.
ISBN 978-0-262-01487-8 (hardcover : alk. paper)
1. Video games. 2. Online journalism. 3. Interactive multimedia. I. Ferrari, Simon.
II. Schweizer, Bobby. III. Title.
GV1469.3.B64   2010
794.8—dc22
                                                                    2010011990

10 9 8 7 6 5 4 3 2 1

Contents

Acknowledgments

Research for this book was made possible by a generous grant from the John S. and James L. Knight Foundation. We'd like to extend special thanks to the journalism program staff at the foundation, and particularly to Alberto Ibargüen, Eric Newton, Jessica Goldfin, Gary Kebbel, and Jenne Hebert.

Additional gratitude goes to graduate students in the Georgia Tech Digital Media program who participated in this research: Mariam Asad, Ayoka Chenzira, Nick Diakopoulos, Tom Gibes, Sergio Goldenberg, Cinqué Hicks, Tanyoung Kim, Adam Rice, Digdem Sezen, Tonguç Sezen, Ray Vichot, and Douglas Wilson. We are indebted to their many thoughtful suggestions, many of which shed light on subjects that would have otherwise escaped notice.

Of these researchers, Goldenberg, Vichot, and Wilson require special credit for contributions that have been incorporated into this book. Where needed, these have been indicated in the notes.

1 Newsgames

Piracy off the coast of the east African nation of Somalia has run rampant since the start of a civil war in the early 1990s, but attacks have become more frequent and more daring in recent years. By the spring of 2008, pirates were venturing well away from the Somali coast in order to reach the higher-value vessels that enter and exit the Gulf of Aden, gateway to the Red Sea and eventually the Suez Canal and the Mediterranean.

With numerous international governments concerned about the safety and viability of their shipping routes, the United Nations Security Council established Resolution 1838 in October 2008, calling on member nations to "deploy naval vessels and military aircraft" in support of maritime security in the region.[1] Regular conflict spurred an increase in worldwide coverage of Somali pirating. Most news outlets filed stories under international politics, as reporters cut the hull of a nation in anarchy through the waves of global commerce, defense, and other bastions of centralized authority.[2] Others offered human interest stories about the "fear and terror" that accompanied lengthy hostage situations on overtaken vessels.[3]

But *Wired* magazine's writers sailed a different tack in their July 2009 feature on Somali pirates, choosing to focus on economics over politics or personality.[4] In "Cutthroat Capitalism: An Economic Analysis of the Somali Pirate Business Model," Scott Carney observes that Somali pirating expeditions had become not only more frequent, but also more profitable. Payouts from ransom and plunder surged to levels one hundred times greater in 2009 than they were just four years earlier.[5] It stands to reason, argues Carney, that this escalation had arisen not from the depths of new wickedness and anarchy, but from the changing economic dynamics of piracy itself.

Unlike its more mainstream counterparts in the *New York Times* or the *Guardian*, *Wired*'s coverage looks more like a spreadsheet than an investigative report. It features eight full-color pages of text, infographics, and diagrams, all meticulously illustrated and annotated by Siggi Eggertsson and Michael Doret. The graphics are playful, their rounded-edged pixel art abstracting boats, people, and maps into actors in an economic system (figure 1.1). The coverage itself takes a procedural rather than a narrative approach: it is divided into sections that describe the different steps of an attack, each section offering a textual description, an infographic, and a ledger or algorithm describing the economic dynamics of the topic.

The article's infographics run the gamut from mundane to remarkable, from bar graphs and pie charts to fever charts and a full-page map. The piece also deploys unusually complex typography to highlight different economic forces. Taken together, the spreads illustrate how a piratical Chief Financial Officer might witness a highjack-and-ransom attack from the vantage point of a ledger rather than a skiff. Each step calculates and summarizes its value proposition, and in so doing the feature explains the risk-reward system of ransom piracy by showing how the Somali pirates act according to a highly logical, if disruptive, self-interest.

Much about "Cutthroat Capitalism" reminds the reader of a videogame. Its visual design riffs off the blocky art of early coin-op and home console games, a method commonly used on screen and in print to apply video-game aesthetics to serious topics. But something else makes this decidedly static print feature resemble a game more than a column. Good games depict system dynamics rather than narrating specific accounts. Instead of telling a *story* about a particular pirate crew or hijacked freighter, the article characterizes the economic *system* of Somali piracy in general.

Of course, "Cutthroat Capitalism" isn't a game. It's a set of descriptions, formulas, and tabular data that *describes* the behavior of a system rather than *simulating* the system directly. A reader of *Wired* could get out a pencil and paper to determine a strategy for a hypothetical pirate raid, but it would be much easier to let a computer do the work.

Wired realized as much, so they paired "Cutthroat Capitalism," the article, with a Web-based game of the same name, one that operates under the same mathematical logic the article describes. The game puts the reader at the helm: "You are a pirate commander staked with $50,000 from local tribal leaders and other investors. Your job is to guide your pirate crew through raids in and around the Gulf of Aden, attack and capture a ship, and successfully negotiate a ransom."[6] The result effectively simulates capture and negotiation, synthesizing the principles of the print spread into an experience rather than a description.

The player begins on a map of coastal Somalia. The ship—represented by a skull token—starts in the city of Eyl, a pirate haven north of the capital

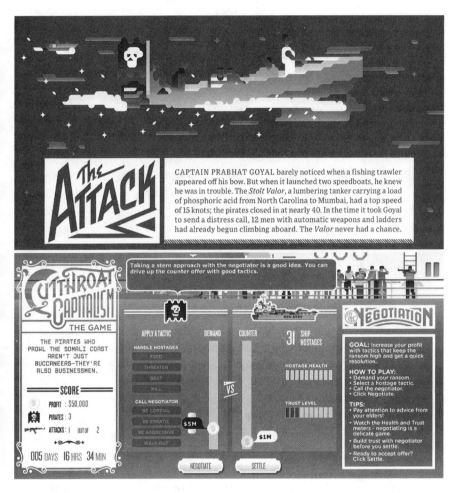

Figure 1.1

The similarities between "Cutthroat Capitalism" the magazine spread and *Cutthroat Capitalism* the game go beyond their visual design. Each describes the economic system of piracy off the coast of Somalia: one with words, the other through play.

of Mogadishu. When the player clicks on a part of the map, the pirate ship moves. Once in the Gulf of Aden, players click on passing ships—depicted as colored dots representing different classes—moving the pirate vessel toward a target. If the player's skull token intersects with one of these dots—be it container ship, cargo ship, cruise ship, tugboat, or one of five other classes—the game presents a chance to capture the ship and proceed with ransom negotiations. If the player fails to intercept, the crew is forced to sail back up the coast to try again.

The negotiation process consists of turns in which the player can choose a behavior to exhibit toward the hostages aboard the ship (feed, threaten, beat, or kill), a stance to take with the negotiating party (be cordial, erratic, aggressive, or walk out), and a ransom demand of up to $30 million. The game rules remind the player that the highest ransom ever paid was only $3 million.[7] A complex calculus of these choices determines the health of the hostages, the mood of the negotiators, and the likelihood of a counteroffer.

Hijacking a ship turns out to be a process just as methodical as buying a car. Negotiation proves effective only when the player quickly divines the value of the ship and its hostages, and then works carefully and methodically toward that monetary goal. If the player successfully negotiates a ransom, the reward (covered by the vessel's insurer) is split between the local government, the tribal leaders and investors who staked the journey, and the crew. But if the pirate crew abandons ship or the player's forces are overrun, the negotiation ends in failure.

A smart player will rarely fail—and that is the strongest rhetorical point presented in the negotiation process. If a ship can be captured, its hostages and cargo are always worth *something*. Failure arises mostly from poor planning or greed. The game helps players recognize this fact, encouraging them to optimize for many small bounties of one or two million dollars instead of fewer, larger ones—a realization that also frames the increasing number of attacks as matters of economics rather than wickedness. A $5 million settlement from a particularly lucky negotiation provides a smug sense of satisfaction, but it's rarely worth the risk of getting caught or losing bounties in order to spend the time needed to negotiate a ransom of that size.

Admittedly, the game does not simulate all of the elements of Somali pirating discussed in the article. The risk of capture after a ransom has been paid doesn't make it into the game, nor do the costs of maintaining a crew or mounting an unsuccessful attack (a real mission costs $30,000 per crew member, but normally only a quarter of missions are successful).[8] Some of the subtleties that make the system rich (and make the article fascinating) are lost in the game—a situation probably attributable to the designers' desire to make the game manageable, learnable, and playable in short sessions. Nevertheless, the article provides only a disconnected, mathematical account of piracy, while the game offers a synthetic experience of the practice, one that unifies the disconnected algorithms of the print piece into a holistic account.

Cutthroat Capitalism (the game) explains how a pirate crew's modest, persistent efforts will produce significant results within the economic and social system of sea commerce that it disrupts. The print article addresses the issue from the perspective of the shipping industry. Somali piracy is just a modest cost of doing business for global freight. The time and money saved by going through the Suez Canal rather than around the Cape of Good Hope, combined with the relatively low cost of insurance compared to that of private security, makes good business sense for shippers. The game makes the case from the other side—that of the pirates. But it does something more, too: the game forces players to understand piracy by *experiencing* it in abstraction. The player quickly learns that the pirate's best strategy is to attempt a series of small ransoms, making the total cost to each ship low. Only 0.2 percent of vessels passing through the Gulf of Aden are successfully boarded by pirates, a fact that feels much more startling for the player of *Cutthroat Capitalism* than it does for the reader of its companion article.[9]

Newsgames

Cutthroat Capitalism shows that videogames can do good journalism, both as an independent medium for news and as a supplement to traditional forms of coverage. But what methods exist for creating and using such game in journalism? Are there different genres, forms, or styles? What are the editorial and publishing considerations for a news organization interested in pursuing such games? And why would such organizations want to take up such a practice in the first place?

Given the financial state of journalism today, everyone knows that a change is coming. Newspaper advertising revenue was down nearly 30 percent in 2009.[10] Some papers, especially smaller ones, have had to cut staff or shut down completely. Community bloggers and big city newspaper publishers may not agree on the best format for news, but they do agree that digital media will play an important role in its future. Yet, most of the discourse about the way news and computers go together has focused on translations of existing approaches to journalism for the Web.

For that matter, despite the differences in popularity and accessibility afforded by Web publication, much journalism practice remains the same online. Online news sites large and small still publish written stories similar to those inked onto newsprint. They upload video segments like those broadcast for television. They stream monologues and interviews like those sent over the radio airwaves. The tools that make the creation and dissemination of news possible have become more simple and widespread, but the process remains almost identical: stories still have to be written and edited, films shot and cut, audio recorded and uplinked.

But as *Cutthroat Capitalism* suggests, there is something different about videogames. Unlike stories written for newsprint or programs edited for television, videogames are computer software rather than a digitized form of earlier media. Games display text, images, sounds, and video, but they also do much more: *games simulate how things work* by constructing models that people can interact with, a capacity Bogost has given the name *procedural rhetoric*.[11] This is a type of experience irreducible to any other, earlier medium.

For this reason it is necessary to understand the uses of games in the news, both new and old, on different terms. This book offers an introduction to *newsgames*, a term that names a broad body of work produced at the intersection of videogames and journalism. In the chapters that follow, we explore the ways games have been used in the news from past to present, covering the different applications, methods, and styles of newsgames. We also make projections and suggestions for how newsgames might be applied to journalistic practice now and in the future. Each chapter takes up one key genre of newsgames. Some will feel like adaptations of traditional news content, while others take the first steps into unfamiliar terrain.

In 2003, Uruguayan game studio Powerful Robot released a game called *September 12th*, about the war on terror.[12] Its lead designer Gonzalo Frasca envisioned short, quickly produced, and widely distributed newsgames about *current events*, the subject of chapter 2. *Editorial* games like *September 12th* offer the videogame equivalent of columns and editorial cartoons, conveying an opinion with the goal of persuading players to agree with embedded bias—or at least to consider an issue in a different light. Other forms have emerged as well, from *tabloid games* that offer a cruder form of opinion to *reportage* games that strive to reproduce the unvarnished goals and style of daily news coverage. This chapter also covers the many issues that arise when creating current event games, including timeliness, accessibility, and editorial line. Creators of these games typically strive to release such a game while the story it covers is still relevant, a challenge that increases with the depth of the simulation and the complexity of the event.

Chapter 3 explores *infographic newsgames*. Visual matter has long done journalistic work by visually representing data and thus synthesizing information. At the start of the twentieth century, larger newspapers began integrating visual representations of data into papers to help the reader draw connections between complex networks of information and events. The resulting "information graphics" come in many formats, from the traditional forms of pie chart, line graph, data map, and diagram to more experimental forms produced for digital consumption. The adaptation of infographics into computational forms has broadened their scope in addition to changing their methods of authorship. As digital infographics mature and become more interactive, they are becoming more like games. Players can explore information to find surprising new revelations, engage with processes that depict how information arises or interacts, reconfigure information to replay possible scenarios, or experiment with information for the simple enjoyment of play itself. Some infographics might take the form of proper games, while others are merely gamelike, adopting some of the conventions and sensations of games.

Current event games cover isolated stories in a short and accessible way, but longer, more detailed treatments of the news are also possible. In chapter 4 we present *documentary newsgames*, titles that engage broader historical and current events in a manner similar to documentary photography, cinema, and investigative reporting. Usually larger in scale and scope, these games offer experiences of newsworthy events, something impossible to capture in print or broadcast news. In the case of past events, they recreate times, spaces, and systems that one can otherwise only understand from archival film footage or imagination. We discuss different types of documentary games, including those that recreate the setting and progression of particular events and those that attempt to create procedural (rule-based) accounts of the logics of social and political situations.

Serious news coverage notwithstanding, it's worth remembering that games have been a part of the news for almost a century, since the first "word-cross" puzzles appeared in the *New York Sunday World* in 1913.[13] By the 1920s, the crossword was a sensation, becoming so popular that it even incited a moral panic. When the *New York Times* finally revised the form and made it more "literate" at the end of World War II, the public was sold. Since then, many newspaper readers look forward to the puzzles as a joyous and intellectually engaging part of the day. Puzzles have not always carried news content, but experiments such as editorial crosswords and news quizzes have tried to do so. The past, present, and future uses of such *puzzle newsgames* are covered in chapter 5, from digital adaptations of traditional news puzzles and quizzes to the popular online casual games that represent both a threat to and an opportunity for news publishers.

Journalism comprises a set of values and skills that must be learned somehow—it is a literacy, a set of rules for reading, writing, and critiquing a particular domain of knowledge.[14] The first steps of journalism practice are traditionally taken in classrooms or at school newspapers, but certain qualities of videogames make them ideal supplementary media for a journalistic education. In chapter 6, we discuss *literacy newsgames*, those that offer direct or indirect education in how to become a good journalist, or for understanding why journalism is important to citizens and their communities.

Speaking of communities, at first blush videogames might seem to oppose cooperative action. When we think of games, from tabletop games like *Dungeons and Dragons* to board games like chess and *Risk* to videogames like *Super Mario Bros.* and *The Sims*, we normally think of them as private affairs. We play games indoors, at tables or televisions or computers. Even if we play with others, it is only in small groups. And while recent innovations in massively multiplayer online games (MMOGs) can support many hundreds or thousands of simultaneous players at a time, those players are usually widely distributed geographically. In chapter 7, we explore new genres of *community newsgames* that create and nurture local populations—often by situating games wholly or partly in the real world rather than in front of the screen.

As the technology with which news is created and disseminated changes, the very form of journalism alters itself. While the genres of newsgame just mentioned represent immediate opportunities for news organizations, many more might be developed in the future, either in response to technological shifts or as entirely new inventions. In chapter 8, we explore *newsgame platforms*, systems for the creation of new forms of game-based journalism that might supplement or replace current coverage in the future. In its most basic form, a platform is something that makes it easier to build other things.[15] The newspaper itself is a platform that supports research, writing, printing, distribution, and feedback from the public. The format of the evening news is a platform that describes how to order stories in a useful or compelling way, how to integrate advertising, and how to consistently produce a televised show. Starting from familiar yet alternative platforms for news like fantasy sports, we speculate on the novel newsgaming platforms (and new applications of existing computational platforms) that might support journalism in the future. They range from the familiar to the bizarre—what if a news organization released a documentary game "yearbook" about the changes in a local community? What if Yoshi the dinosaur from *Super Mario World* needed health care, and he had to buy insurance at the going rates? What if the dynamics of New York City racketeering laws could be operationalized in *Grand Theft Auto*? These possibilities suggest how journalists might think about what they do in new ways, instead of simply translating old media for digital distribution. It is on this note that we conclude the book, with a call to action for journalists and news organizations in chapter 9.

Many of the types of newsgames this book covers are already established forms. *Cutthroat Capitalism* matches five of the seven genres of promising newsgames just mentioned: infographics, editorial, documentary, puzzles, and platforms. Though it might not be the best possible example of any of these individually, the amalgam shows how *Wired* attempted to integrate a game into actual journalistic coverage of a topic, not just to supplement a print edition with an online throwaway.[16]

The game's connection to infographics is obvious. The article makes extensive use of information displays, and the game's map draws on the tradition of abstracted information set geographically. While the link to infographics is primarily aesthetic, the fundamental purpose of both article and game satisfies noted information designer Edward Tufte's goals for information visualization: inform the reader, reveal insights into information that would otherwise be obscured, and synthesize complicated information into a legible format.[17] The infographic transforms raw data into visuals, while the game transforms that data into mechanics.

Wired's approach takes up documentarian goals as well. Stories about piracy off the coast of Somalia mostly enjoy coverage in the United States when events directly affect its citizenry and commerce. The seizure and subsequent standoff on the *Maersk Alabama* in April 2009 was notable for its violent resolution—Navy SEAL snipers shot and killed three pirates. Coverage of this incident certainly brought the issue of piracy directly to the American public's attention. But rather than pursue the issue further, the three pirate deaths and one capture provided journalistic closure: the evildoers "got what was coming to them." *Cutthroat Capitalism* directly challenges this tale, examining the structures of global trade that embed pirate attacks as a part of doing business.

The piracy game serves as both investigation and exposé. Its documentarian stance may not appear to take on the traditional firsthand infiltration of a global situation in progress, but it very much does: by uncovering the dynamics and injustices of an economic system. At a rudimentary level, it even provides a "day in the life" account by putting the player in the shoes of one of its actors. By taking the role of a single pirate embedded in a complex network, the player comes to understand the logic by which all other pirates in that same system operate.

Cutthroat Capitalism might not seem much like a puzzle, because newspaper puzzles take very specific forms. But if puzzles refer to simple, abstract logic games pursued for mental pleasure, then aspects of the game start to fit the bill. The negotiation phase is reminiscent of a game of probabilities like rock-paper-scissors. The player plays three cards, the computer plays three, and the outcome alters the dynamics of the negotiation. Something more complex is at work here, too: the system boasts a preexisting state, as if the player is playing his or her cards against a given (but hidden) hand. The player must then reason about the state of the freight owners, and how they might respond. This casual noodling bears a resemblance to the chess or bridge problems that often appear alongside the crossword or cryptoquip. Negotiation in *Cutthroat Capitalism* satisfies our desires to outwit a system by finding the optimal moves.

The relevance and interest of piracy notwithstanding, the game's journalistic significance comes from more than its content. By publishing a print story tied directly to a game, in which each is based on the same factors, *Wired* has shown how a periodical can integrate games into its workflow. This workflow can become a model that might enable the regular production of these kinds of artifacts through organizational, rather than technical advances. The print and digital versions tell the story in two different but complimentary ways, allowing the writers, artists, and designers to share more than just a topic. Given journalism's troubled present and uncertain future, proving the feasibility of producing new and different media artifacts is perhaps even more important a task than creating new media artifacts themselves.

All of the topics discussed in this book make a common assumption: that journalism can and will embrace new modes of *thinking* about news in addition to new modes of production. Rather than just tack-on a games desk or hire an occasional developer on contract, we contend that newsgames will offer valuable contributions only when they are embraced as a viable method of practicing journalism—albeit a different kind of journalism than newspapers, television, and Web pages offer. Newsgames are not a charmed salve that will cure the ills of news organizations overnight. But they do represent a real and viable opportunity to help citizens form beliefs and make decisions.

2 Current Events

From somewhere in the sky, you peer down onto a bustling town in the Middle East. Among the women and children going about their daily routine in the marketplace, you spot the caricature of a familiar figure: white keffiyeh bound tightly to his forehead, shrouded in a black robe, AK-47 in hand. You control a reticle with your mouse, the kind of crosshair seen when playing a first-person shooter. Your targeting circle is relatively large, much bigger than the buildings and people below, who move rapidly as they go about their business. Carefully isolating your target, you wait for the terrorist to walk into an uninhabited sector of the city and you click, expecting instant gratification and success. Instead, there is a delay. The terrorist begins moving away. A woman, two children, and a dog walk into the targeted area.

Finally, a missile strikes the marketplace. It does not discriminate, shattering bodies and buildings alike. Bloodied human limbs litter the streets. Smoke settles from the rubble. When civilians pass by the dead, they drop to their knees, crying. Eventually, mourning turns to anger, and a citizen morphs into a figure with black robe, keffiyeh, and automatic rifle—a new terrorist is born (figure 2.1).

The game is called *September 12th*, and the only way to win it is not to play in the first place. For every terrorist the player kills, many more rise to fill his place, indignant at the thoughtless slaughter of innocent passersby. It's an argument against "tactical" missile strikes, conveyed in game form. And its opinion is clear: terrorism cannot be attacked surgically, and violence begets more violence. The elegance, directness, and novelty of *September 12th* were exceeded only by its timeliness. Released in the autumn of 2003, six months after the start of the Iraq War, the game enjoyed considerable coverage in the mainstream news.[1] *September 12th* also enjoyed considerable attention in scholarly and exhibition contexts. Bogost offers it as an example of a procedural *rhetoric of failure*, a design that comments

Figure 2.1
Every missile strike in *September 12th* triggers the conversion of new terrorists, illustrating the cycle of retribution as innocent civilians are killed in "surgical" attacks.

upon a political situation by denying players a victory condition.[2] Miguel Sicart argues that the game has the ability to turn its player into a moral being, by stimulating ethical reasoning rather than telling the players its message outright.[3] Six years after its creation, lead designer Gonzalo Frasca received a lifetime achievement award at the Games for Change festival's Knight News Game Awards.[4]

Political games have been around since the early days of computer gaming. Titles like *Balance of Power*, a cold war diplomacy game, and *Hidden Agenda*, a postrevolutionary simulation set in Central America, enjoyed commercial success in the 1980s. Indeed, politically themed board games have been common for decades, among them 1959's *Diplomacy*, a pre–World War I strategy board game that John F. Kennedy and Henry Kissinger both called their favorite.[5]

But such games had disappeared from the public imagination by the early 1990s. *Balance of Power* and *Diplomacy* are games for adults, about adult topics, an audience the commercial videogame industry had abandoned in favor of titles for children and adolescents. Tepid, forgettable "edutainment" titles had further marred the public perception of games beyond entertainment.

It took the open publishing environment of the World Wide Web and the turbulent politics of the post–September 11 world to make such games viable again. Al Qaeda's attack on American soil and the preemptive wars in Afghanistan and Iraq that followed became the most visible public policy issue in the United States and abroad, leading to an explosion of opinions online. This was the fertile soil into which Gonzalo Frasca planted *September 12th*, and the genre he named to house it.

Frasca called them *newsgames*, a genre he described as "simulation meets political cartoons."[6] We have adopted Frasca's term, but we also expand its scope: for us, "newsgame" suggests *any* intersection of journalism and gaming. Frasca's games do engage with the news, of course, in the same way as do reporting, editorial, and cartooning. This specialization in mind, we suggest the name *current event games* to describe titles like *September 12th*. Current event games are short, bite-sized works, usually embedded in Web sites, used to convey small bits of news information or opinion. They are the newsgame equivalent of an article or column.

Types of Current Event Games

Frasca's first experiment with this challenge came before *September 12th*, although it was inspired by the same events. Frasca had been on a plane during the attacks. Just before boarding again to return home, he had heard a news report about the war in Afghanistan, in which American supply drops had crushed people and structures as they fell from the sky.[7] Outraged at this mix of violence and humanitarianism, but charmed by the black comedy of the situation, Frasca created *Kabul Kaboom*. It is a simple game that asks the player to catch falling hamburgers while avoiding bombs. The name *Kaboom* comes from the game's inspiration, an Atari 2600 title from 1982 called *Kaboom!*, in which the player moves water buckets across the bottom of the screen to catch bombs thrown by a prisoner at the top. *Kabul Kaboom* changes the water buckets to an iconic figure from Picasso's *Guernica* and adds hamburgers in addition to bombs. Picasso painted his masterwork in response to the bombing of the city of Guernica by German and Italian warplanes during the Spanish Civil War. Frasca's piece thus makes explicit historical connections—U.S. airstrikes and funding of the Northern Alliance in order to topple the Taliban are analogous to the involvement of foreign air forces in the Spanish Civil War.

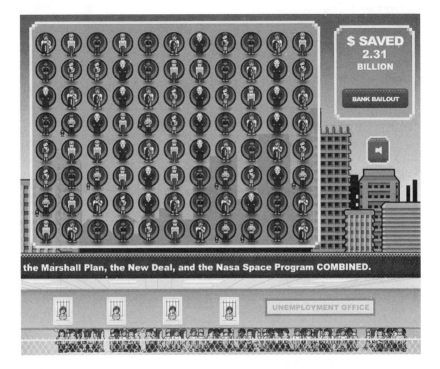

Figure 2.2
Tiltfactor's *Layoff!* illustrates how hundreds of workers with individualized stories have been reduced to simple color-coded types for easy elimination through redundancy. Note the number of "banker" tiles that have begun to dominate the grid.

Like *Kabul Kaboom*, many current event games borrow from simple arcade, home console, and casual games. *Layoff!*, created by Mary Flanagan's Tiltfactor Lab at Dartmouth College, offers another example. It comments upon the economic effects of the 2008–2009 recession on the workforce. Borrowing the mechanics of the popular match-three game *Bejeweled*, *Layoff!* editorializes about the mindset of the corporate downsizing specialist (figure 2.2). Players match "redundant" worker units (those with similar job descriptions) to clear them from the board into the unemployment line. The game generates a name and a backstory for each worker matched and fired, personalizing the experience. *Layoff!* adds another constraint atop the *Bejeweled* ruleset: the banker, who cannot be moved or matched. The combination of personalized workers and impersonal, immovable bankers forms the game's commentary: honest workers lose their jobs in order to preserve the livelihood of the same fraudulent economists who caused the downturn in the first place.

September 12th, *Kabul Kaboom*, and *Layoff!* are modest games. It takes no longer to play them than it does to read a news article or to peruse a comic. But current event games can also take more complex forms, the equivalent of features instead of columns.

Killer Flu offers such an example. The game was commissioned by the UK Clinical Virology Network (the British equivalent of the U.S. Centers for Disease Control and Prevention) to educate the public about pandemic influenza. Originally conceived to explore both seasonal and avian flu, the game was released in time for the H1N1 "swine flu" panic of 2009. *Killer Flu* offers a serious, factual treatment of flu in a surprising way: rather than managing the response of health professionals or government officials, the player controls the spread of the virus itself, by enhancing its capabilities and guiding it between populations. Critiquing the manufactured pandemic flu panic that swept the world, *Killer Flu* shows players just how difficult it is for pandemic flu to mutate and propagate. The game also explains how seasonal flu spreads, and why it affects so many more people than animal flus. With generated geography and hundreds of simulated characters, *Killer Flu* is more technically complex than *Layoff!* and *September 12th*. Yet, it can still be played in a Web browser, just like the latter two games.

Current event games have low system requirements and wide distribution at online game portals in addition to the Web sites of their sponsoring organizations. They are often created in Adobe Flash, a multimedia technology with nearly universal access that can be embedded directly in Web pages.[8] Producing a current event game does not pose technical challenges, but logistical ones. Their creators must balance timeliness with quality, deciding whether games should cover an isolated political issue or an ongoing social issue. Because they are short and compact, current event games have to work hard to ensure their players immediately understand the context and constraints of the topic and the game's approach to it. Some current event games explicitly state the facts via text or video, whereas others follow Frasca's lead and attempt to sway opinion through play alone.

We distinguish between three subtypes of current event games: *editorial games*, *tabloid games*, and *reportage games*.

Editorial games are current event games with an argument, or those that attempt to persuade their players in some way. *September 12th* and *Layoff!* offer examples, as do titles from independent developers Persuasive Games and La Molleindustria. Editorial game makers feel strongly about the issues they cover and use their games to express opinions. Some editorial games offer simple, one-note commentary (*Kabul Kaboom*) akin to an editorial cartoon, whereas others make a more complex statement, like an op-ed column (*McDonald's Videogame*, discussed below). These games can take anywhere from one day to a few months to create.

Tabloid games are playable versions of soft news—particularly celebrity, sports, or political gossip. Within hours of Zinedine Zidane's disgraceful head butt at the end of the 2006 World Cup final, an anonymous Italian football fan created *Hothead Zidane*. Players control the titular antihero, who can be moved around a part of the pitch as clones of his Italian adversary Marco Materazzi come at him waves. After a few successful head butts, a red card is thrown and the game is over. The result offers neither entertainment nor commentary (the game lacks even a score), but it does capitalize on public interest, earning traffic as a result. Within a week of its creation, online game portal AddictingGames.com revamped the game with a score system and multiple levels of hit detection, better graphical fidelity, and enhanced sound effects. They also released the source code so other designers could make their own versions.[9] Tabloid games, because they are so easy to make, are often improved and reinterpreted by other amateur game designers.[10]

Reportage games fall somewhere between editorial and tabloid games. They strive to emulate factual reporting, producing the videogame version of a written article or televised segment. Reportage games are carefully researched, with an eye toward factual description. For this reason, they are far less common than editorial and tabloid games. Unlike editorial games, they seek not to persuade players, but to educate them. And unlike documentary games (discussed in chapter 4), they are of smaller scale, and released while an issue is still current.

Although they were published in the paper's op-ed section, two games created by Persuasive Games for the *New York Times* offer good examples of reportage. The first, *Food Import Folly*, deals with insufficient numbers of FDA inspection personnel and their inadvertent role in food contamination outbreaks. The game challenges players to inspect agricultural imports at ports nationwide. Each level corresponds with a year in the decade 1997–2007, during which food imports increased from two million to nine million shipments, while FDA personnel and resources remained roughly constant.[11] By experiencing the increasing mismatch between imported goods and inspection resources, the player develops an abstract sense of the problem, independent of any opinion about its cause or solution.

Another game, *Points of Entry*, clarifies the behavior of the merit-based green card award system proposed in the 2007 McCain–Kennedy immigration bill. The bill proposed a federal standard for worker visa awards, based not on individual achievement, but on a single, standardized system for all immigrants. Some criticized the bill for rejecting family ties, others for putting business interests in the hands of the government. The bill never passed, but during debate about it, details were infrequently covered in the press beyond isolated examples.[12] The game goes further, asking players to configure hypothetical immigrants within a time limit such that they just outqualify a competing candidate (figure 2.3). By playing through many scenarios, citizens develop a more sophisticated understanding of the legislation the bill proposes, without the baggage of a particular opinion on the matter.

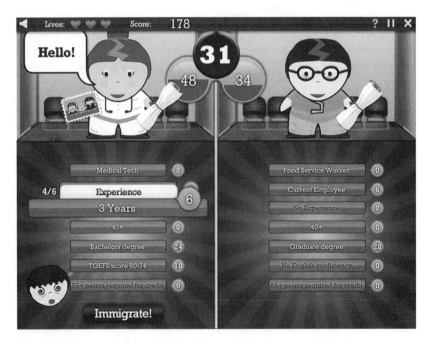

Figure 2.3
This match-up from *Points of Entry* visualizes the reductive force of the proposed immigration scoring system. Clothing and accessories change as the player alters values in order to attain a desired score, here matching a food service worker with a graduate degree against the "more desirable" medical technician with a bachelor's degree.

Easy to Pick Up and Easy to Put Down

Before citizens tuned in or logged on for the news, they picked up a paper, reading it at the breakfast table, in the recliner, or on the commuter rail. Newsstands sprung up on street corners throughout the cities of the world for a reason: news must be widely available and highly visible in order to draw the attention of busy pedestrians. All newsgames face the challenge of distribution in a noisy market, but only current event games demand *timely* distribution to ensure their relevance.

Although Frasca created his own Web site to host *September 12th*, he relied on links from news Web sites and blogs to generate traffic. Still, the game's primary purpose was to editorialize, not to generate revenue. By contrast, tabloid games often take advantage of a popular controversy to turn traffic into ad impressions. During the 2004 U.S. elections, innumerable political "whack-a-mole" clones appeared, allowing players to bonk their favorite foreign enemy or least favorite politician.[13] AddictingGames .com—owned by media conglomerate Viacom—often seeks out games like *Hothead Zidane*, paying developers small fees (around $500) for rights to publish the games with pre-roll video ads. More recently, independent creators of current event games have been able to take advantage of user-contributed game portals like Kongregate.com, where they can earn a share of revenue from advertising.

Not only are current event games easy to create and distribute, they are also easy to play. And for good reason: they need to appeal both to people who regularly play games for entertainment and to people who don't. One strategy for drawing in potential players is to borrow tried-and-true game mechanics: match puzzle pieces, avoid falling objects, run and jump, point, shoot, and click. If players already know how to play a game, they might better absorb the news it contains.

This in mind, some current event games deliberately copy commercial games. Released just before Thanksgiving 2008, *Cooking Mama: Mama Kills Animals* is an "unauthorized PETA [People for the Ethical Treatment of Animals] edition" of the popular Majesco cooking simulation series. The game urges Majesco to create a vegetarian version of *Cooking Mama*, while educating players about the consequences of their upcoming Thanksgiving feasts. Through a series of sequences that ape the Nintendo Wii platform's motion control system, players pluck and gorge a turkey while mixing spare parts into stuffing and gravy. The process is presented as disgustingly as possible: blood, feathers, and offal drip out of everything (even the chicken eggs). The game's cartoon gruesomeness is juxtaposed with real footage of the American turkey industry, including depictions of animal drugging and live slaughter.

After preparing the bird, mixing the stuffing, and rendering spare parts into gravy, the player unlocks a "bonus round" wherein Mama decides to go vegetarian by preparing a meal of Tofurkey and steamed vegetables in one-third of the time it took to cook the traditional meal. It argues both for the humanity and the relative ease of the vegetarian lifestyle. Accompanying links distribute vegetarian recipes and a pledge to "go veg." PETA, never an organization to be upstaged in public relations, rewards players who complete the experience with wallpapers, banner ads, and the ability to download the game or host it on their own Web pages.

Mama Kills Animals is both editorial game and reportage game. On the one hand, it offers openly biased commentary against meat eating, simulating processes that don't usually concern the Thanksgiving chef, such as the plucking and beheading of the bird. On the other hand, the game uses the platform of commentary to showcase extensive research in an accessible manner. It also manages to be fun in a way that many games of this genre aren't, copying the mechanics of a popular children's game exactly while making the player conscious of and complicit in a grotesque act that we all take for granted.

PETA's game is timely because it takes advantage of a cyclical event, the Thanksgiving holiday. Following this lesson, current event game publishers can plan for the creation of games in the same way they might plan for traditional stories. New York City's *Gotham Gazette*, an online newspaper published by the Citizens Union Foundation, was one of the earliest news sources to start producing editorial games. In 2004, they created a suite of games on the theme of that year's upcoming election, called *Voting Arcade*. The hook: New York City's voting booths had been around since before Atari released *Pong* in 1972. As shown in figure 2.4, these games reskin arcade classics (*Pong*, *Pac-Man*, *Donkey Kong*, and *Dig Dug*), and they mix trivia content with procedural rhetoric to great effect.

Dig Dug Kellner is a stripped-down version of the classic coin-op, featuring the iconic mining protagonist and theme music but none of its other mechanics. The player moves around, running into rocks that represent the ridiculous aspects of the voting apparatus: language limitations, a mandatory twenty-five-day preregistration period, misplaced registration applications, and untrained poll workers. The lack of authentic *Dig Dug* mechanics breaks the game in a purposeful way. It argues by extension that the voting system itself is missing key functionalities required to make the process fair and democratic.

Figure 2.4
In Gotham Gazette's remake of *Donkey Kong*, a political incumbent becomes a buffoonish ape who throws paperwork and media influence down the rafters toward the ascending challenger. Nestled in a recliner atop the tower sleeps the undecided voter.

Donkey Con (Elephant Evasion) is a *Donkey Kong* clone about tackling incumbent officeholders for the hearts and minds of lazy constituents. Each tier of Kong's tower represents a different set of obstacles for the challenger: ballot access, party politics, name recognition, the incumbent powers of media relationships, and campaign cash. Unlike the original, the challenger can't get a hammer power-up to smash through the descending perils. There is a custom death message for each tier, contextualizing abstract obstacles through concrete examples. The game also features a curious exploit: an invisible ladder, which represents running as a Reform candidate, provides a protected route from the bottom level to the top. The game seems to suggest that most of the obstacles of incumbency are surface effects of the two-party system. For somebody running on a Reform ticket, the *Gazette* argues, campaign cash is the only major concern.

These simple arcade games forsake complex narratives in favor of familiar and evocative experiences. In so doing, they encourage reflection rather than enjoyment. Following playwright Bertolt Brecht's practice of breaking down theater's fourth wall, Gonzalo Frasca argues that players must be able to maintain a critical distance from the subject matter of a political game.[14] In commercial games, immersion threatens this distance, often through complex, carefully crafted narrative structures.[15] One of the ways games can immerse players is through a well-crafted narrative structure; therefore, Frasca suggests focusing on simulation instead of storytelling. Simulation lends itself to multiple playthroughs, a wide variety of end states, and a flexibility of values. This is why Frasca made *September 12th* an abstract simulation of the origins of terrorism, not a narrative on the same subject. Avoiding narrative also contributes to the casual nature of current event games, making them "easy to pick up and easy to put down." Simulation often distinguishes editorial or reportage games from tabloid games; the former two tend to offer an experience of a model (the economics of Somali pirating), whereas the latter often recreate an event through a short narrative (a head butt at a World Cup match).

Timeliness

In the videogame industry, conversations about business ethics and quality of life are common.[16] In particular, game studios often demand extremely long hours at the end of a videogame's development cycle to complete a title in time for a predetermined ship date. Industry insiders call it "crunch time." These standards seem especially cruel when compared to the labor conditions of other industrial arts, film and television, whose practitioners enjoy union protection and overtime pay. Yet long before game corporations concocted crunch time, reporters burned the midnight oil to bring breaking news to the public. In a way, this shared understanding of the lived condition of largely thankless over-work is a unique way in which journalists and game designers are linked.

The twenty-four-hour news cycle puts a strain on current event games. Although game designers are no strangers to toil, few current event games are actually released within a day or two of the event they cover—a key period, after which many stories reach saturation.[17] Even veteran designers and programmers would be hard pressed to craft a game worth playing overnight. Gonzalo Frasca was able to create *Kabul Kaboom* in only a few hours, not bad for a videogame cartoon. But more complex procedural arguments require more time. Even though it may seem fairly simple, *September 12th* took three months to perfect.[18] Perhaps the most successful rapidly produced current event game is *Madrid*, which Frasca and his studio Powerful Robot Games created in the forty-eight hours following the terrorist bombing of a subway train in Spain's capital on March 11, 2004. Instead of depicting the event or mounting an argument, *Madrid* solemnly asks its player to remember the tragedy that transpired.

The game presents one screen to the player: a candlelight vigil. Its attendants wear T-shirts commemorating major cities that have suffered a prominent bombing: Madrid, Baghdad, Oklahoma City, and Buenos Aires, among others. A steady wind is *Madrid*'s only sound effect, cueing the player to the slowly dimming candlelight. The player must click the candles to keep them lit, and doing so methodically for an extended period results in "victory." It is actually quite difficult to keep the candles lit and reach the win state, and for many players the game offers a poignant lesson that remembrance requires non-trivial effort.

Madrid provides no information about the bombing itself; players have to come equipped from previous news coverage to comprehend it. The same could be said of *Hothead Zidane*, which also offers no context or explanation. Should a current event game be held to the same standards of timeliness as the news? Perhaps, although commentary takes time to develop. A current event game need not be timely in the way a breaking story is timely. Frasca envisioned current event games as adaptations of editorial cartoons rather than features, but other options suggest themselves.[19] Mike Treanor and Michael Mateas have suggested that current event games need not release when a story breaks, but only while the issues they cover are still pertinent, a sentiment that dovetails with a journalist's duty to "make the significant interesting and relevant."[20] Treanor and Mateas expand on Frasca's proposal for playable editorial cartoons by differentiating between *social comment cartoons* and *political cartoons*.

Social comment cartoons, they explain, focus on a broad and easily identifiable social issue, such as global warming, and encourage the viewer to acknowledge the issue with a smile.[21] Political cartoons, by contrast, take a specific news event and use it to comment on a larger issue. A videogame analogue of the social comment cartoon would enjoy a much more leisurely production schedule than a political cartoon game, because it could tap into an ongoing issue able to maintain public interest over time.[22]

The tabloid game *So You Think You Can Drive, Mel?* illustrates the difference clearly. Created by the Game Show Network in the aftermath of

Mel Gibson's widely publicized ethnic-slur-riddled DUI, it is perhaps the most well-designed celebrity sleaze tabloid game ever. A caricature of Mel's face hangs out of his car window as he speeds down the highway. The screen scrolls to the side, and the player can only control the car's vertical motion. The player's score rises slowly as the game wears on. Grabbing bottles of whiskey increases the score considerably, but it also raises Mel's blood alcohol level. In turn, it becomes more difficult to control player movement as the car lags behind, jumps forward, and bounces up and down.

There are two enemies in the game: Hasidic Jews and cops. The Hasidim throw Stars of David at Mel's car from the top of the screen, and if they score a hit the player loses twenty-five points. Running over a cop doesn't decrease the score, but once the player hits five of them the game is over. The rhetoric is clear: Mel has a single-minded obsession to drink, he despises "Hollywood Jews," and he sees the law as little more than an inconvenient obstacle.

It is ironic that a game about an isolated celebrity blunder might offer the best example of timeliness in political cartoon games. One can't imagine it helping players make decisions about their own lives, yet *So You Think You Can Drive, Mel?* is not only timely, but also a timeless documentation of an event now forgotten by most of the media and public. By contrast, a social comment rendition of this tabloid piece would require a broader perspective; the fallibility of celebrities could serve as a hook to draw attention to the fact that no one is immune to the dangers of drunk driving.

Timeliness in other current event games follows this model. *Madrid's* poignant commemoration of tragedy is more likely to become unplayable due to changes in technology than it is to become irrelevant, while *Kabul Kaboom* is inscrutable absent supplementary information about airdrops during the Afghan war. Social comment games often cover highly visible, ongoing public policy issues; thus, they remain relevant as long as the situation covered persists. In the case of *September 12th*, the war on terror itself has remained a pressing issue long after September 11. The game can continue to be played as long as civilian deaths from missile strikes remain a part of the contemporary milieu. Additionally, daily newspapers serve an archival purpose. More so than even popular and academic history books, archived newspapers preserve a record of daily, lived experience. Any current event game created becomes a peculiar ludic commentary on the trials and tribulations of a specific moment in time.

Editorial Line

Whether editorial or reportage, cartoon or social comment, all current event games derive their content from actual events. Just as news stories don't reinvent common forms of composition like the inverted pyramid with every publication, so newsgames don't always reinvent forms of the videogame. Today's commercial videogames may sell millions of copies, but they still reach a far narrower population than a major news broadcast or Web site. As many of the games discussed above show, current event games can focus their players on journalistic messages by borrowing from classic videogames.

Consider a plaintive example. In his book on game design, Raph Koster imagines how the experience of playing *Tetris* might be different if its iconic tetrimino blocks were transformed into the bodies of genocide victims being packed into a mass grave.[23] Some years later, Brazilian artists realized a similar idea in a political game about execution, *Calabouço Tétrico (Dungeon Tetris)*. The game can only be "won" by allowing the torture victims to climb out of their pit and assault the player's avatar, driving home a moral rhetoric: one can never undo the atrocities one commits. In game development, reskinning is generally denigrated as uncreative derivativism. But *Calabouço Tétrico* shows that serious commentary can arise from repurposing familiar games.

Less graphic examples exist, too. One widely circulated current event game of the 2008 U.S. presidential election was *Super Obama World*, a reimagining of Nintendo's *Super Mario World*. The game replaced Mario with Senator Obama, goombas with corporate crooks, and koopas with pork barrel politicking pigs. Each zone in the game covers a foible of the McCain campaign. In one, Obama trounces villains while leaping over a series of high-end clothing stores, commenting on Cindy McCain's wealth and Sarah Palin's then-scandalous use of campaign funds to buy clothes for public appearances. In another, the player runs for an annoying length of time on an empty bridge that abruptly dead-ends into a ravine, highlighting the absurdity of the "bridge to nowhere" Palin backed as Governor of Alaska.

Controlling an Obama avatar as he stomps on crooks offers a reasonably effective message, but adopting the form or mechanics of a familiar game hardly guarantees journalistic relevance. Years before creating his first current event games, Frasca remarked that "the design of consciousness-raising videogames is not as simple as replacing Nintendo's Mario and Luigi with Sacco and Vanzetti."[24] To trade gimmickry in favor of commentary, a current event game must tightly couple its content to its mechanics. A current event game takes a mechanic that is primarily *expressive* (communicating a feeling from the game to the player) and makes it *persuasive* (communicating the operation of an idea), thus creating the videogame equivalent of an editorial line.

Simulations have varied complexities. Much of their meaning rests on which facts an author decides to include and exclude. Journalists embrace objectivity by including all the reliable facts, whereas editorialists pick and choose in order to persuade their readers.

When creating a simulation game, a designer accepts the need to omit some facts or possibilities from the model. Instead of hard-coding each important aspect, the programmer crafts algorithms that create an *impression* of the represented system, along with a gulf between it and its real referent. Bogost has called this gulf between the real system and the game's model of it the "simulation gap."[25] With this representational chasm in mind, Miguel Sicart argues that the "ideology of a newsgame ... can be found in the way the original topic of the news has been translated into the game system."[26] Creating an editorial line in a current event game involves a process of including or excluding specific information from the model, of creating a simulation gap. In the case of the pro-Palestinian editorial game *Raid Gaza!*, much relevant information is excluded to make a succinct political point. The game addresses neither Palestinian terrorists' reasons for shooting missiles at settlements nor the motivations of rogue Israeli settlers. Instead, *Raid Gaza!* focuses all its effort on claims that Israel uses undue force and that the United States will never cease military and fiscal support of the country. The game carefully picks its fight and then plumbs the depths of possible, relevant consequences.

There is much work left to be done to accomplish such tasks successfully. Failure is still common. Persuasive Games' Arcade Wire series, published on AddictingGames.com and Shockwave.com, attempts to contextualize its editorial heft by beginning games with the image of a newspaper's front page, the headline presenting a comedic one-liner on the subject matter at hand (figure 2.5). These games also feature extensive tutorials that ease players into the experience. Yet despite this effort, a short glance at the comments on the Web pages containing the games shows that a significant number of players expect vanilla leisure, not thoughtful commentary.

One of the greatest examples of cinema's failure to convey an idea to its audience was the "intellectual montage" Sergei Eisenstein employed in many of his films. Eisenstein contended that the essence of cinema could

Figure 2.5

The splash screen from *The Arcade Wire: Oil God* apes the front page of the Gray Lady while encapsulating the editorial thrust of the gameplay: by manipulating nature and humankind, the player attempts to drive up oil prices as quickly as possible.

be found in the juxtapositions made possible by linear editing. One of his first proofs-of-concept was a scene in *The Strike*: he intercut the Tsar's slaughter of revolutionary workers with images of the butchering of a steer. In Eisenstein's mind, this simple cross-editing would communicate directly to his viewers the idea that the revolters had been senselessly slaughtered without any means to defend themselves.[27] Upon viewing the film, audiences were confused or infuriated. Why? Eisenstein was an intellectual, his audience the Russian peasantry. In rural communities, the slaughtering of a steer was a happy occasion resulting in a rare dinner of meat instead of grain. It is a misunderstanding akin to that of the AddictingGames.com audience expecting a casual distraction and receiving an editorial exegesis. These games must be carefully framed to avoid confusion.

Perhaps the best example of the clash between a designer's ideology and player expectations can be found in La Molleindustria's *McDonald's*

Figure 2.6
This four-panel view of La Molleindustria's *McDonald's Videogame* displays the different fast-food business domains players can manipulate. What to do first: corrupt children with advertising or destroy an Amazonian village with a tractor?

Videogame. Its designer, a young Italian subversive named Paolo Pedercini, harbors anticonglomerate and prolabor politics, advocating strikes and corporate sabotage in his life outside making games.[28] *McDonald's Videogame* hopes to demonstrate the abject corruption required to maintain the profitability of a multinational fast-food organization. In the game, players control fields in South America where cattle are raised and soy is grown, a factory farm where cows are fed and controlled for disease, a restaurant where workers have to be hired and managed, and a corporate office where advertising campaigns and board members set corporate policy (figure 2.6). The game starts out like most business simulations—set up a steady supply of meat and soy, build a workforce, run television advertising. Costs quickly outstrip revenue, and the player must take advantage of more seedy business practices. These include razing rainforests to expand crops, mixing waste as filler in the cow feed, censuring or firing unruly employees, and corrupting government officials to minimize public outcry against the above actions.

Interestingly, many players—especially those who are technically minded and enjoy mastering their videogames—find themselves lamenting the difficult job of McDonald's executives, rather than incensed by their corrupt corporate policies. Keep in mind that Molleindustria's games are well contextualized, both on their own Web site and on game portals, thanks to sophisticated introductory statements about the political opinions of the game and its creator. Still, players manage to recast their contexts; well-crafted simulation gaps always admit unexpected reactions. The incredible difficulty of *Madrid* has lead players to conclude that it addresses the *futility* of remembrance rather than its necessity.[29] And *September 12th* could be read as a call for a full-scale military invasion—bombing creates more terrorists, and they're not going away on their own, so a ground strike might be the only path to success.

Exploits—loopholes or modes of play unforeseen by the design team—pose additional trouble. Since a game requires player interaction, it is never possible to anticipate the myriad ways someone might "break" a game. Treanor and Mateas note such an exploit in Persuasive Games's *Bacteria Salad*, which addresses issues of food safety in industrial farming.[30] In it, the player must maintain the crops of five contiguous farms, defending them from agro-terrorists and disease as they attempt to provide a steady stock of two types of vegetables to consumers. But the game is easily compromised and mined for points: players can just raze a farm and quickly replace it every time a contamination event occurs. A critical player may ask whether this behavior is part of the game's commentary or an unintended effect of the system. The power of interpretation, present in the experience of all other media, is amplified by the participatory nature of computational media.

Public Debate

Here's a question anyone using videogames for purposes outside entertainment will eventually hear: is a *game* really an appropriate way to address a serious issue? In the short history of current event games, the greatest fallout from such a query blighted *Faith Fighter*, a game about religious intolerance.[31] La Molleindustria created the game in order to comment upon a string of anti-Islamic editorial cartoons in Danish newspapers.[32] In the game, Molleindustria attempts to expand prejudicial claims about the Muslim penchant for violence to include every major creed, showing that those in positions of power use religion instrumentally, usually by inciting hatred among the faithful. The game even provides explicit instructions for how it should be used, as a cathartic way to exorcise religious hatred without actually doing real-life violence against others.

A number of concerned parties spoke out against the game, including mass media outlets and the Organization of the Islamic Conference (OIC). When negative attention for the game reached critical mass, designer Paolo

Pedercini removed the game from his Web site and replaced it with a letter to visitors. In addition to linking to some of the many versions of the game others had posted online, Pedercini also accused the OIC of not having played his game before denouncing it. He found it impossible that they had played it, based on the statements made by the organization that the game could *only* be seen as inciting hatred between Muslims and Christians: "This phenomenon is related to the still marginal role of the medium," writes Pedercini. "Commentators feel authorized to judge a game without playing it and just conforming to the common narrative depicting video games as violence generators."[33]

It's a common sentiment among the creators of current event games that the vanguard of privileged media uses its position of power to prevent the public acceptance of gaming as a form of sophisticated speech. But the *Faith Fighter* controversy also underscores a major problem for games as advocacy, because it shows that the parties a game addresses are the most likely to be offended. Pedercini understood the dilemma, and he created a sequel to share his insight. The result was *Faith Fighter 2*, a parodic appropriation of Frasca's mechanic of commemoration in *Madrid*: click on numerous gods from the first game to feed them with love and prevent their memories from fading away (see figure 2.7 for a comparison of the two games). Upon inevitable failure, the player is treated to the claim that many made against Pedercini himself: "Game Over: You failed to respect a religion, and now the world is a total mess!" It may be possible to keep a game of *Faith Fighter 2* going indefinitely, as it doesn't appear to arrive at a natural conclusion. At some point the player must slow down or give up, a meditation on the possible futility of the endeavor.

According to many editorial cartoonists, a publication that apologizes for a cartoon or removes it from their archives commits journalistic treachery.[34] The purpose of a cartoon is to inspire heated discussion, and suppression does just as much of a disservice to detractors as it does to the artist. Pedercini was heavily criticized by some of his fans for "caving" to the demands of what they saw as a bullying OIC; in reply, he insisted that the removal of the game didn't constitute self-censorship, but recognition that the game had missed its mark completely. Prominent editorial cartoonists, deploring the current state of the art, admit that most of the cartoons that never make it off the drafting table probably deserve to remain there.[35] The greatest weakness of most rejected cartoons is their lack of clarity. In Pedercini's case, he set out to critique the negative treatment of Muslims in Danish political cartoons and ended up upsetting the OIC instead. He apologized not for making the game, but for the

Figure 2.7
At the top, from *Faith Fighter*, Buddha uses his "dharma wheel" secret move to slam a cartoon Jesus into the city below. In the sequel, on the bottom, gods of the multireligious pantheon stand around giving thumbs-up and peace signs, vying for love in the form of clicks.

unfortunate circumstances leading up to its removal. Both his letter and the follow-up game further poke fun at the ridiculous mass media manufactured outrage, making the apology easier to stomach.

In both tabloid games and tabloid journalism, a fine line separates earnestness from sensationalism. The "red tops" of the United Kingdom, papers that focus on celebrity, sports, and political gossip with transparent ideological bias, might exemplify the former. For the latter, one need go no further than the supermarket checkout, where gossip rags publish outright fiction, selling sensationalism by means of the nastiest rumor possible. *Hothead Zidane* offers an example of the former, but relatively few examples of the latter seem to exist.

Perhaps a close cousin to supermarket tabloid schlock in current event games is *Terri Irwin's Revenge*, a game about "Crocodile Hunter" Steve Irwin's death. The game, originally circulated by email, features Terri Irwin snorkeling through stingray-infested waters in a quest to slaughter the animals that killed her husband. Compared to *Hothead Zidane, Terri Irwin's Revenge* is much more complex—featuring opening and closing titles, two types of enemies, a "Croc bomb" attack that summons a beloved crocodile ally to clear the screen of rays, a life and health pack system, and a steadily increasing difficulty. Despite its polish, the game was so tasteless to most players that a significant outcry resulted in its total removal from the Web. Yet, even *Terri Irwin's Revenge* doesn't hold a candle to the offense of celebrity rumor papers.

Tastefulness is a long-standing problem among even the best editorial cartoonists, so it's no surprise that the challenges of refinement extend to current event games. Even bad taste is sometimes a good thing: in the case of editorial cartoons, crossing the line is often necessary in order to determine exactly where the line is.[36] Political correctness is helpful when it protects oppressed minorities from the often unconscious denigration of the privileged, but it also tends to limit the playful expression that can elucidate unseen facets of an issue. Sometimes, generating public debate about an underexplored issue is the whole point of the enterprise.

Turn to the Games Section

Bias is inherent to opinion journalism. When flipping to the editorial page of a newspaper, one knows that facts take a backseat to persuasion. One must muster the same attitude when playing editorial games. Therein lies the difference: the editorial page provides a recognized context for opinion, often by highlighting a spectrum of differing viewpoints on a single page.[37]

Editorial cartoons are refined, clarified, and expanded by accompanying columns, and vice versa. But no such setting yet exists for the editorial videogame.

Editorial games have been denied much of this organic discourse and oversight because of their relative isolation from other news. Most current event games have been relegated to curious corners of the Web, primarily sites specializing in casual games. Few efforts have combined editorial games with traditional online reporting and editorial. Even if heavy-hitters like the *New York Times* and CNN have dabbled in the form, none has offered more support than parenthetical hyperlinks to related articles for accompaniment. The series of articles and infographics on Somali pirates that accompany *Cutthroat Capitalism* may be the best integration of games into wider reporting to date.

Perhaps innovation in current event games will not take place in the United States at all, but in scrappier news markets. In 2009, the *New York Times* and the *Washington Post* published not a single game, but Brazilian newspaper *Estado* created two under the title *Jogos de Sustentabilidade* ("Sustainability Games"). These titles were produced for a series on recycling and conservation, and the editors embedded them in pages carrying informational articles, columns, and graphics on the same subject. One is a clone of the arcade game *Elevator Action*, the other a reskinning and revision of *Kaboom!*. The latter simply educates players about the types of materials that go into each color-coded recycle bin, but the former uses a quiz format to test the player's knowledge of energy conservation in an apartment building. Halfway around the world, *Madrid* was cloned into the Turkish current event game *Huys* ("Hope"), a game that invites players to remember the murder of an outspoken Turkish journalist and the importance of journalistic freedom and integrity.

Divorced from their natural habitat of the front page or the editorial page, current event games are used all too often as rudimentary Web site traffic-grabbers. Most current event games are loss leaders, a way to draw visitors to the "real news" and to generate revenue through advertising viewership. The relative novelty of current event games ensures that blogs, forums, and even mainstream news outlets will circulate information about these games, particularly if they are controversial. Current event games can thus be used instrumentally, as attention-grabbers rather than as earnest journalism.

Nadya Suleman, the single mother of octuplets who dominated human interest coverage in early 2009, suffered no dearth of editorial criticism.[38] Among the many editorial cartoons that critiqued her plight, one riffs off the widely published photograph of Suleman's enormous pregnant stomach, slapping ads and emblems on it, including donation requests via PayPal and Visa.[39] Others connect her with a contemporary event, the Obama economic stimulus plan. One suggests that a large litter might help bear the burden of the stimulus plan's debt; the other compares the irresponsibility of Suleman with that of the Democrats by applying an overstretched womb to a donkey.[40]

All of these cartoons are biting in their own way, but not one of them addresses the fate of the mother or the children. Other forms of written and spoken editorial took on this topic more than any other, puzzling over how one could care for fourteen children and what ill effects eight babies might have in the hands of a human mother designed to care for two at most.

The Octuplet's Game picks up here. The game's subtitle declares, "now you can be a milk machine!" Gameplay mimics *Space Invaders*, the player controlling the two breasts of a lactation device rather than a defensive laser. Eight babies line the top of the screen, each nestled into a color-coded test-tube to match its gender. Occasionally the babies cry, inching their way down the screen. Pressing spacebar fires milk, which placates the crying babies above. If an unfed baby makes its way to the bottom of the screen, the game ends. There's one catch: the milk machine can't operate continuously. A pump at screen right shows the machine's current power. Once it's depleted, the player must press the B and G keys in alternation to refill it.

As coverage and commentary, the game effectively communicates a few points. It highlights the inhuman act of technological medicine, which transforms mother into machine. It questions whether such a machine can ably tend to so many children in the way a mother can, mirroring the concern expressed in other media about Suleman's ability to mother such a large brood. And it depersonalizes the children themselves, absurdly extending their test-tube conception to a cyborg-childhood. Indeed, it is hard not to see the babies just as fluid-sinks rather than human beings.

Even if it might not be the most sophisticated, scathing, or insightful example of public commentary, *The Octuplet's Game* functions effectively. Yet it wasn't created as news at all. The French interactive agency L'Agence Toriche whipped it up not on behalf of a journalism client but as a demonstration of their own services in e-marketing, realizing their prowess at "getting buzz" online by performing the act with their own product.

The Octuplet's Game isn't quite yellow journalism, but it's hardly Pulitzer Prize material either. A journalist might want to present a more even-handed view of the Suleman situation. For example, tending to eight infants at once as a single mother is an idea worth experiencing rather than just pondering. Perhaps the most interesting aspect of the game has nothing to do with its journalistic quality, but with its context: a marketing agency rather than a news organization chose to produce and distribute it. The three types of current event games suggest a continuum, from tabloid sensationalism, through balanced reportage, to the biased conviction of editorial. Within this spectrum, newsmakers will have to make deliberate investments, lest the potential for earnest counsel in current event games become subsumed by crass marketing.

3 Infographics

"If you ever wanted to control where your tax dollars go, here's your chance to decide," proclaims *Budget Hero*, a game created by American Public Media. *Budget Hero* challenges players to plan for the nation's future by picking and choosing programs that reduce or raise government spending while avoiding excess debt and fulfilling player-chosen promises. Play involves reallocating funds from different budget categories, each allotment altering a twenty-year projection of the country's financial situation. Since budgets imply values, the player chooses goals in the form of "badges," among them health and wellness, national security, economic stimulus, and efficient government. The game judges the player's performance based on how well these chosen areas are developed over time.

Budget Hero's interface is a bar graph drawn to look like a cityscape (figure 3.1). It uses the skyline bar graph as a metaphor for the nation's health, stability, and size. By raising and lowering the constituent structures, the player helps to "define tomorrow's skyline." When the player clicks on a building, the game reveals a series of cards with budgetary subitems. One might choose to "Bring troops home soon" to save $210 billion, fund "diplomacy and foreign aid" at the cost of $390 billion, "increase mass transit funding" for $33 billion, or give a "tax break for first time home buyers" at the expense of $4 billion. There are 154 policy options in all.

The heights of the buildings change when the player selects a card or drags a marker across a timeline, displaying the projected budget over a twenty-year period. Players can see their progress on three meters measuring the deficit/surplus level, the relative size of the government, and the national debt. Another display shows the "Budget Bust," the year when the combined costs of health care, Social Security, and debt interest overtake revenue, breaking the bank. After selecting budget options, the player submits the budget to see what results it would produce. The game then

Figure 3.1
Budget Hero dresses up a simple bar graph of government spending in a city skyline adorned with symbolic illustrations. Success is measured not only by a balanced budget, but by how well the player lives up to chosen values, indicated by the "badges" at right.

passes judgment on the budget, evaluating the three categories just mentioned, as well as the goals chosen at the start of the game. The player can then go back and tweak settings to achieve better scores or to fulfill more completely the promises represented by the badges.

Budget Hero extends beyond the cityscape as well. American Public Media provides detailed explanations about its assumptions on the Web site that hosts the game, including an extensive FAQ that discusses how they got their numbers, why different categories were chosen or omitted, and how results were calculated.[1] They also describe the uses of data culled from playthroughs of the game, analyzing trends such as player demographics, the most frequently pursued badges, popular bipartisan badges, and the policies and decisions that most players enacted.

At its heart, *Budget Hero* is a spreadsheet with a fancy skin. It is but one of many types of *information graphics* or *infographics*—visual depictions of data used for reasoning about information.[2] *Budget Hero* offers a good example of what can make an infographic playable. With its bar graph and timeline, it incorporates a deep data set that can be manipulated on multiple axes. The graphical display itself is dynamic, changing in real time to provide visual feedback. One does not manipulate the display haphazardly, but with a goal in mind: a budget with the greatest longevity and highest compatibility with player values. It is an example of *directed activity*: a graphic that guides the user through the information so that the component parts can be synthesized for understanding. The measures of success—deficit/surplus, government size, and national debt—provide universal goals, while the badges make the effort of playing personally relevant. And it offers an example of free-form *exploration*, thanks to the large space of information around the game's primary goals of budget longevity and badge values. Replaying the game encourages the user to explore the depths of the data, examining the causes and effects of decisions or trying out different badge goals. The sheer number of possible priorities that arise from replay may make the game's most important statement about the national budget: it's complex, and riddled with conflict.

Infographics and Journalism

To understand the relationship between infographics, journalism, and play, it is useful to look at the history of the infographic's form and function. Infographics have appeared regularly in the news since the late 1930s.[3] It was *USA Today* who popularized the infographic among newsreaders with their "Snapshots," graphics appearing in a sidebar below the fold on the front page of every issue. Compiled from national surveys, the daily snapshot usually displays the results in a simple fashion that visually evokes the topic in question. For example, a snapshot printed in the November 24, 2008, *USA Today* explains changes in radio listening habits among 14- to 24-year-olds, based on a survey.[4] The results are rendered as a pie chart on the circular top of a studio broadcast microphone. Though the infographic makes for front-page eye candy, *USA Today* hardly takes full advantage of this technique as a tool for explaining issues.

Statistician and information designer Edward Tufte helps us understand why. Whether artist-drawn or computer-produced, Tufte warns, information graphics should not be used to "show the obvious to the ignorant"; instead, he urges us to see them as "instruments for reasoning about quantitative information."[5] Good infographics make sense of data through visual display, illuminating insights typically obscured in text and numbers. They transform raw data through statistics and design, making complex ideas clear and precise. Charts like the *USA Today* Snapshots *present* information, but they fail to provide *instrumentation* or to inspire *reasoning*. *Budget Hero*, by contrast, offers a detailed context for budgetary information, as well as a set of challenges that inspire players to reason about that data.

Tufte studies the use of information graphics in any domain, but *Budget Hero* suggests that journalism offers a particularly salient domain for making sense of information. As designer Alberto Cairo explains, news infographics demand sound journalistic effort as much as they require competent information design.[6] Infographics place data in context to assess cause and effect, to allow for quantitative comparisons, to present alternatives and contrary cases, and to assist in decision making.[7] They are used to inform, to reveal details in information that would otherwise be obscured, and even to persuade readers to see new relationships between actors and systems in the world. The news infographic designer thus embraces the journalistic value of synthesis, condensing complicated information into a legible format.[8]

Tufte's and Cairo's ideas are hardly new. William Playfair, an infographics pioneer of the late eighteenth century, published tracts on economics and politics in an attempt to eke out a living as an independent journalist.[9] Over the course of his career, Playfair pioneered the graphical forms that are now familiar parts of our mathematical education: line charts, bar graphs, and pie charts. The beautiful charts in Playfair's *Commercial and Political Atlas* inspired Charles Joseph Maynard, designer of the famous map of Napoleon's 1812 march into Russia.[10] Maynard transformed a plotted course of Napoleon's path into a statistical map representing the dwindling size of his army, valuing data over geography. Edward Tufte claims that this map "may well be the best statistical graphic ever drawn."[11]

Most early infographics were used in economics, mathematics, and the sciences, but it was not long before they found broader application. In the 1920s Otto Neurath, inspired by Swiss modernist design, espoused information graphics as a form of communication that could potentially rival the written word.[12] His *isotype* movement sought to create a universal language of symbols featuring abstracted shapes best compared to the human silhouettes on the doors of restrooms. The purpose of the movement was to find the most effective form of visual communication—a kind of "prose graphic."[13]

At the same time Neurath worked to popularize pictorial language, infographics began to appear in American newspapers. On the front page of its November 3, 1920 edition, the *New York Times* demonstrated the results of the presidential race by mapping them onto an image of the United States in the familiar style of today's election returns maps.[14] Rather than using an alphabetical list of states and their polling results, the map makes visual connections between geographic areas and their political alignment. According to the map, the America of the roaring twenties was split along an old geographic wound—the South voted for Cox while the rest of the nation voted for Harding. Simple maps like these were the most prevalent infographics until the influx of immigrants in the 1930s brought the European style of infographic design to the United States.

Thanks in part to Czech information designer Ladislav Sutnar's role in the 1939 New York World's Fair, continental graphic design took off in America by the outset of World War II.[15] That year, *Fortune* magazine published a page of graphical bar charts based on a business survey it had conducted, using simple outlines of people to illustrate the survey's choices.[16] While major publishers possessed both the resources and the technology to pursue infographics, the field remained untouched by smaller newspapers and publishing outlets.

As the war years gave way to the prosperous 1950s and 1960s, a more creative take on infographics unseated the isotype style. The New York School "chartoon" style, popularized by Nigel Holmes in the 1960s and 1970s, reacted against the overly functionalist graphics of the mid-century. Chartoons dress up displays of graphical data with cartoon-like illustrations and extraneous detail to make the graphics more visually appealing, a precursor to the high-gloss, low-synthesis graphics of the *USA Today*.[17]

A large supply of professional artists entering the rapidly expanding fields of print publishing and advertising further emphasized illustration over information.[18] Edmund Arnold, considered by many the father of modern newspaper design, was among them. A graphic designer and journalist, Arnold incorporated images and infographics into the routine of the newsroom and into the more than one thousand newspapers he designed.[19] In 1977, *Time* magazine underwent a redesign that included frequent pop-data graphics contributions from another news diagram innovator, Nigel Holmes. Even though he deployed a less technical style than Playfair had two centuries earlier, Holmes reinvigorated infographics as a legitimate branch of journalistic endeavor.[20] Between 1965 and 1980, the *New York Times* frequently published sophisticated infographics, becoming the main proponent of the form in newspapers for decades.[21] But the infographics in the *Times* of this period, and the purposes they served, were altogether different from those the *USA Today* would popularize in the early 1980s by publishing them daily. The latter's need for daily data forced the paper to turn to simple polls, trite little info-nibbles. It was part of a move that earned the *USA Today* the name "McPaper" for its focus on soft and inconsequential questions. Figure 3.2 shows examples from the evolution of journalistic infographics.

Despite their questionable value, the *USA Today*'s daily graphics raised the bar on the form by changing expectations. The growing accessibility of desktop computers in the 1980s led to the faster production of more affordable graphics, but early software was still too primitive to be used quickly in newsrooms. By 1988 editors were clamoring for graphics, and news wire services entered the race.[22] Moving from telephone lines to satellite delivery systems, the Associated Press, the Knight-Ridder-Tribune News Service, the New York Times News Service, and the Gannett News Service began offering graphics just as they offered news stories by wire. Infographics not only improved readers' comprehension of information, they also sold papers, adding visual flare to an otherwise text-heavy medium.

The journalistic yang to *USA Today*'s yin would emerge in the digital age. The *South Florida Sun-Sentinel* brought on Don Wittekind in 1996 to head their interactive graphics department. Wittekind expanded the department to create infographics to complement stories from the print and online news departments. Another early adopter of digital infographics, the online edition of Spain's second largest newspaper *El Mundo* (elmundo.es) founded its online graphics department in 1999. Alberto Cairo, a founder of the department, has written extensively on the transition from print to digital infographics, with a focus on journalistic integrity over novelty of implementation.[23]

Uses of Digital Infographics

In print, infographics are static by necessity. *Digital infographics*, by contrast, involve computation and user manipulation of underlying information. At its simplest, a digital infographic might layer ancillary information visually, such that additional detail is revealed when a user moves the mouse pointer over a particular object. But genuine digital infographics make interaction a part of understanding: analog infographics are *read*, whereas digital infographics are *operated*. Maish Nichani and Venkat Rajamanickam coin the term *interactives* to underscore the difference—explanation through interaction.[24]

According to Nichani and Rajamanickam, the interactive has the potential to free information from the rigid constraints of the printed word. They offer four categories of interactive graphics: *narrative, instructive, explorative,*

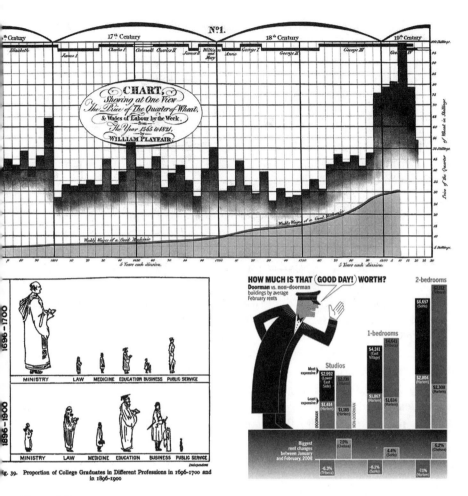

Figure 3.2

The changing aesthetic of infographics as depicted in a series of bar graphs. Plotted data are transformed by illustrations to provide additional information while making the graphic more appealing. Top: William Playfair, *Commercial and Political Atlas* (1786); bottom left: Willard C. Brinton, *Graphic Methods for Presenting Facts* (1914); bottom right: Nigel Holmes, *New York Observer* (2008).

and *simulative*. Narratives are used for telling straightforward stories, instructives provide step-by-step directions to reach a single goal, exploratives allow the user to engage in their own processes of sense-making, and simulatives allow the reader to grasp the processes of a system.[25]

By becoming active participants in the unfolding of information, readers can develop a deeper understanding of the underlying logic of an issue. *Budget Hero* offers an object lesson: instead of depicting trivial details about the budget as would a *USA Today* snapshot or even a static bar graph, *Budget Hero* allows players to *experience* the difficult trade-offs required to promote particular social programs. Nichani and Rajamanickam's categories may offer useful ways to group examples or guide production, but we prefer to focus on the possible uses of infographics.

We propose three primary patterns of use for infographics, both digital and nondigital. *Explanatory* infographics depict specific data for simultaneous consumption. *Exploratory* (or free-form) infographics allow participants to draw a variety of conclusions by manipulating data according to personal goals or ideas. And *directed* infographics guide readers through data in a specific way, leading to a shared experience of synthesis.

Explanatory graphics display synthesized information in a relatively static form. They value results over processes, abstracting discussions about how a journalist arrived at a particular conclusion. Such information might be quantitative, qualitative, or narrative in form. Consider the *New York Times* front-page graphic from December 16, 1965, which shows a diagram of the *Gemini 6* and *7* flight crews' rendezvous while orbiting Earth.[26] It illustrates the orbital paths of the two ships, and comment boxes attached to points on the paths describe key steps in the process. A single reading of all the details offers sufficient explanation.

Portfolio.com's May 2009 feature on the construction of the Boeing 787 Dreamliner aircraft offers a digital example of an explanatory infographic. An exploded view of the 787 makes its constituent parts easier to identify.[27] Lines direct the eye to these elements, and hovering over dots on the graphic reveals information about where a particular part is manufactured. The purpose of the graphic is to illustrate the global production of the aircraft, a business decision that had been required to accomplish Boeing's engineering goals, but which had also introduced unexpected logistical delays.

Exploratory (free-form) graphics show data that is meant to be synthesized by the user independently of the creator's expectations. Both Tufte and Benjamin Schneiderman encourage the use of information graphics to offer multiple levels of granularity for maximum flexibility. Tools or controls allow the reader to arrange, filter, or zoom data. For example, a map of the world produced by Dan Smith in *The State of the World Atlas* represents a country's size not by its geographic mass but by its population.[28] A few textual notes detail general trends in population growth, but it is up to readers to discover how the maps might clarify their particular situations. The graphic features a high density of information presented in multiple formats that encourage the reader to explore, make comparisons using the different graphics, and draw conclusions about the world's population.

USA Today's 2008 "Presidential Primary Delegate Tracker" graphic offers a commendable example of an exploratory digital infographic.[29] The graphic depicts a map of the United States, timelines of Democrat and Republican events, and a bar graph with the total number of delegate votes cast for each presidential candidate. Rolling over states on the map shows how many votes each delegate won. Mousing over points on the timeline highlights the states whose primaries approached, while also masking previously decided states. As users approach the map by means of these different tools, they develop a better sense of the unfolding drama of the primary.

Directed infographics guide the reader through a dynamic data set toward a conclusion synthesized beforehand by the designer or journalist. Spatial, temporal, or process-heavy stories often lend themselves to directed graphical rendition. The front page of the January 26, 1986, *USA Today* features a large color graphic explaining the tragic explosion of the Space Shuttle *Challenger*.[30] An explanation of liftoff appears, with increments of time detailing the one minute and fifty-one seconds before the shuttle exploded. It uses an insert map of the Cape Canaveral area to situate the event, and two cut-away diagrams of the shuttle—one of the rockets and one of the shuttle's cockpit—to add detail. Directed activity encourages constrained exploration. The *Challenger* infographic guides the reader through the chronology of the tragedy, while providing supplementary information that might offer detail and context.

In digital infographics, direction can prompt the user to explore abstract or generic information from the perspective of his or her personal situation. Imagine a hypothetical family that lives in East Orange, New Jersey. A wife, husband, and their one child have been renting a house, but the wife has been offered an opportunity to be transferred to her engineering firm's new branch in Reston, Virginia. Her husband is self-employed, so he has the freedom to work from anywhere. When they first moved to East Orange they assumed they wouldn't be able to afford a house, but a few years of savings plus the raise she would receive upon transferring have turned their attention to the possibility of home ownership. Does it make financial sense to try to buy a home in Virginia? They would rather not see a financial planner without first exploring some options, so they search the Web for information. There are thousands of generic mortgage calculators online, but they stumble on a more robust tool: the *New York Times* rent–buy calculator, "Is It Better to Buy or Rent?"[31]

The calculator is an interactive infographic that compares the relative costs of renting and buying equivalent homes. The graphic contains fields to enter rent cost, home price, down payment, mortgage rate, and annual property taxes. Additionally, it uses two sliders to adjust annual changes in home value and rent. As shown in figure 3.3, a timeline at the center shows how many years it would take to justify the cost of buying a home, paying property taxes, and settling a mortgage versus simply renting. The calculator even accounts for more specific costs: condo or home-owners association fees, costs of selling a home, maintenance costs, rent deposit, rate of return on investment if the money used to buy a home were invested elsewhere, and so on. Though the results of the calculator shouldn't be taken as gospel, they offer a concrete starting point for people looking for homes in an uncertain housing market. The tool directs use by prompting the user to enter personalized information.

Information graphics find a close relative in the world of computing: *information visualization* or *infovis*. While both fields concern the visual representation of data, information visualization values computational innovation first, elucidation second.[32] It is used to for "exploiting the dynamic, interactive, inexpensive medium of graphical computers to devise new external aids enhancing cognitive abilities."[33] Whereas information graphics generally entail hand-drawn materials produced by an artist, infovis artifacts use computers both for processing large quantities of data and for rendering that data. In a data set with thousands or millions of individual elements, a computer's speed, power, and accuracy are required to produce a viable rendering. As such, infovis has traditionally taken place among computer professionals—experts with experience analyzing problems in a specific domain, and with the know-how to write software to render the results of that analysis.

By and large, infovis has found root in highly technical contexts, where scientific information is both large and complex. However, Zachary Pousman, John Stasko, and Michael Mateas have coined the term "casual infovis" to suggest a broader role for information visualization in less professional contexts.[34] Examples abound, aggregated from the corners of the

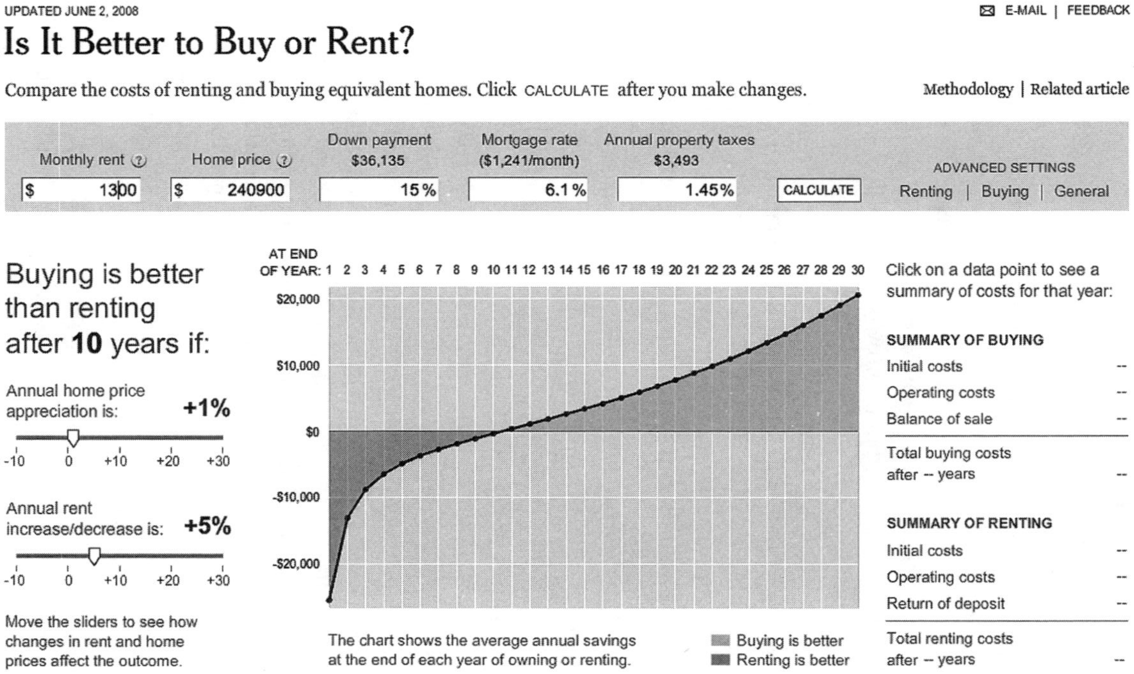

UPDATED JUNE 2, 2008

✉ E-MAIL | FEEDBACK

Is It Better to Buy or Rent?

Compare the costs of renting and buying equivalent homes. Click CALCULATE after you make changes.

Methodology | Related article

Monthly rent ②	Home price ②	Down payment	Mortgage rate	Annual property taxes
$ 1300	$ 240900	$36,135 15%	($1,241/month) 6.1%	$3,493 1.45% CALCULATE

ADVANCED SETTINGS
Renting | Buying | General

Click on a data point to see a summary of costs for that year:

Buying is better than renting after **10** years if:

SUMMARY OF BUYING

Initial costs	--
Operating costs	--
Balance of sale	--

Total buying costs after -- years   --

SUMMARY OF RENTING

Initial costs	--
Operating costs	--
Return of deposit	--

Total renting costs after -- years   --

AT END
OF YEAR: 1 2 3 4 5 6 7 8 9 10 11 12 13 14 15 16 17 18 19 20 21 22 23 24 25 26 27 28 29 30

$20,000

$10,000

$0

-$10,000

-$20,000

The chart shows the average annual savings at the end of each year of owning or renting.

■ Buying is better
■ Renting is better

Annual home price appreciation is: **+1%**

-10   0   +10   +20   +30

Annual rent increase/decrease is: **+5%**

-10   0   +10   +20   +30

Move the sliders to see how changes in rent and home prices affect the outcome.

Figure 3.3

Not only does the Web application "Is It Better to Buy or Rent?" let users enter a large range of data to produce a graph that determines the year a person is better off buying a home than renting, it also demonstrates the importance of exploring data through manipulable sliders and input. In this example, a user can see how increased rental rates might influence buying decisions.

Web on sites like FlowingData.com. Their "5 Best Data Visualization Projects of the Year" for 2008 features a static infographic, dynamic infovis, and even two video projects.[35]

The wider availability of both graphic design software and software development tools has drawn the practices of both infographics and information visualization into increasing overlap, despite their differences. On the one hand, infographics deploy the artist/journalist as an information synthesizer. The author of the graphic provides direction and prompts specific user engagement. Infovis, on the other hand, makes use of large data sets that can reveal underlying patterns that might be difficult to identify without visual arrangement. But because infographics have a long tradition in journalism, we have chosen to use the term inclusively, to encompass both traditional applications of infographics as well as the increasingly complex information-processing techniques of information visualization.

Playing with Infographics

The history of journalistic infographics highlights not only their on-again, off-again relationship with intricacy over simplicity, but also the changing attitudes toward their purpose and execution. Infographics started as a tool for economists, sociologists, and scientists—serious data depicted seriously. The rigidity of the form loosened as designers sought to make visual presentation more compelling for popular audiences—the silhouetted outline of an iconic woman from a pictographic language transformed into a style of popular cartoons and comics. Today, infographics range from graphically formal to stylized, rational to emotional, serious to inconsequential. Their power for visual appeal and explanation is well acknowledged in journalism, but infographics still have not fully exploited computation as a medium for *behavior* as well as visualization.

Videogames offer a new model for infographics, one that might combine the analytical sophistication of Playfair's and Maynard's early infographics with the emotional context of later approaches. Digital infographics intersect with the world of games when we can *play* with them.

Play has been defined in many ways. Anthropologist Johan Huizinga called it a "free activity" standing "outside 'ordinary' life," one that is "not serious" but at the same time absorbs the player intensely and utterly.[36] Roger Caillois refined Huizinga's definition: play is "free, separate, uncertain, unproductive, governed by rules, and make-believe."[37] But game designers Katie Salen and Eric Zimmerman offer the best general definition of play: "free movement within a more rigid structure."[38] Even if they are not games quite like *Pac-Man* or *The Sims*, infographics can become *game-like*, exploiting the properties of games in numerous ways: to encourage the manipulation of information for replayability, to allow pleasurable engagement with a system, or to invite exploration.

We might call them *playable infographics*: works that adopt infographics' principles but add layers of gameplay around them. In particular, playable infographics embrace a synthetic amalgam of directed and exploratory infographic design principles. Consider *Budget Hero* once more. The game offers a directed experience, in which the player must create a budget that extends as far into the future as possible without going bust, while maintaining a reasonable debt ratio and accomplishing personal political goals. Players cannot simply move budget sliders around willy-nilly, as if budgetary commitments existed only on an annual basis. Nor can they make allocations without the appropriate tax receipts or debt obligations to support them.

At the same time, *Budget Hero* offers an exploratory experience. Unlike explanatory infographics, which offer no choice whatsoever, and unlike narrative games, which offer a progression through a set of challenges that tell a story, *Budget Hero* won't do anything without player intervention. The player can make a range of choices: exploring the requirements of different budget-goal badges, browsing the policy and taxation cards, and researching the pros, cons, and impact of public policies associated with those cards. The player can pursue some, all, or none of these options at any time. The best playable infographics offer specific direction in the context of broader information exploration, using the space of experimentation as the "free movement" that produces play.

Budget Hero is instructive, but it offers only one example. What other types of playable graphics are possible? In print or online, common infographics formats from the newspaper, television, and the Web take different forms for different functions. Eric K. Meyer summarized these forms in his guide to designing infographics. We have modified them slightly to better apply to interactive digital infographics (see figure 3.4 for the forms in practice).

Graphs compare quantities of information in familiar formats: bar graph, line graph, a pie chart, fever chart, or in more complex combinations. *Sequential graphics*, which take the form of *chronological* and *process graphics*, allow the order of the data to take a central place in unfolding information.

NATURE'S ULTIMATE WEAPON

Whether they're called hurricanes, typhoons or cyclones, they are the most devastating weather events — churning masses of wind and rain that cause swaths of damage up to hundreds of miles wide at points along paths a thousand miles long. Beginning as thunderstorms in equatorial seas, the biggest storms can release as much energy as 15 atomic bombs and send walls of water 30 feet high surging into unprotected coastlines.

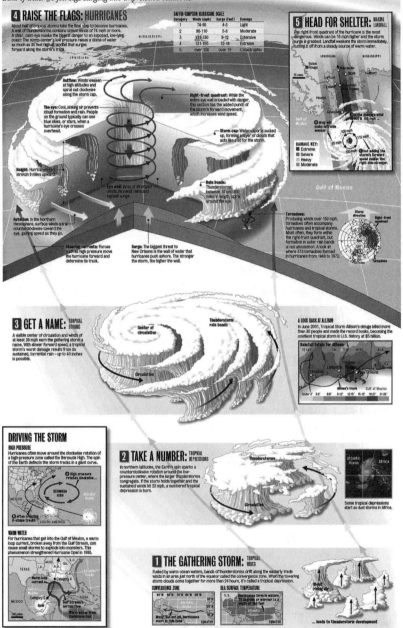

4 RAISE THE FLAGS: HURRICANES

About half of tropical storms take the final step to become hurricanes. A wall of thunderstorms contains violent winds of 74 mph or more. A clear, calm eye masks the biggest danger to an exposed, low-lying coast: The storm center's low pressure raises a dome of water as much as 30 feet high at landfall that surges forward along the storm's track.

SAFFIR-SIMPSON HURRICANE SCALE

Category	Winds (mph)	Surge (feet)	Damage
1	74-95	4-5	Light
2	96-110	5-6	Moderate
3	111-130	8-12	Extensive
4	131-155	12-18	Extreme
5	over 155	over 18	Catastrophic

Outflow: Winds weaken at high altitudes and spiral out clockwise along the storm cap.

The eye: Cool, sinking air prevents cloud formation and rain. People on the ground typically can see blue skies, or stars, when a hurricane's eye crosses overhead.

Right-front quadrant: While the entire eye wall is loaded with danger, this section has the added punch of the storm's forward movement, which increases wind speed.

Storm cap: Water vapor is sucked up, forming a layer of clouds that acts like a lid for the storm.

Height: Hurricanes can stretch 9 miles upward.

Eye wall: Area of strongest winds, heaviest rains and highest surge.

Rain bands: Thunderstorms between 10 and 300 miles in length, spiral around the eye.

Rotation: In the Northern Hemisphere, surface winds spiral counterclockwise toward the eye, gaining speed as they go.

Steering currents: Forces such as high pressure move the hurricane forward and determine its track.

Surge: The biggest threat to New Orleans is the wall of water that hurricanes push ashore. The stronger the storm, the higher the wall.

Tornadoes: Producing winds over 150 mph, tornadoes often accompany hurricanes and tropical storms. Most often, they form within the right-front quadrant, but formation in outer rain bands is not uncommon. A look at where 373 tornadoes formed in hurricanes from 1948 to 1972.

5 HEAD FOR SHELTER: MAKING LANDFALL

The right-front quadrant of the hurricane is the most dangerous. Winds can be 18 mph higher and the storm surge is greatest. Landfall weakens the storm immediately, cutting it off from a steady source of warm water.

DAMAGE KEY:
- ■ Extreme
- ■ Severe
- ■ Heavy
- ■ Moderate

3 GET A NAME: TROPICAL STORMS

A visible center of circulation and winds of at least 39 mph earn the gathering storm a name. With slower forward speed, a tropical storm's worst damage results from its sustained, torrential rain – up to 40 inches is possible.

A LOOK BACK AT ALLISON

In June 2001, Tropical Storm Allison's deluge killed more than 30 people and made the record books, becoming the costliest tropical storm in U.S. history at $5 billion.

Rainfall totals for Allison:

| Under 3" | 3-6" | 6-9" | 9-12" | 12-15" | 15-18" | 18-21" | 21-24" |

DRIVING THE STORM

HIGH PRESSURE

Hurricanes often move around the clockwise rotation of a high-pressure zone called the Bermuda High. The spin of the Earth deflects the storm tracks in a giant curve.

1. High pressure rotates clockwise...
2. ...often creating C-shape tracks

WARM WATER

For hurricanes that get into the Gulf of Mexico, a warm loop current, broken away from the Gulf Stream, can cause small storms to explode into monsters. This phenomenon strengthened Hurricane Opal in 1995.

2 TAKE A NUMBER: TROPICAL DEPRESSIONS

In northern latitudes, the Earth's spin sparks a counterclockwise rotation around the low-pressure center, where the larger thunderstorms congregate. If the storm holds together and the sustained winds hit 23 mph, a numbered tropical depression is born.

Some tropical depressions start as dust storms in Africa.

1 THE GATHERING STORM: TROPICAL WAVES

Fueled by warm ocean waters, bands of thunderstorms drift along the easterly trade winds in an area just north of the equator called the convergence zone. When the towering storm clouds come together for more than 24 hours, it's called a tropical depression.

CONVERGENCE ZONE

Many, but not all, hurricanes start in this zone.

SEA SURFACE TEMPERATURE

Hurricanes form in waters 79 degrees or warmer to a depth of 150 feet.

... leads to thunderstorm development

Maps display geographically situated data rather than physical geography itself. A map might conform to traditional depictions of spatial arrangement, or it might distort the area for aesthetic or informatic effect.

Diagrams present a piece of information in order to explain its individual components. A diagram presents an object, concept, event, or scene, and describes the illustration with labels, comment boxes, iconography, and other explanatory figures. Renderings, exaggerations, exploded views, and cutaways are examples of diagrams.[39]

These formats are not mutually exclusive. Bar graphs can appear on a timeline, process graphics can show geographically situated steps, and a diagram can depict a dynamic process. Furthermore, different formats can explain a subject in different ways. Consider a volcanic eruption. A bar graph might compare the amount of ash thrown into the atmosphere to other eruptions in the past. A volcano's geological birth might form the basis of a process graphic. A temporal graphic might situate the events just after the eruption, such as the dispersal of ash and the movement of the surrounding population in response to it. A map might illustrate the path of a molten lava river, while a diagram might show a cutaway of the volcano's interior and its various geological components.

Playable infographics derive from these common types of traditional or digital infographics, adapting their forms, features, and benefits for use in directed exploration.

Playing with Graphs

When Laura Wattenberg published a book on baby names, her husband Martin, an infovis designer at IBM Research, created a visualization tool called NameVoyager to support its release.[40] Powered by lists of the thousand most popular names for boys and girls from every decade from 1900 to present, NameVoyager graphs complete or partial names on a timeline of popularity, instantly updating its view as the user types (see figure 3.5).

◀ **Figure 3.4**
This full-page spread on the development of a hurricane incorporates different infographic forms to tell its story. As indicated by the bold numbers, "Nature's Ultimate Weapon" is a sequential graphic detailing the order of events as a hurricane forms and makes landfall. Diagrams illustrate the motion of the air as the clouds gather, maps track the motion of the storm and locate rainfall data geographically, and a circular scatterplot reveals the frequency of tornadoes found in the different locations of the swirling storm. Image courtesy of Dan Swenson/The Times-Picayune.

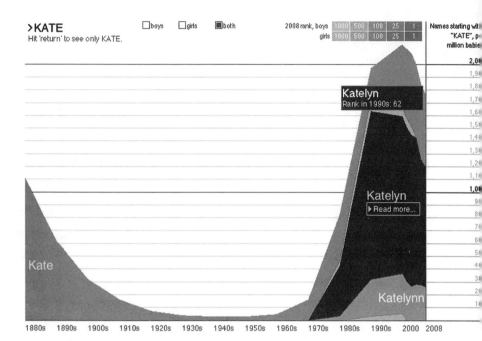

Figure 3.5

Martin Wattenberg's NameVoyager illustrates the decline and rise in popularity of given names. Here we see the ebbs and flows in adoption of the name Kate as well as the meteoric rise of the name Katelyn in the 1970s.

Though NameVoyager is clearly not intended to be a game, as more people used it, Wattenberg noticed that they talked about exploring the data playfully, "identifying trends and anomalies and forming conjectures."[41] For example, one Web site commenter suggested: "For a challenge, try finding a name that was popular at the beginning of the sample, went out of style, then came back into vogue recently." Wattenberg calls the tool's usage patterns "strongly social" and "more closely related to those of online multiplayer games than to a conventional single-user statistical tool."[42]

Wattenberg noticed trends in user activity that he aligned with Richard Bartle's four categories of players in online games—explorers, achievers, socializers, and killers.[43] Such an idea disrupts the traditional view of information visualization as a task-oriented, problem-solving activity. NameVoyager is playable because its users have invented directed goals within the exploratory context of the visualization. The achievers in NameVoyager used the tool for its primary function: to pick out a name for their baby. "We want something slightly retro, nice, and not too popular," one woman wrote, "and this visualization gives us all that." NameVoyager socializers are users "whose main concern is their interactions with others, and who place their data exploration in a personal social context," often searching for their own name or friends and family names and commenting on the results in context of their experiences. Some of the explorers particularly enjoy discovering odd names or unusual groups of names. Finally, the "killers" (aggressive, acerbic players) take pleasure in mocking the names they find, seeking out targets to ridicule. As one killer comments, "Britney, Brittney, Britany, Brittany, Brittani, Britannie, Britni. Enough already."

These behaviors do not quite make the visualization a game, particularly since NameVoyager's "players" have to invent their own goals. But they do suggest that playful, gamelike habits developed around the work. It is not hard to imagine an even more playable implementation of NameVoyager: the graph could be treated as a puzzle, and an author could set specific goals: find a name popular in the 1920s that returned in the 1990s, or find a name equally popular for boys and girls in the 1970s. While the freedom of open exploration might seem preferable, a guided experience would help retain users who might not know where to begin when confronted with an unstructured visualization.

Playing with Sequential Graphics

A vivid example of a *chronological* graphic comes from a news story that rapidly unfolds over a matter of minutes. Built atop the popular flight-simulator *X-Plane*, *Sully's Flight* is an iPhone game that puts the player in the cockpit of US Airways Flight 1549, piloted by Chesley Sullenberger, which was forced to land in the Hudson River on January 15, 2009. The player begins on LaGuardia Airport runway four in the cockpit of an Airbus A320. The path of the flight is outlined on the screen by green reticles, through which the player must pilot the aircraft. The screen animates with objects hitting the windshield at the proper moment the geese were said to have struck the airplane. The engines lose thrust and it is up to the player to make a successful river landing.

Sully's flight was widely covered, but mostly from the vantage point of heroism in general. Understanding the quickly unfolding events of the emergency itself offers a different perspective. The re-creation of the plane's flight path helps, but the game's reproduction of cockpit radio transmissions between US1549 and air traffic control best accentuates the flight's urgency. The live audio is far more effective than a static infographic with a timeline of events or a written transcript. Even with perfect hindsight, successfully making a landing proves challenging, offering a powerful illustration of the improbable accomplishments of Captain Sullenberger.

In other circumstances, chronology is less critical than *process*. Consider the unpredictable dangers of hurricanes to Florida coastal residents. The events of a past disaster might be instructive, but less so than the process by which hurricanes develop and move. What better way to understand such a storm than to make your own? The *South Florida Sun Sentinel*'s Web site offers just such a tool, a "Hurricane Maker."[44] It presents the user with a map of the Atlantic and coastal regions of the Americas. It then invites the user to place a storm on the map, choosing a body of water with a higher average temperature to ensure the hurricane will form. Wind shear can be set at different altitudes, and humidity levels around the storm can be tweaked. Once the player is satisfied, a button press sets the hurricane in motion. If all the proper conditions have been met, the little storm animates into a fearsome hurricane. If not, the infographic explains reasons for the user's failure and offers a chance to try again. Hurricane Maker has playful qualities: players attempt to achieve a goal by adjusting a system. It teaches users through trial and error, by directing their interaction. Still, even if it might satisfy intellectual curiosity, Hurricane Maker disappoints as an overall experience. Its hurricane never moves nor makes landfall, abstracting the average reader's concern about safety and property into an unsatisfying binary of success or failure.

"The Earth Impact Effects Program" (EIEP) offers a better example of a procedural infographic, albeit for a less likely catastrophe.[45] Developed by researchers at the University of Arizona's Lunar and Planetary Laboratory, EIEP is a text-only Web page that allows its users to tweak the parameters of an inbound doomsday asteroid to estimate "the regional environmental consequences of an impact on Earth."[46] Like Hurricane Maker, EIEP plays on our fascination with disasters, daring users to orchestrate the greatest destruction possible. Hurricane Maker makes an all-or-nothing gambit: players either create a hurricane or not. EIEP, by contrast, encourages players to trigger all its various scenarios of destruction, from seismic effects to thermal radiation.

In gaming terms, EIEP is more replayable. While game makers prize the trait as a virtue of good game design, replayability isn't necessarily a journalistic value unless it encourages broader and deeper understanding.[47] EIEP describes the results of the user's input in far greater detail—the size of the crater, seismic activity, scattered debris, and global climate change. It lists the relevant parameters of several famous asteroids to give players a sense of scale, to provide context, and to guide subsequent choices. By playing with it multiple times, one develops a sense of the plausible outcomes of an asteroid cataclysm. In that respect, EIEP's merit as news might seem suspect (until an asteroid actually threatens the Earth). Yet it shows the untapped potential of playable infographics like Hurricane Maker.

Playing with Maps

The ReDistricting Game challenges players to redraw fictional Congressional districts along party lines. Red and blue dots of varying density show concentrations of partisan populations, and colors on the map itself indicate elected officials' current districts. The player must recolor the map such that each official is satisfied with his or her district, districts are of proportional sizes, and a chosen party enjoys election victory. *The ReDistricting Game* focuses on geographic data manipulation as a political strategy, providing directed gerrymandering goals along with an exploratory map.

While *The ReDistricting Game* characterizes a process, the *New York Times'* Hurricane Gustav interactive map and the Minnesota Bridge Collapse map offer event reporting via geographical infographic.[48] Released soon after the tragedies, these maps allow people affected by these events to attach text and multimedia to nodes on a map of the area. The Hurricane Gustav map is simple: it's just a Google Map covering some the states impacted by the hurricane. Users can click on points on the map that link to video, audio, or photos of the disaster. The Minnesota Bridge Collapse map is far more sensational. From a helicopter or satellite's point of view, we look down from the sky at the destroyed bridge. Nodes appear for survivors and victims. Family members can leave messages of grace or sorrow, adding humanity to the traditional list of names and statistics.

While the Minnesota Bridge Collapse memorializes a current event, the Pittsburgh Bike Map aggregates the experiences of user contributions to paint a landscape of the issues of biking in a major city.[49] This map offers a hub for bikers in Pittsburgh to learn about current biking conditions in the city. Different types of information—including nodes for bike shops, trails, and accidents—can be turned on and off. One can zoom in or out to get a better sense of the area. Of particular note are the map's crash reports. Unlike a crime map that reports violations without detail— "burglary, grand theft auto, larceny"—the bike map's reports are fleshed out so others can understand the extent of the problem.

Playable maps like these are not intended to be experienced in a particular order, nor does the user have to engage with all possible data. The user identifies with stories the map traces, constructing relevant meaning from fragments. Story maps like Minnesota Bridge Collapse aren't games in the traditional sense, but their format encourages exploration and narrative construction. The Pittsburgh Bike Map inspires an unusual kind of play, one that takes place both on and off the computer (a topic addressed in detail in chapter 7). Users consult the map to optimize their strategy outdoors in the city. After testing routes and forging new paths, they return to update information and tactics for the benefit of other users.

Playing with Diagrams

The *Sun Sentinel*'s Virtual Butterfly Ballot works like an interactive diagram. Re-creating the experience of the confused Palm Beach County voter during the controversial 2000 U.S. presidential election, the interactive graphic reproduces the ballot used in that county and challenges the user to cast a vote correctly for a specified candidate.[50] If the intended and actual candidates do not match, a message explains possible reasons, clarifying how perceptual conundrums might have caused real voters to make unintended choices: ballot punch holes don't line up well with names and arrows (see figure 3.6). A voter reading top to bottom on the left side easily

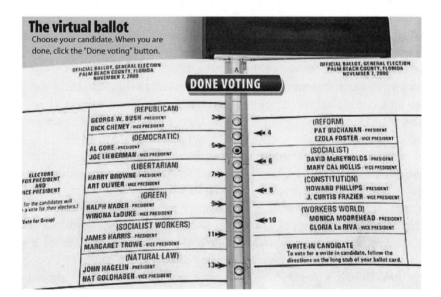

Figure 3.6
A quick glance at the *South Florida Sun Sentinel*'s Butterfly Ballot infographic clarifies why Florida voters might have cast votes for different candidates than they intended.

might have intended to mark the third hole to vote for Al Gore, but inadvertently selected the second, voting for Pat Buchanan instead.

Though not grounded in fact or journalistic intention, *Effing Hail* by Jiggman and Greg Wohlwend of Intuition Games is a Web game that looks like an infographic.[51] It is an isometrically positioned diagram of the atmosphere sliced into fictionally named sections (the cleverly invented Aiesphere through Effingsphere). The player's mouse-clicks create strong updrafts of wind that can lift falling precipitation into the upper atmosphere to form large hailstones, which then pound the defenseless buildings on the ground. The game asks players to craft armies of hail, pummeling an increasingly stronger set of buildings and objects in the sky within a time limit.

Though the game is not intended to teach users about the meteorological phenomenon, it (imprecisely) uses the process that builds hail in the atmosphere as a physics mechanic and indirectly (and again imprecisely) educates the player about such conditions. This educational facade arises largely from the game's infographic aesthetics. It is not only the type of design one might find in a popular magazine or Earth studies textbook, but also what we might see in a newspaper article about a recent storm.

Synthesis in Playable Data

Bill Kovach and Tom Rosenstiel have argued that fast access to detailed information, particularly information gathered online, has made it too easy to ignore the foundation of a news story.[52] The lurid dissonance of comments, blog posts, tweets, and other speculation can occlude the important elements of a topic. Infographics offer a possible reprieve from the anonymity of information, particularly when the exploratory and directed uses of the form are combined.

At first blush, journalists might think exploratory infographics like "Is It Better to Buy or Rent?" work best when they are unfettered, when users can do whatever they want with them. They certainly seem more flexible that way, too: an individual can configure the infographic for any purpose whatsoever. But total freedom is not always illuminating. It can fail to point out the particular examples of a system, such as home ownership, that might offer punctuations of clarity.

For example, what if the Rent–Buy Calculator offered optional but explicit goals, like the ones Wattenberg catalogs from NameVoyager adopters? "Find a city with a population larger than 500,000 where buying a $250,000 home won't pay off in five years," or "Find the town in Idaho where home ownership is the most effective for families with a monthly housing budget of $1,200." By acting more like a game, the infographic could provide insights into the situations of particular citizens, while still allowing users to apply it to their own situations.

When authorial direction guides exploratory activities, the author can "sift out the rumor, the innuendo, the insignificant, and the spin," while focusing effort on what makes the story important and relevant.[53] The journalist's role is to make sense of facts, but without author synthesis the data remain raw and undigestible. Though an interesting visualization may be visually appealing, forcing the user to do all the work putting it together results in research, not journalism.

Another *New York Times* infographic, "How Different Groups Spend Their Day," offers an interactive graph of daily activities performed by eighteen demographic groups in twenty categories of daily activities, chronicling them over the day in ten-minute intervals.[54] It has enjoyed the sort of "viral" response on blogs and Twitter that many publishers and citizens mistake for journalistic impact. Among those who commented on the link, game designer Raph Koster wrote that "it invites exploration; it feels fun to investigate."[55] Others underscored the "fascinating" results that emerge from the large quantities of information in the data set.[56] Yet, the graphic itself does little more than compile a lot of data in one place, wrapped in a clever interface (figure 3.7).

Why, then, do people like it so much? Each reader has some stake in the data presented by the visualization. Although its use is not directed by instructions, the graphic's categories suggest goals—everyone fits into at least some part of the demographic survey. An employed white male aged 25–64, with an advanced degree and zero children, has five initial categories to start exploring. He might then branch out to other demographic groups, perhaps those of friends and family, to compare results. Users can drag a mouse over the graph for more detailed information, or click on areas of the chart to isolate them for examination. Perhaps that is what people are attracted to: the sheer amount of seemingly precise data.

In the end, it is difficult to say what a reader is supposed to take away from the visualization. Does it reveal something important? Will the average reader even remember what he or she saw in the graphic? Ought it to be used for scheduling? For self-improvement? For mockery? The *New York Times* puts all the data in one place, yet fails to synthesize its meaning. The accompanying article says little about the results of the survey, and the textual information displayed while browsing the graph amounts to little more than "fun facts," which may or may not be related to the data

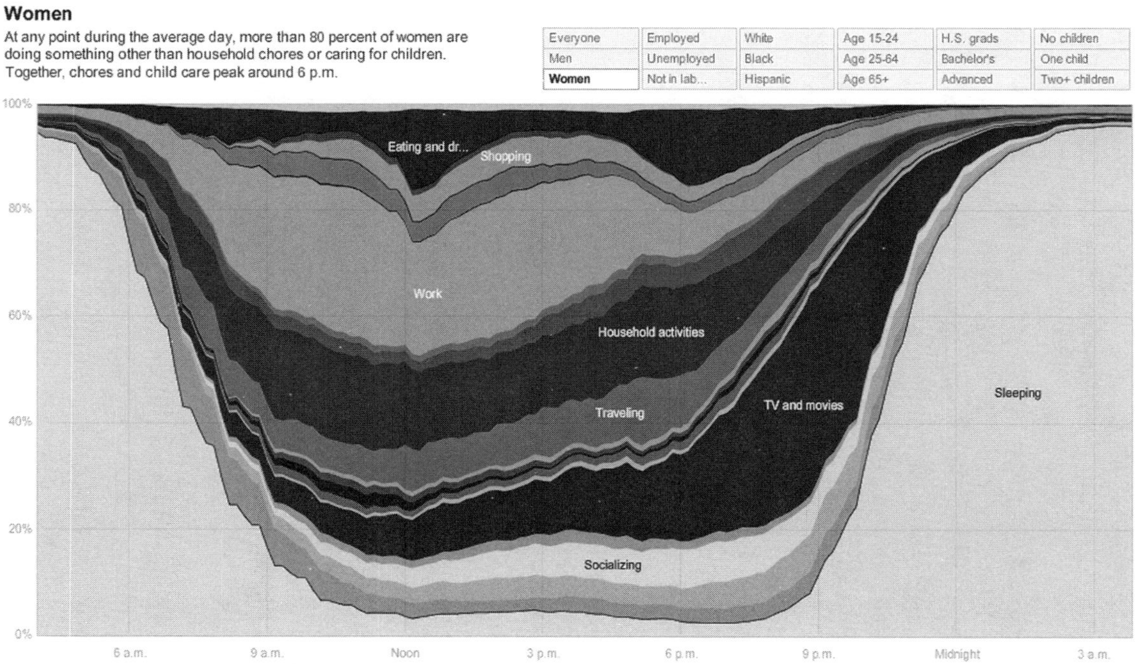

Figure 3.7

A wealth of data lies below the surface of the *New York Times'* "How Different Groups Spend Their Day" info-graphic, but extracting relevant information is an arduous task. In addition to providing the tool, journalists must synthesize data meaningfully.

being examined.[57] The article describes the results of the survey as "strik-ing," yet there is no effort to expand on what counts as striking in this context.

An experiment on CNN shows how context can add synthesis to raw data. During the 2008 U.S. presidential primary elections, CNN premiered its "Magic Wall," a large interactive screen on which current and historical electoral information, mostly in the form of maps, could be displayed.[58] Like Apple's iPhone and iPad, the screen offers multitouch capability for fluid, tactile operation. Instead of leaping from one bit of data to another by clicking a hyperlink, the user transforms the screen's image by direct application of several fingers.

Because elections are complex, media outlets have tried to help citizens understand the electoral process using graphical representations of the electoral data—most frequently in the form of maps and charts. CNN deployed the Magic Wall for just this purpose, to better explain the dynam-ics of election data using a technology that allowed for fluid transitions between different levels of information.[59] During the 2008 primary, CNN National Correspondent John King seemed more interested in the novelty of the system than its potential as a reporting tool. He played with the multitouch features like a child with a new toy on Christmas morning, moving the map around to show off the technology rather than to use it for information. Criticisms, including a *Saturday Night Live* send-up, may have inspired the network to reconsider their use of the map.[60]

By election day, King had moved past the device's novelty and began to use the screen for information analysis. As polling returns flowed in over the course of the evening, King used the screen to show regions—including individual counties—with the potential to influence the election's outcome. Calling up data from previous elections, King compared historical results with projections and polls to form hypotheses on the magical screen. In a climactic moment, King used the map to show viewers why Republican candidate John McCain could not win the election based on returns alone, rather than projections. King used the screen as a data simulator but treated it as a puzzle, in which he played with states that the Republican candidate might earn in order to reach the needed 270 electoral votes. The presenter even gave states to McCain that were predicted to be won by the Democrats as a way to show that in the unlikely event the candidate might win those states, McCain still could not emerge victorious.

This simulation made the outcome of the 2008 presidential election visually clear, but it also showed how technology can be used to clarify the meaning of data, not just as newfangled gimmickry. The screen helped

King discover and explain the unseen details of the process while unveiling patterns that would be invisible on a static map. This multitouch interactive infographic worked because it facilitated the journalist's process of performing this synthesis through dynamic contextual material on a live broadcast.

The frequent absence of synthesis draws attention to a quandary in contemporary information journalism. In recent years, technology advocates have called for "open data"—systems or services that publish the data they use, giving anyone the ability to download, evaluate, modify, and reuse the information as they please.[61] In October 2008, the *New York Times* launched its Visualization Lab, which "allows readers to create compelling interactive charts, graphs, maps and other types of graphical presentations from data made available by *Times* editors."[62] Built atop IBM Research's Many Eyes platform, readers of the *Times* can download data, create their own visualizations, and share them on the Web. The *Times* proclaims that "users could bring their insight to the process of interpreting data and information and discovering new and innovative ways of presenting them. Just as readers' comments on articles and blogs enhance our journalism, these visualizations—and the sparks they generate—can take on new value in a social setting and become a catalyst for discussion."[63]

It sounds great in theory. But in practice, the output of these visualizations is less insightful: tag clouds of frequently used words in the Democratic and Republican national convention speeches, basic line graphs of infant mortality rates, and word trees of political party affiliation by religious tradition fill the pages of the Visualization Lab's community Web site.[64] Few visualizations have been rated by members, and even fewer have elicited comments. Users have the option to look at visualizations made by the community or visualizations from the editors of the *New York Times*, but the content of both sections looks identical. With a limited number of data sets available and the finite number of Many Eyes output formats, the "democratic" open data appears to offer little more than good publicity. The mere availability of data is not enough to qualify as good journalism.

To be fair, the *Times'* visualization system is limited; users can match one of twenty data sets to an output graph. They cannot manipulate the data outside the template, nor can they introduce new data to the existing data for comparison or correction. But even open data without such limitations often suffers the same synthetic failing. Creators of playable infographics should take care to heed the advice of Edward Tufte, who warns against needless, misleading, and deceptive graphics.[65] Thanks to the rising popularity of infographics online, Web sites like Flowing Data and the aptly named Chartporn.org spread visualizations as entertainment. A "cool" visualization with a strong graphic design will just as readily spread as one that illuminates something fascinating and important about the data.

Playable infographics won't solve the problems of data synthesis, but they can contribute to a solution. By addressing a set of information as a context for specific types of actions and goals in the context of broader exploration, data can gain both context and relevance. Infographic games like *Budget Hero* offer both freedom and perspective. It is not only the source of the data that is important, but also why the output format was chosen, what tools were used to produce it, how they might affect the outcome, and what service the resulting artifact claims to provide for citizens.

We might conclude that infographic games help players distinguish data from information. Data describe raw sensor readings, direct observations, and collected metrics. Information adds context and interpretation to the data, imbuing them with meaning. Creating an infographic is no longer just a matter of making data visual. Instead, it involves the creation of a tool to help understand that visual data by synthesizing it through play.

4   Documentary

Peering through the scope of a rifle, you focus on a turn in the road. You look up from the scope and out the window to the street six floors below. A vehicle turns the corner, moving toward you. The window of opportunity is small, so you must act more quickly than in most videogames. Police motorcycles pass by, followed by a few cars, and then you see your target: John Fitzgerald Kennedy. After you've squeezed the trigger a few times, the heart-thumping authenticity of the situation turns to cold statistics: a breakdown of the projectile ballistics of your shots, where each bullet struck, and what damage it caused (figure 4.1). You've just attempted to recreate Lee Harvey Oswald's assassination of the president on November 22, 1963. The game is called *JFK Reloaded*, and its creators offered a reward of up to $100,000 to the player who most closely matched the ballistic data in the Warren Commission reports.[1] Traffic Games hoped to put to rest the many conspiracy theories about JFK's murder by inviting thousands of players to accurately re-create the single gunman account of the assassination.

Five years later, at the 2009 Games for Change Festival in New York City, University of Southern California professor Tracy Fullerton announced her plans to re-create Thoreau's *Walden* as a game. A year into the design process, Fullerton described her intention to translate events from Thoreau's story into plot points within the game, while crafting game mechanics that would force players to live by the rules of his personal experiment. She hopes to avoid reward-based gameplay or "simulated material gain," which would be antithetical to Thoreau's goals when he went to live away from society.[2] The structure provided by the historical events and mechanics might re-create and interrogate Thoreau's philosophy of simple living.

On the surface, *Walden* and *JFK Reloaded* might seem to have little in common. But the games share similar goals: they seek to record an event, its space, and its stakeholders for posterity. Following their cinematic

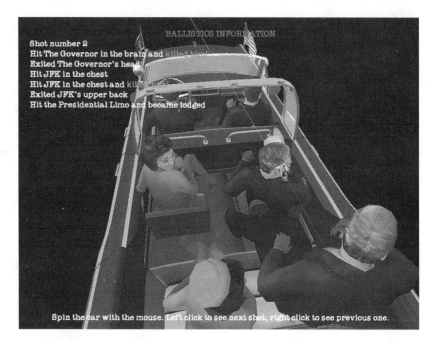

Figure 4.1

The scoring screen of *JFK Reloaded* is used to compare ballistics data in an investigative simulation of the event. Controversially, the game re-creates the assassination of John F. Kennedy from the perspective of the gunman.

counterparts, we might call them *documentary games*. In an early article on the form, Fullerton uses the genre as an umbrella term for commercial war games that feature fictional recreations of World War II battles, like *Medal of Honor*, as well as with shorter, independent games that stage historical events, like *JFK Reloaded*.[3] The notion suggests a question: can videogames represent actuality in the way that cinema, photography, and nonfiction writing have done?

In videogames, "realism" has typically referred to the way something looks. Continuous advances in real-time 3D graphics since the mid-1980s have made it possible to create immense, verisimilitudinous environments. Such capabilities are impressive, but documentary does not necessarily rely on visual fidelity to capture the truth of a situation or event. Alexander Galloway has suggested that videogames are also capable of *social realism*, a kind of realism orthogonal to visual realisticness.[4] Social realism finds its roots in photography and film, where it refers to artistic attempts to render the gritty reality of lived experience—not just the gloss of perfection found in Hollywood blockbusters or lifestyle magazine spreads, but also the trials and failures of hardship.

Social realism has often entailed social critique, a feature documentary photographers and photojournalists have long embraced.[5] Consider, for example, Dorothea Lange's famous images of the Depression, or any of the many journalistic photographs awarded the Pulitzer Prize since the inception of a photography category in 1942. Though it is still uncommon, Galloway suggests a few examples of social realism in games, including the rioting game *State of Emergency*. He insists that this form of realism in games comes not from presenting realistic environments or stories, but from affording realistic player action.[6]

Along with theater, documentary is one of the two origins of cinema. Edison's first Kinetoscope films, relegated to peeping booths in the turn-of-the-century version of the arcade, were little more than recordings of staged dancing and pantomime. Because Edison's camera was hefty, it was confined to his New Jersey studio. When the father of Auguste and Louis Lumière first viewed an Edison film, he returned to his factory in Lyon, France, and demanded that his sons conceive of some way to "get the image out of the box."[7] The result was the Cinématographe, a combination camera, projector, and printer that could be picked up and carried by a single operator. The Lumière brothers recorded snippets of French daily life; films of farmers, dockhands, soldiers, and factory workers recorded the mundane lived realities of the working class. Eventually the brothers hired operators to take the camera abroad, allowing international audiences to enjoy moving images of faraway lands such as Egypt and Vietnam.

Unlike cinema, videogames arose from the histories of recreational play and computing. Perhaps these different media genealogies explain why social realism has taken so long to gain a foothold in games. As media coexist more closely, they bleed into one another. Joost Raessens suggests that the early development of documentary games has relied partly on naïve popular conceptions of documentary film as an "objective" depiction of reality.[8] And scholars at the University of Abertay Dundee argue that the form has emerged from a larger media environment of interactive television documentaries and "quick-time event" games such as the laser-disc coin-op *Dragon's Lair*.[9]

Playable Realities

Games enjoy good company among media that discovered social realism when they were already mature, among them literature and journalism.

The muckraking of the Gilded Age is perhaps best exemplified by author/ journalist Upton Sinclair's 1906 novel *The Jungle*, which offers an extended, fictionalized editorial on labor conditions among the immigrant working class.[10] Muckraking of this kind developed into journalistic watchdogging, a practice best known by the name *investigative reporting*.[11] Investigative reporting has earned a bad reputation in recent decades, however. Local television news is a prime culprit, offering stories of consumer protection, local business, and personal safety that frequently devolve into sensationalistic fear-mongering. The same has taken place in film documentary, the cinema verité documentaries of the 1970s having given way to the flagrantly manipulative work of Michael Moore. Perhaps journalists and game designers can root out the popular mistrust of investigative reportage and documentary by reinventing it in videogame form.

Here we consider three ways that videogames can engage actuality: through explorable *spatial reality*, which makes the environments of events navigable; through experiential *operational reality* that re-creates the events themselves; and through *procedural reality*, or interactions with the behaviors that drive the systems in which particular events take place.

Spatial Reality

Four decades before *Schindler's List* recaptured the horrors of life in Nazi concentration camps, Alain Resnais's famous documentary *Night and Fog* took viewers through the halls of Auschwitz with a series of steady tracking shots.[12] Many had read about the immensity of the tragedy, but the camera's ability to slowly capture row upon row of bunks, furnaces, and housing blocks made its horror simultaneously immediate and incomprehensible. Space provides a context for actions and systems; its contours hold the memories of past events and the possibility of future occurrences. Although the cinema's camera has the ability to dissect a space, doing so requires rigorous planning through storyboarding, complex camera setups, and multiple takes. A documentary crew must transport gear to a site, make decisions about lighting and film stock, and edit footage together to recreate a space faithfully. These working realities are something that television news crews can relate to as well.

With the advent of real-time 3D game engines, spatial exploration has become an intrinsic feature of videogames. Long takes and depth of field— painstakingly chased-after ideals of André Bazin's cinematic theory of objective reality—are a native and mundane actuality for players, no matter the game.[13] Even a relatively early 3D game like *Doom* offers a freedom of movement far greater than the Steadicam.[14] Later games allowed players

Figure 4.2
The Berlin Wall, fashioned using the Source engine game modification tool *Garry's Mod*, re-creates the physical structure and atmosphere of the cold war edifice. Despite its visual realism, the player's actions and movement in the space are severely restricted.

to pan and tilt at their own volition, uprooting the camera from its tracks to let it bob and weave through space.

Documentary games allow players to experience spaces of conflict that are difficult to engage with in the abstract. A basic example shows how the experience of space itself can be clarifying. *Berlin Wall* re-creates a stretch of the infamous wall that divided East and West Berlin, including watchtowers, Checkpoint Charlie, the Death Strip, and an underground network of refugee tunnels (figure 4.2).[15] Players are encouraged to experiment crossing from East to West by jumping the wall, going through the checkpoint, or using underground tunnels, although the game does not accurately convey the danger of the crossing. *Berlin Wall* features the location's architecture, but it doesn't educate the player about the political purpose these civic projects served for the Soviet government. Likewise, it's detailed with the results of political resistance (a small section of graffiti on the Wall, for example), but it does not allow the player to enact such guerrilla maneuvers and experience the consequences. Instead, *Berlin Wall* is a minimally playable 3D recreation of a space that attempts to preserve a sense of what it would have been like to be present in a Berlin now decades gone.

Spatial documentary games extend cinematic *mise-en-scène*, or "things on the stage." All game development involves some aspect of mise-en-scène, but it is normally relegated to a secondary aspect of design, subordinate to the more central concerns of playability and exploration.[16] In some genres, such as adventure games that rely heavily on object interaction for the discovery of secrets, mise-en-scène serves a central role. In a text adventure, a room description might mention curtains, which would prompt players to experiment with commands such as "pull curtain" to reveal a hidden passageway. In graphical adventure games such as the *King's Quest* series, mise-en-scène becomes visually important because the player is often confronted with a room full of objects, some small or otherwise occluded, that might need to be moved or used. Of course, even the most sophisticated 3D engines cannot render a virtual scene in its entirety, down to every last detail. Choices must be made about which features are to be excluded, but how does a designer decide?

Imagine that you are modeling a college campus. Is it enough for the building facades to be the right color, or is the texture more important? Is the covered roof on a bus stop important, or just its benches? Should the space include pathways that pedestrians create by walking and matting down the grass, or just the concrete sidewalks? And how do you represent the people that typically populate such a space?

In his discussions of the development of news infographics, Alberto Cairo argues that a level of abstraction is necessary to preserve journalistic integrity when information is missing.[17] Abstraction offers a method for both transparency and verification, preventing the work from claiming more than its creator knows. But abstraction offers more than an ethics check; it is also a design tool. Abstraction allows a work to focus attention on one aspect of an experience over another. From the perspective of social realism, it is less important to fill a space with photorealistic textures and high-polygon 3D models than it is to fill a less technologically advanced space with meaningful, naturally arranged objects.

Operational Reality

Berlin Wall creates a spatial situation for the player, one that offers navigational flexibility but relatively limited interaction. *JFK Reloaded* provides a similar environment, but it also offers guided activity for the player. By allowing the player to enact the role of a specific figure during an actual historical moment, these games avoid accusations of bias or fiction. It creates an operational reality, one that allows players to *enact* specific events, rather than explore them haphazardly.

The documentary game *9-11 Survivor* abstracts considerable architectural detail from its re-creation of an emotionally charged space.[18] The game puts players in the shoes of someone trapped on a high floor of the World Trade Center during the September 11 terrorist attacks. Players can attempt to find an open stairwell, provided no fallen debris has blocked it, and run down dozens of flights to the bottom of the building, or they can do what many others did when faced with the same reality: jump.

News footage that fateful day captured the small specks that were office workers leaping from the towers as they collapsed. The sight was horrifying, comprehensible only through intellectualization. One could *imagine* the intense heat of jet fuel fires inspiring egress into the cool air, even as it meant certain death. But one couldn't really fathom what it would feel like to be faced with the decision to accept death and choose this method. At the time of its release, *9-11 Survivor* was denounced by many as callous and exploitative, though its motive was to commemorate the memories of those lost by sharing the operational reality of their unrepeatable experience. In this respect, the game was a success, allowing the public to come one step closer to understanding what friends, loved ones, and strangers had felt in their last moments.

9-11 Survivor invites reflection about a traumatic event for the sake of memory rather than decision making. But traditionally, documentary has also invited viewers to examine an issue in order to form an opinion. Kuma Reality Games made such an effort to interrogate a contested historical record in one of the episodes of their news-inspired war game, *Kuma\War*.[19]

John Kerry's 2004 presidential bid was marred by controversy surrounding the circumstances under which he was awarded the Silver Star during his service in Vietnam. As the official record would indicate, Kerry had strategically piloted a swift boat on the Cua Lon River toward a shore occupied by hostiles, thus reducing the impact of Viet Cong gunfire by narrowing the target and protecting the vessel's crew with the hull of the ship. But many veterans claimed that Kerry's strategic prowess had been greatly exaggerated by Naval command. The *Kuma\War* simulation offers a playable recreation of the mission, suggesting that players could "decide for themselves" whether Kerry deserved his commendation.

As the mission begins, the player controls Kerry but has the ability to switch between three other unnamed "swifties" (see figure 4.3). The user interface features a few subtitles that set the exact time and place of the mission, as well as a simple display consisting of a mini-map, ammo, and health information. The foliage surrounding the river implies an expansive

Figure 4.3
Behold Senator John Kerry's face, texture mapped onto a 3D model. *Kuma\War's*
John Kerry's Silver Star puts the player in the 2004 presidential candidate's infamous
Vietnam swift boat.

jungle, but the playable level deliberately constrains player action by
means of invisible boundaries. The game feeds the player a series of objectives, just as a commercial tactical shooter might.

The first objective is to patrol the river on watch, examining the locals
while looking for Viet Cong. If the player shoots an innocent fisherman,
the game ends abruptly—a design decision that reinforces the player's
moral alignment with the game character.[20] In the game, as in the actual
guerilla conflict, it is often hard to tell the difference between innocents
and the Viet Cong, no matter how noble a soldier's intent. Thus, the game
expresses the difficulty of making decisions about the terrain and people
in a guerilla conflict.

Continuing down the river, the player runs into trouble on one of the
banks and has to shoot enemies from the mounted turret on the swift boat.
After killing a few hostiles, the objective display orders a beach landing.
Steering the swift boat toward the shore, the game prompts the player to
exit the boat and engage hostiles on the ground. Once the player and crew
have eliminated the Viet Cong, a new objective requires the destruction
of a weapon cache. Finding a rocket propelled grenade launcher on the
body of a downed hostile, the player blows up covered munitions boxes.

In the mission's final objective, the player must return to U.S.-controlled docks at the river's start without suffering any casualties.

This sequence of events precisely follows Kerry's own account of the mission. Instead of letting players manipulate the space to explore its dynamics or figure things out for themselves, *Kuma\War* forces the player to experience the mission according to the official record. One might question Kuma's affirmation of neutrality ("the players can decide for themselves"), since the game appears to endorse openly Kerry's own account. At the very least, it doesn't present opposing accounts. Still, unlike a cinematic rendition, these documentaries make their spaces operational.

Procedural Reality

Documentary games collide with a problem of participation. Can something qualify as historical documentation if the player is able to modify the actual course of events as they are known to have occurred? The *Kuma\War Silver Star* mission addresses the problem by making the experience entirely linear: a progression down the river, a series of mandatory objectives, and a variety of failure states to enforce those mandates. However, linearity doesn't do justice to videogames' capacity to represent the behavior of complex systems. Linearity pushes a singular, official version of events that discounts other possible readings. But procedural documentary games use rules to model the *behaviors underlying a situation*, rather than merely telling stories of their effects.[21] It is procedural reality that holds the most promising future of documentary games.

Journalistic interest in the processes underlying news events developed slowly. In the 1960s and '70s, two journalistic traditions—literary storytelling and muckraking—coalesced. Both traditions eschew objectivity in favor of ideals native to each form: writing a good story and uncovering the truth, respectively. Popular magazines like *Rolling Stone* added depth and personality to popular culture, while hard-boiled scrutiny like that of Seymour Hersh, Bob Woodward, and Carl Bernstein put investigative reporting at the forefront of the American popular imagination.[22] In 1967, *Newsday* established a team of dedicated investigative reporters whose sole job was to produce three stories a year, each of which ran over five days.[23] The *Boston Globe* and *New York Times* also formed investigative teams in the latter part of the decade to satisfy the journalist's watchdog role.

Most commonly, investigative journalism weaves vivid stories of corruption, abuse, incompetence, or an institution's failure to serve the public, while ignoring the Kafkaesque processes of the system that gave rise to these problems. The Pulitzer Prize for investigative reporting has been awarded since 1953, and its recipients—hard-boiled journalists like Gene Goltz of the *Houston Post*, who won the prize in 1965 for an exposé of government corruption in Pasadena, Texas—have enjoyed well-deserved praise for probing malfeasance and revealing wrongdoing.[24] Yet, even though stories like Goltz's overflow with detailed and irrefutable facts, they don't necessarily explain how a problem came to be, how it perpetuates in the structure of a social system, and what effects it has on the surrounding community beyond a few examples. Investigative reporting requires journalists to uncover the seedy underbellies of situations to derive their behavior, but the result of such reporting usually involves descriptions of *specific* injustices rather than discussions of the *general* processes that underwrite the injustices themselves.

In 2008, one of the two Pulitzers for investigative reporting was awarded to the authors of a series of *Chicago Tribune* articles on the faulty government regulation of toys, car seats, and cribs. Dubbed "Hidden Hazards," the stories are ghastly and sad, chronicling the avoidable deaths of infants at the hands of faulty goods. In one piece, Maurice Possley details the underlying structural causes of the neglect, attributing them to undermanned staffs at the regulatory agencies.[25] These effects are hard to grasp. When Possley explains that the Consumer Product Safety Commission had recalled over a million cribs in response to the *Tribune*'s investigation, readers and policymakers alike might consider the loop closed. But questions remain: how and why are government agencies understaffed? Is staffing really the problem, or is apathy and inaction the inevitable result of bureaucracy? Is there any reason to believe that a similar problem won't arise soon enough in another agency or corporation operating under similar logics?

A journalist's story is fashioned not only from facts, but also from vibrant examples that stir emotion. Consider the lede for Possley's article: "Photographs taken of Liam Johns' crib by the Sacramento County Coroner's Office clearly show where it came apart." Emotional hooks like this may absorb, but they do not satisfy. No one would deny that the death of Liam Johns was both tragic and needless. It is easy to assign blame and call for reform, but change is complex. It is institutional. It cannot be interviewed one on one or filmed, head down, exiting a county court. A news article can describe a poignant story that exemplifies the problem, but it cannot handle the multitude of possible issues at stake.

Games excel at handling multitudes. The rules and parameters of game systems can be used to dramatically reveal information, to make concepts tangible, and to produce alternative scenarios for further exploration or comparison. Games thus offer a compelling form for the issues approached by investigative journalism, if those issues are unpacked into the behaviors of a simulation. The player of a procedural documentary game would come to understand not only the facts and outcomes of a story but also the underlying systems that caused it to come to pass.

The practice of *doing* investigative reporting is procedural, but creating procedural investigations is simultaneously familiar and unfamiliar. On the one hand, everything that goes into a good filmic or written investigation also applies to a good ludic one: collecting evidence, performing interviews, examining situations from multiple perspectives, and looking for relevant archive material. Good investigative journalism not only asks not only the "five Ws"—who, what, when, where, and why—but also the procedural question: "how." Good reporting should elucidate how a situation arose, not just uncover the actors, events, and consequences of that situation.

On the other hand, a procedural documentary does not weave a path through evidence like a film or an article does, telling a story the viewer or reader grasps through empathy with its characters. Instead, a videogame models the behavior and dynamics of a situation, treating character, setting, and events as side effects of an overall logic.

Consider Eric Schlosser's 2001 book *Fast Food Nation: What the All-American Meal Is Doing to the World*, an example of what John Pilger calls "investigative journalism that changed the world."[26] Schlosser's tale features characters, both human and corporate, who perform specific acts that the author narrates as a story. As all good stories do, the book begins with a human character, in this case Carl's Jr. founder Carl Karcher. Schlosser tells the riveting tale of the restaurant chain's humble roots, early success, and inevitable excess. But, as Pilger summarizes, the book is not a story of men or companies; it is an account of "how industrial food production has transformed and endangered not only our diet, but our environment, economy and culture, and even our basic human rights."[27]

Explanations of *how something works* can be described in written or visual argument, by mustering explanations and examples. This is precisely what Schlosser does in *Fast Food Nation*, and most documentaries and investigative reports do the same. But *models* can also address how things work, not through explanation or example, but by showing the operation of a source system directly. If writing and film best realize their potential when they tell stories, then computers realize theirs when they model behavior, when they depict worldly processes through computation.[28]

Think of a simulation game like *SimCity*. It dispenses with stories about particular citizens, bureaucrats, or corporations in favor of a rendition of city management. Even though it simplifies urban planning considerably, the game addresses the social and political factors that encourage or discourage growth and prosperity. A documentary film set in *SimCity* might tell the story of how a small town neighborhood became a slum as new zoning policies encouraged the development of industry nearby. It might depict the life of one or more families in the neighborhood over time, showing how a once idyllic borough became a crime- and pollution-ridden backwater. It may well be moving and upsetting. But such a film would cover matters of bureaucracy and planning primarily to advance human interest. *SimCity*, as a game, works exactly in reverse: it abstracts specific human elements in favor of urban dynamics themselves.

Fast Food Nation begins with and returns to individuals by necessity: storytelling requires characterization. Indeed, in the 2006 film adaptation that fictionalized Schlosser's account of the fast-food industry, the specific experiences of various characters (illegal immigrant workers, cattle ranchers, corporate executives) rule the roost. But if the book and the film intended to cover the *processes and consequences* of industrial food production, then another approach might do a better job: putting the business, social, and political dynamics of industrialized food at the forefront, rather than in the subtext of the work.

We can find the start of such a design in *Freedom Fighter '56!* (*FF56*), a game about of the Hungarian Revolution of 1956. Through the experiences of three fictionalized "freedom fighters," players learn the dynamics of the revolt against the Stalinist government of Hungary, which killed 2,500 Hungarians and inspired another 200,000 to flee the country.[29]

At first, the game seems like a digital adaptation of a graphic novel. It borrows that form's visual and narrative conventions, with hand-painted frames and inset text, narrated by voice actors in English or Magyar. As the game begins on October 22, 1956, an introductory scene sets the stage historically, covering the descent of Hungary into Stalinism after World War II and the resulting oppression by the secret police (Államvédelmi Hatóság, or ÁVH), state censorship, and religious persecution. The player is cast as a young student present at the protests that started the revolution. Clickable objects in the scenes reveal additional information, and the game also allows the player to collect items for later use (e.g., the student manifesto, a Hungarian flag armband).

The game casts events as activities with specific behavior and consequences, not just as factual statements of historical progression. For example, when players begin the student march to Parliament on October 23, they can traverse the city by any means they choose, rather than via a prescribed route. Historical events do make an appearance, including the toppling of the statue of Stalin near Városliget park, the detention of students entering the Radio Budapest building to broadcast their demands, the ÁVH flash point that erupted soon after, and the general worker's strike that followed. But as these events unfold, the player must build a larger faction by persuading new participants to join the cause. To do so, the player must make a convincing argument using the inventory items previously collected as "premises." Once the player constructs an argument, the game shows the interlocutor's current alignment, the persuasive effect of the evidence mustered, and the resulting likelihood that the resulting argument will win him or her over (figure 4.4).

FF56 still bears traces of spatial and operational reality. The player moves around a simplified version of Budapest and carries out actions that

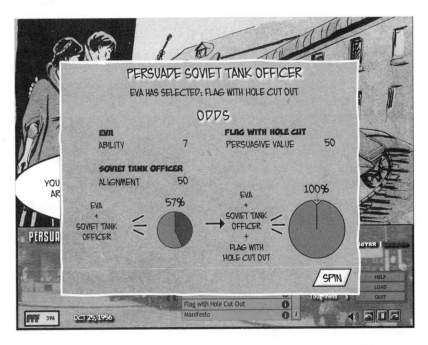

Figure 4.4
A player reasons with a tank driver in the Hungarian Revolution documentary game *Freedom Fighter '56* by showing a Hungarian flag with a hole cut in it (a symbol of a nation with its heart cut out). The move appeals to the tank officer's patriotism, and as a result the player's odds of persuading the driver increase to 100 percent.

a '56er might have done. But within this context, the player comes to understand the specific challenges of the resistance by experiencing their dynamics, rather than just by listening to their description or following along step by step. As they progress, players earn "Freedom Fighter Factor" points to show how well they have mastered the *behavior* of a freedom fighter, rather than how well their results match the outcomes of the revolution itself. Still, *FF56* does not dip as deeply as it could into the procedural register of the Hungarian Revolution. Though the dynamics of the revolution itself appear in the game, the politics of Soviet-controlled Budapest remain in the background.

Another documentary game about geopolitical conflict does the reverse. *PeaceMaker* is a game about the contemporary Israeli–Palestinian conflict created by independent developer ImpactGames. The player can take the role of either the Israeli prime minister or the president of the Palestinian Authority. In either case, the goal is to bring peace to the Middle East by establishing a diplomatic resolution suitable to both parties. Here the game takes a strong position, as a two-state solution is the only one that the game affords.[30]

To succeed, the player must win over the support of both their home and neighboring publics by building infrastructure, amassing political support, and, when necessary, meeting the demands of the opposing leader. Meanwhile, random events like insurrections, attacks, and protests often throw a wrench in one's plans, requiring the player to attend to local protests or to respond to unexpected attacks before returning to negotiations.

Play is abstract. On each turn the player can take action in response to a local event or take a variety of other measures in the categories of security, politics, and construction. Each leader sees things differently. The Palestinian president, for example, has to satisfy the world community (or at least avoid offending it), while the Israeli prime minister only has to satisfy the local citizenry. Moreover, the Israelis have more resources and can execute more direct actions, including bulldozing settlements and launching missile strikes.

Even though *PeaceMaker* includes real images and video to illustrate in-game events, the game primarily characterizes the diplomatic process of the conflict and its possible resolution, rather than particular historical events that have occurred within it. By so doing, it offers a lesson about the dynamics of international politics in Middle East conflict. As designer and critic Ernest Adams explains,

PeaceMaker illustrates some of the hardest lessons of leadership of all: that tough decisions are not always popular; that what the public demand in the short run isn't necessarily the right answer in the long run; that responding with overwhelming force to punish every outrage produces nothing but more outrages. Knee-jerk reactions usually fail.[31]

In games like *PeaceMaker*, players do not ask, "What can I do next?" but instead, "How do the dynamics of this situation operate?" A procedural reality goes beyond the spaces or actions of an event, exploring the reality of a situation's behavior.

Human Interest

The promise of procedural documentary notwithstanding, games also have the ability to reconstruct personal emotional experiences rather than just describing them. Sometimes a newsworthy experience involves events and how they took place, as in the case of a timeline of the Mumbai terrorist attacks that occurred in late 2008.[32] But in other cases, experience means something much more abstract: the emotional sensation of an event—what it felt like to cower in fear for hours in a guest room at the Taj Hotel. A news story might become relevant only in the aftermath of an experience, whether it be tinged with joy, fear, desperation, or loss. Indeed, if citizens were able to experience the sensations of an experience through simulation rather than by description, perhaps they would better connect world events with the joys, fears, desperations, or losses in their own lives. *Human interest games*, we might call them.

All too often, the journalistic human interest story exudes cloying manipulation instead of earnest characterization. A personal touch should make a story human, rather than melodramatic. Perhaps surprisingly, home movies offer a better example of documentarian human interest than most lifestyle pieces. In 1959, Stan Brakhage shot *Window Water Baby Moving*, a film that documents his wife's first childbirth while conveying his own emotional experience of the event through editing and exposure effects. Brakhage uses a handheld camera and 8mm film stock, tools whose lo-fi aesthetic further personalizes his subject matter.

We can see traces of similar designs in the autobiographical games of Jason Rohrer, whose work reflects his own emotional experiences of certain events and processes in his life using a similar lo-fi, 8-bit visual style. Rohrer's *Gravitation* tells the sort of story one might hear on National Public Radio, a moral tale mixing sadness and joy before reaching a tiny revelation. A close friend of Rohrer's had fallen ill, lying "effectively brain dead" in a hospital bed while her son and Rohrer's family researched the affliction and the decision whether or not to pull life support.[33] His previous game *Passage* was at that time experiencing its first bits of popular attention, so he was stealing time away to reply to new fans and critics. The complexity of these tragedies and triumphs led him to reflect on his own passions as an artist, what he calls his "mania," and how his moods and creative cycles affected his family. With another child on the way, he realized that the particular dynamics of the three-person family formed by himself, his wife, and his son Mez would soon be lost to him.

Gravitation interprets these sensations through the challenge of abstract, difficult work, and its interplay with the inspiration that comes from family interaction. Players begin in a largely dark, cold game world with two characters on screen: the player and a child. Playing catch with the child, the player expands the view around the avatar, melting the snow, exposing flowers, and expanding the soundtrack to an uplifting crescendo. Once the player successfully bounces enough balls back and forth, the avatar's "mania" overtakes him in the form of a fiery crown, allowing the player to leap great distances through a tight vertical maze in order to collect stars. The stars fall down and turn into blocks on the ground, which the player can push into a furnace to further fuel the artistic mania and increase the score. But the more blocks the player accumulates at once, the harder it becomes to shove them into the furnace, and the less time one has to play with the child to revitalize (figure 4.5). Eventually, after a third or fourth search for stars, the player returns "home" to the boy, but finds only his bright red ball lying alone on the ground.

On radio, television, and in print, human interest stories lack synthesis. Recounting heart-wrenching facts through emotionally charged voices separates the story from its telling. *This American Life*, hosted by Ira Glass of Chicago Public Radio, manages to avoid most of these pitfalls. An episode at the end of the second season of the show's television incarnation offers lessons for human interest games.

In the episode, Glass weaves together the lives of seven men named John Smith throughout various stages of life. He compares their childhoods, their marriages, and their experiences with raising children. Montage is necessary here, as it would be impossible to track the life of one John Smith in its entirety. Part of the show covers the various Johns' experiences with videogames. One, age eight, unwinds with PlayStation 2 after frolicking in the yard. Another, age twenty-three, lingers in an arcade after being fired from his job as a line cook. A third, in his thirties, toils

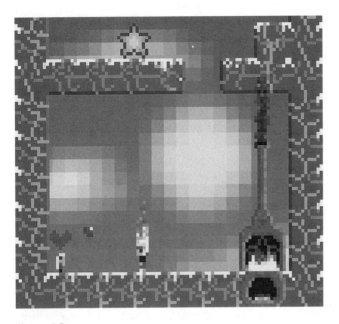

Figure 4.5
Players of Jason Rohrer's *Gravitation* struggle to balance inspiration, work, and family. Unconventional and abstract, it offers an example of a game of universal human interest.

through another day of work at Microsoft's Xbox division. Glass cuts to a story of the child at school, playing a game in which everyone creates a small city in the gym and takes on ordinary jobs, "the jobs no adults actually want." The boy describes what amounts to a predigital version of the popular videogame series *The Sims*.

Much of the emotional power of the John Smith episode comes from editing together common or incongruous moments in the lives of the numerous men. Unlike narration, games like *The Sims* are capable of tracing the life of a single John Smith in its entirety. They can manipulate space and time. Although *The Sims* is temporally and spatially linear, one can imagine another version in which the player can jump between different moments in an avatar's life. Games create rule-based interactions that can underwrite a succession of emotional moments that the player can experience directly, instead of simply identifying with them abstractly.

Such models of mental or emotional space have even been attempted in mainstream videogames, such as *Psychonauts* and *Dreamkiller*, both of which invite entry into the brains of psychiatric patients confronting their personal demons. An early example of a documentary game attempting the same mental exploration is Mary Flanagan's [domestic], a first-person shooter modification (or "mod") that allows the player to confront the artist's traumatic childhood memory of her home burning down while she was at church.[34] Working through a labyrinth of burning rooms, the walls of the virtual world of walls textured with photographic images and intro-spective text, the player attempts to extinguish the rising flames with a gun that shoots "coping mechanisms." Medieval Unreality, a collection of personal reflections on the infamous blood feuds of Albania, takes the same approach, but in a different context: a collaboration between game design-ers and the victims of the tragedy themselves.[35] Both games use a violent first-person shooter to create nonviolent, personal meditations on loss and reconciliation, through the use of metaphor, evocative imagery, and spatial exploration.

Controversy

Documentary games still struggle for legitimacy. Scholars like Fullerton and Raessans recount the challenges these games face in the popular imagi-nation: they are seen as exploitative cash-grabs with little regard for human decency and historiographical intent.[36] Some grumble in private or in the obscurity of blogs and Web forums, but others deride the genre in public. The most prominent might be late senator Ted Kennedy's one-word reac-tion to JFK Reloaded: "despicable."[37] Kennedy's objection boils down to an accusation of bad taste, but it also carries tinges of ignorance and closed-mindedness. Fullerton wonders, "Why don't we have the same reaction to a film like Oliver Stone's JFK, which goes so far as to use the much-derided filmic 'recreation?'"[38] Clearly, the general public is not yet ready for vid-eogames that reenact charged events and memories.

   The most controversial documentary game by far is Super Columbine Massacre RPG!, a painstakingly detailed reconstruction of the Columbine High School massacre created by young Colorado film student Danny Ledonne, who had been deeply, personally affected by the tragedy. The game re-created Eric Harris and Dylan Klebold's preparations that morning, their tactical takeover of the school, the murders and maimings they committed, their eventual suicide, and a fictional imagining of their descent into hell (figure 4.6). The game enjoyed considerable praise from prominent critics, as well as widespread scorn, including earning the number two spot on PC World's list of the ten worst games of all time.[39] Two years earlier, Gus Van Sant's film Elephant, a fictionalized account

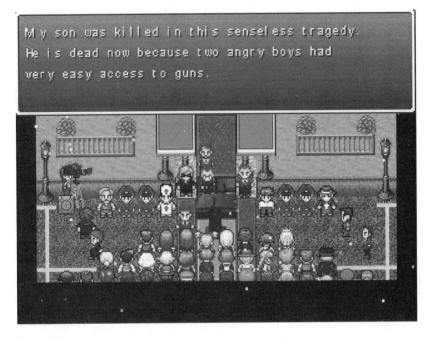

Figure 4.6
Taken from *Super Columbine Massacre RPG*, this re-creation of the tragedy's famous memorial service reaffirms the game's critical stance in its exploration of the shooting tragedy at Columbine High School.

of a school shooting inspired by Columbine, had won the Palme d'Or at the Cannes International Film Festival. Ledonne's game, by contrast, was ejected from the independent film and game festival Slamdance, despite earning a special commendation from the festival's film documentary jury.[40] Eventually, Ledonne showed his work at the AFI Fest in Los Angeles. It wasn't the videogame he premiered this second time, but a documentary film he had made about the game's controversy, entitled *Playing Columbine*.

JFK Reloaded and *Super Columbine Massacre RPG!* are independent games that endured mass-market controversy. In 2009, the first attempt at a mainstream documentary game was revealed to similar contentiousness. *Six Days in Fallujah* appears to be a first-person shooter much like any other. Almost a decade after the September 11 terrorist attacks, the Middle Eastern setting had become old hat in commercial games.[41] But, instead of hiding behind generic locations and scenarios in the interest of escapism and anonymity, the game explicitly casts itself as a playable documentary of the Second Battle of Fallujah—one of the bloodiest encounters of the Iraq War. Konami, a major videogame publisher, had initially funded the game's development and planned to distribute the title worldwide. But in the wake of widespread negative sentiment from politicians, military personnel, and the parents of soldiers killed during the operation, Konami pulled out of the project, casting doubt on whether it might eventually be released at all.[42]

Controversy is nothing new for videogames—it is a medium that has been accused of inspiring prurience, brutality, and sloth for decades. Industry publishers often milk controversy, taking a "no press is bad press" position. But *Six Days in Fallujah* was different: it elicited a negative political reaction, not just a negative social one.

Developer Atomic Games made missteps in their early publicity efforts. Their first error was rhetorical. Peter Tamte, the game's producer, foolishly proclaimed that the game would mix entertainment with education. Critics were suspicious of the appropriateness of turning a major battle into idle fun.[43] Military personnel and families of the deceased objected particularly, arguing that having "fun" during a bloodbath would disrespect the memories of men and women lost.[44] Of course, it might be entirely possible to create an engaging videogame about the Battle of Fallujah that would not produce enjoyment, but distress and reflection—a game more like *Black Hawk Down* than like *Independence Day*. But once the studio let the conversation turn toward "the entertainment problem," they had a hard time reframing the discussion.

After Konami pulled its publishing agreement, the public conversation about the game turned to realism and accuracy. On June 11, 2009, Fox News aired a panel with Tamte, the game's military advisor, and the mother of a fallen soldier from the Fallujah operation. Although the Fox pundits attempted to derail the conversation with inflammatory remarks about profiting at soldiers' expense, the discussion between the panelists focused on a different question: could a game realistically portray the horrors of war? What then would have to be done to ensure accuracy and yet engage players, making them want to keep playing the game?

As details emerged, two more problems arose for Atomic Games. First, the game was reported to implement a common first-person shooter mechanic: a refilling health bar.[45] After taking damage in the game, a player can withdraw from the line of fire for a short time in order to fully heal. Even the military personnel supportive of the game's production were concerned that an unrealistic health bar would fail to convey the sense of real danger faced each day by soldiers.

Second, it was revealed that the game had been described as a "survival horror" game in marketing materials—a genre typically concerned with the slaughter of zombies, mutants, and other supernatural entities. Was the game meant to cast Iraqi civilians and insurgents as the undead or the inhuman, akin to stereotypical waves of mindless monsters? If so, it would surely offer a jingoistic view of Western involvement in complex foreign affairs.

In response, Tamte observed that a realistic portrayal of the battle must frighten the player, like a horror game might do. Soldiers in Fallujah had to comb city streets for insurgents, entering every building to root out strongholds. They would search numerous buildings futilely, but the occasional breach would reveal the barrel of a rifle. Tamte wanted to convey this reality with the game. Additional realism would come from fully destructible environments, a feature that would allow players to blow out walls selectively to reveal hiding insurgents. Finally, in an effort to make the game as fair as possible, Tamte revealed that Atomic Games consulted with a number of insurgents involved in the Battle of Fallujah. Though this knowledge would be necessary for a faithful account of the operation, it also instantly garnered accusations of "treason" from conservative pundits.[46] Accuracy turns out to be a double-edged sword.

Atomic Games was forced to lay off a significant part of its staff in order to move forward with its production schedule without a major publisher.[47] Supporters, and even some detractors, argued that the game ought to be completed, even if it didn't live up to the expectations of fairness, reality, and respect. As the prospects of the project reaching its full potential dwindled, another realization arose: it might be enough for the game to have been attempted and discussed, with or without a release. Although Fox's Gretchen Carlson dismissed the idea of a documentary game, the mother of a fallen soldier turned the conversation around when she expressed hope that the game, if made properly, might in fact honor her son's memory. Game developers might not yet have proven themselves as responsible commentators on public issues, but with cooperation between the gaming and nongaming publics, videogames may yet become documentarian.

5 Puzzles

Boot up *Scoop!*, a casual downloadable game by developer Red Mercury, and a familiar image appears onscreen: a crossword puzzle. It's a simple puzzle, and a colorful one, more like the kind one might see in a kids' activity book than in the Sunday *New York Times*. But even though the game looks like a crossword, it doesn't exactly play like one (see figure 5.1). It downloads headlines from the Internet and selects words from those headlines to form crossword answers. The headlines themselves become the clues, with the word that serves as the answer blanked out.

To play, the puzzler must guess the missing word. For example, a head-line clue like "Iran's embattled supreme leader: a test for ☐☐☐☐☐☐☐☐☐ Khameni" would take a correct response of "Ayatollah." *Scoop!* makes this process easier than it might be in a traditional crossword: instead of typing in the answer, the player clicks on one of the squares in a solution. Clicking reveals a choice of three letters, one of which the player selects. Points are awarded for correct answers. When the player completes a word, bonus letters explode and fill in hints in other words. *Scoop!* recalls the original connection between games and the news: puzzles, especially the crossword puzzle.

A complete chronicle of the crossword is better left to books devoted entirely to that project, but an overview is in order, if only to underscore the surprisingly long history of this familiar riddle.[1] The crossword is around a century old (the first was penned in 1913), but the tradition of riddles from which it derives extends back millennia.[2] A riddle is a state-ment with a double meaning, one that poses the challenge of discovering or deciphering its veiled message. Riddles have graced literature and legend form every age, from Odysseus and the Cyclops to the ancient Norse Eddur. The crossword is a descendent of verbal riddles like these, and it also owes a debt to the rebus (a message in which pictures take the place of parts of words) and the anagram (a word made from the rearranged letters of

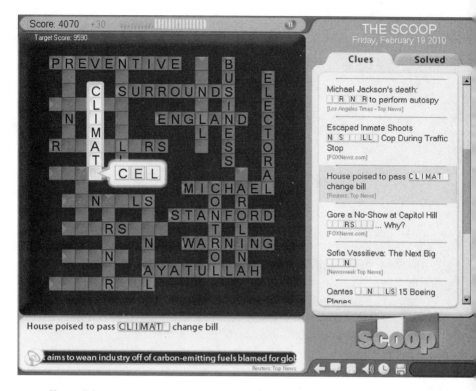

Figure 5.1
The hinting system in *Scoop!* helps players fill in the blanks while a news ticker drawn from the original source of the question streams the article in full to provide contextual information.

another word). But the most important precursors to the crossword are the word square and the acrostic.

The *word square* is an ancient structure with a symmetrical grid of letters radiating out from a central core. To decipher the square, a reader begins at the center and progresses outward, letter by letter, in a zig-zag pattern. Word squares seem to have been popular forms for puzzles, graffiti, and inscriptions since ancient Rome, and they were among the artifacts preserved at Pompeii. The *acrostic* is a composition in which certain letters in each horizontal line (usually the first and the last) form a word or phrase when read vertically. They were first used as divination aids in ancient Greece, and then reemerged as a popular form of love poem in the Renaissance.[3] In nineteenth-century Britain, the form's ability to carry a slightly hidden payload made it useful for delivering morality lessons.

Thanks in large part to the word square and acrostic, puzzles had become an addictive pastime of the Victorian era; even the Queen herself appeared to have been enamored of them.[4] At this time, puzzles were valued for mental relaxation, for intellectual challenge, and for engendering a spirit of collegiality (thanks to the need for collaboration to solve them).[5] Obsession with puzzles extended across the pond, too. By the turn of the century, Americans were crazy about puzzles. Reactions were mixed, with some celebrating the benefits of the "puzzle brain" and others lamenting the fact that "some men prefer solving puzzles to an evening at the theater or a thorough reading of the newspaper."[6]

It wouldn't be necessary to give up the one for the other. In 1913, Arthur Wynne, editor of the "fun" supplement of the New York Sunday *World*, set out to create something different for the Christmas issue. He constructed a diamond-shaped grid that eliminated the tedium of the word square, which required solving for the same words in both directions. Lines in each end of rows and columns were numbered, and Wynne composed clues for each pair. He called the puzzle *word-cross*, a name that was later transposed into *crossword*.[7]

The word-cross got a slow start, partly because of a lack of examples and partly because of the many errors Wynne's office had allowed into the puzzles. Wynne's solution to the former problem was prescient: he prompted his readers to make their own crosswords, arguing that "it is more difficult to make a cross-word than to solve one."[8] The result was a nearly endless supply of puzzles, had at very low cost: an early example of what Web 2.0 proponents call *user-generated content*.

Still, as the years passed, the paper began neglecting the crossword. By the 1920s, Wynne had recruited a friend of the family as a replacement, a young woman called Margaret Petherbridge Farrar. She remedied Wynne's other problem, eliminating typographical errors and other defects that had made some of the *World*'s puzzles unsolvable. Farrar also revised the description of clues to their current form, referring to locations by origin ("2 Down") rather than by start and endpoint ("2-5"). Further, the diamond shape was evolved into a square with its familiar conventions of interlocking letters.

By the mid-1920s the crossword craze had reached fever pitch. Farrar and colleagues published an anthology that sealed the puzzle's fate, allowing players to solve them anywhere (a lesson Will Shortz would not forget decades later when he popularized the Sudoku). Crosswords were everywhere. The *World* began running daily puzzles in the autumn of 1924 in response to demand. A Pittsburgh preacher presented his sermon in

Figure 5.2
The crossword is a form evolved from puzzles like the word square, acrostic, and word-cross, which rely on letters arranged on a grid. The form has been popular for nearly a century. This example depicts an inscription the Sator Square, a word square of a Latin palindrome. Photo by M. Disdero.

crossword form. Checkered fabrics became popular.[9] The puzzle had taken the world by storm.

A moral panic even set in, of the same kind that would later lament the "dangerous" popularity of comic books and videogames. In an accusation that would later reek of irony, the *New York Times* called the pursuit of crossword puzzles a "sinful waste."[10] Others had more measured reactions. Columbia University psychologists theorized that the crossword might serve as a type of intelligence test. Others touted the puzzle's benefits to vocabulary and esoteric information. The *London Times* echoed its stateside counterpart, running a story on the fad with the headline "An Enslaved America." Physicians noted a new kind of eyestrain caused by "compulsive puzzle solving," prefiguring clinical conditions like "Nintendo thumb" a century later.[11]

It wasn't until 1941 that the *New York Times* got into the game. World War II Army papers had included puzzles as a means to pass the time for bored soldiers, and the form's seriousness and popularity got a subsequent boost. Picking up on the untested connection between puzzles and current events, the *Times* hired Margaret Farrar in 1942 to edit news-based puzzles for the *Times*, reflecting "issues of the day."[12] For a time, the *Times* offered two puzzles, a news-oriented one and a more "whimsical" one.[13]

Farrar also made a few changes to the puzzle that gave it the final form we know today. She reduced the number of black squares to less than one-sixth of the total area, and she introduced a larger size for the Sunday edition. Under her watch, the puzzle shifted from an educational reference book hunt to a challenge of wits. As the *Times* printed in 1953, puzzles were to offer a "gentle brain jog" to accompany a morning cup of coffee or a quiet Sunday afternoon.[14]

Puzzles and Journalism

Anyone who enjoys even a casual relationship with crosswords will quickly realize that the videogame *Scoop!* bears only a perfunctory relationship to the crossword puzzle. The videogame does draw on the familiar form of interlocking clues. But the work required to solve the puzzles in *Scoop!* is quite different. Gone is the dictionary searching of the early word-cross, yet gone too is the hunt for the inner riddle of the contemporary crossword. *Scoop!* essentially gives the player the correct answers, letter by letter. Errors bear no real consequence: when the player chooses the wrong letter from the choice of three presented for each square, the selection is marked with an "X," although the game imposes no point deduction.

It is tempting to lament *Scoop!* as a watering-down—or perhaps even a violent disfigurement—of the crossword. But something else is going on, too. Just as the crossword drew its form from the acrostic and the word square, so the crossword itself is now becoming an inspiration for new forms of puzzles. These alterations are evolutionary, and they signal changes in the purposes puzzles serve. To understand this shift better, we might to return to a warning Margaret Petherbridge issued in the third printing of the original crossword compilation during the height of crossword fever of the mid-1920s:

If you want to do any more work the rest of the day, put down this book now. If you insist on going ahead, say good-bye to everything else. This is your problem: Do you wish to own a book which will delight and distract you, and perhaps shatter the serenity of your home, for at least one hundred hours?[15]

From the nineteenth century through the mid-twentieth, puzzles had primarily provided comfort and distraction. Despite early word puzzlers who advocated for their educational benefits, it was the *New York Times* that solidified the intellectual merits of the puzzle as its primary purpose, unseating comfort as a primary reason for puzzling. But even in the haughty intellectual environment of the *Times*, Farrar had the suspicion that the crossword might serve a purpose beyond, or even before enlightenment. Such is the reason she had dampened the paper's charge in the 1940s to elevate the puzzle to the rest of the publication's high journalistic standards, opting instead for softer though still intellectual fare.

A pattern emerges from Farrar's approach. Even if puzzles don't always provide serenity, they do offer logical consistency. The world is a messy place where solutions often elude one's grasp, but a crossword is always neat and tidy. Michelle Arnot even closes her history of the crossword with such a sentiment: "By presenting a solvable problem, the puzzle offers comfort to a chaotic world."[16] A sense of psychic comfort rises above matters of politics and current events in the minds of crossword constructors and players. In this respect, *Scoop!* may embody the experience of the crossword, even if it does not deliver its intellectual bounty.

Another factor separates the crossword and its progeny from the content of news and culture. Puzzle constructor Merle Reagle argues that Farrar established the "Sunday Morning" standard of decorum in the *Times* puzzle.[17] This rule of polite company may explain why political and controversial topics are typically excluded from crossword clues or content, even as the puzzle itself has been considered a high-culture intellectual pursuit. The community of crossword creators is, as expected, focused on wordplay and language.[18] Most discussion about the construction of puzzles focuses not on rhetoric or theme, but on the use of words. Crossword construction site Cruciverb.com, for example, covers issues like "theme entry length versus non-theme entry" or "obvious" clues versus "obtuse" or "too reliant on wordplay" clues. Crosswords focus on the form and meaning of words rather than their status or context. Here too, *Scoop!* follows in the tradition of the crossword surprisingly well, with its focus on the structure of words over their use.

Even if a puzzle-maker wanted to focus expressly on news content, the relatively slow construction process strains the crossword as a form for timely reporting (the typical puzzle takes more than a week to construct). Still, examples of such puzzles do exist. In the July 5, 2003, *New York Times* Opinion page, a large puzzle took the place of the usual daily columns. Entitled "Patriot Games," it is one of ten so-called *op-ed puzzles* created by

Puzzability, a firm made up of three veteran crossword and puzzle constructors: *Wall Street Journal* crossword editor Mike Shenk, former *Games* magazine managing editor Amy Goldstein, and puzzle constructor and illustrator
Robert Leighton.

The puzzles are divided into subpuzzles, each with its own theme—
usually a holiday or event, such as the United Nations Day Puzzle, "Country
Club."[19] The answers to these smaller puzzles are then used as entries in
the final puzzle, which answers a question posed by the writers at the start.
For example, in "Patriot Games," the question asked is: "our vote for the
best way to spend Fourth of July holiday weekend." The answer for this
puzzle is "Join a Party," which, as many word puzzles tend to be, is a pun
on the word "party" as both a festivity and a political group.[20] See figure
5.3 for more detail.

Whether working professionally or not, journalists strive to inform a
citizenry. Do creators like the Puzzability trio consider themselves to be
operating in such a capacity? According to Amy Goldstein, *Times* Op-Ed
editor David Shipley approached her and her colleagues with the idea of
putting puzzles on the page, apparently "as part of his plan to lighten and
broaden the page in general."[21] Goldstein explains that Shipley did consult
crossword editor Will Shortz about the ethical issues of separating editorial
from other aspects of the paper, and Shortz and Shipley agreed that the
former ought not to be involved with these new op-ed puzzles for ethical
reasons.

Despite their more newsworthy content, the construction of the puzzles
is more or less the same as it might be for an ordinary puzzle. Goldstein
explains:

We start by choosing the overall theme, which must be approved by Shipley. We
did a number of holiday themes at first—Independence Day, Christmas, Halloween,
New Year's—but have moved at Shipley's request to quirkier "holidays" or tie-ins,
like Tax Day and the recent Fashion Week. We do two puzzle sets a year, which
means we have done twelve total [as of late 2008].

We start at the end, with a theme-based riddle that has a clever, punny answer—
the "punchline" to the whole set of puzzles. This is often the hardest part of the
process. Once the riddle is approved by Shipley, we continue to work backward,
constructing the final puzzle that will give solvers the riddle's answer after they plug
in all the answers from the main puzzles on the page. We try to use as many theme-
related words in that final puzzle as possible—the words that will be answers to the
six main puzzles. (We have used six main puzzles plus the one final puzzle on the
page for quite some time now. We used to do more puzzles, but the 6+1 size has
worked best for the *Times*.)

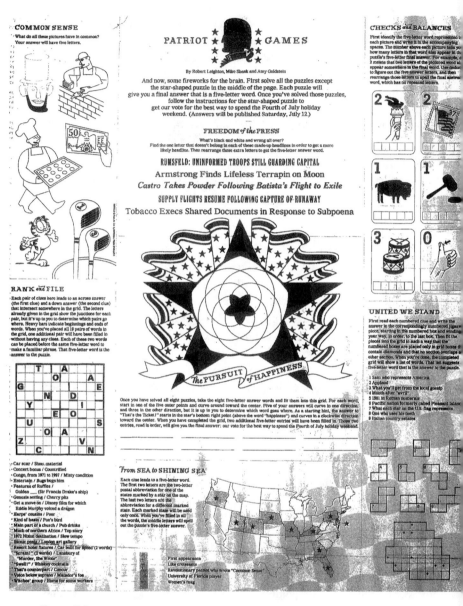

Figure 5.3

A family of "Patriot Games" puzzles occupies the majority of page A11 in the July 5, 2003, issue of the *New York Times*. Each puzzle offers part of the solution to a central puzzle, which takes the form of a star in the middle of the page.

Once we have a good list of answer words for the final puzzle, we construct the rest of the puzzles, each of which uses one of those answer words as its final answer. Each of the puzzles must have some relation to the page's theme, and we also make sure that there is a good variety of puzzle types—one or two picture puzzles; one light, funny text puzzle; a couple of variety grid puzzles.

The basic idea of these puzzle pages is, in a sense, adapted from live team-solving puzzle competitions, which similarly intertwine a variety of puzzles based on some theme. We are most familiar with the competitions that take place annually at the National Puzzlers' League convention and with similar competitions that used to take place at the annual crossword tournament that Will Shortz runs (now in Brooklyn, formerly in Stamford). There are other puzzle competitions, and there have been other puzzle sets like ours published in *Games* magazine over the years. The idea is certainly not original with us.

As the reference to team-solving puzzle competitions suggests, Goldstein and her colleagues believe that the influences for their puzzles are primarily derived from other puzzles, rather than from trends or techniques in editorial or reporting. "Freshness and originality" drive their construction, rather than more traditional journalistic values. Goldstein clarifies that she sees puzzles as "strictly entertainment, and light entertainment at that. They are meant to be fun for anyone who enjoys solving puzzles, and alienating any solver serves no purpose." When matters engage the news, as they will do unavoidably in the case of puzzles of this sort, any connection to positions, events, and outcomes are strictly matters of factual convenience. Goldstein explains:

When it comes to the use of a politician's name, say, we are only interested in whether that person is well-enough known for the name to be recognized by the average solver. We might avoid extreme examples, like Hitler, as being distasteful, but beyond that, our interest is more in the wordplay potential of the names. We recently ran a Common Knowledge puzzle on our website that played off the fact that Sarah Palin's children all have names that are essentially words with other meanings. This was by no means a political endorsement, nor would any solver take it as one.

These "Op-Ed Puzzles" are so named not because they carry an opinion, like the editorial games discussed in chapter 2, but because they appear on the Op-Ed page. Goldstein is clear about her role, which is that of a puzzle creator, not that of a newsperson or a pundit. Interestingly, the paper itself seems to have a similar opinion. Goldstein notes that her puzzles are "reviewed very carefully by the *Times* Op-Ed page staff," but that their comments are always limited to "small matters of copyediting style." In light of the journalistic timidity of crossword authors, we might reconsider the editorial disconnectedness of *Scoop!*. By drawing only from the head-lines, it positions itself as a method of disseminating facts, not of synthe-sizing information.

A more journalistically engaged puzzle is *Crickler*, another crossword-derived digital puzzle game named for its creators, Michael and Barbara Crick. *Crickler* puzzles retain the verbal clues and one-word responses of crosswords, but they explode the layout of the puzzle into a list rather than a grid. When players type an answer, letters from one response automati-cally fill certain cells in other responses down the page, mimicking the way a crossword's answers provide clues for orthogonal solutions. The Cricks explain why this arrangement makes for a better puzzle:

Traditional crossword puzzles are incredibly successful but they have several serious drawbacks: (1) They are difficult to construct, (2) Most words are short and often silly—chosen only because they fit, (3) Matching clues to numbers is a distraction, and (4) A given puzzle is usually either too easy or too hard. Cricklers solve all of these problems while retaining the essence and feel of a traditional crossword puzzle.[22]

As the Cricks suggest, one of their puzzle's benefits is its decoupling of clues from puzzle arrangement. This feature allows *Cricklers* to be more easily and more meaningfully themed than other word puzzles. The Cricks also rightly underscore the fact that this improvement would be difficult to accomplish without computational assistance. (As it turns out, computa-tion and puzzles are in Michael Crick's blood. In addition to having built portions of the Microsoft Windows operating system in the 1980s, he is the son of another great puzzle solver, Nobel Laureate Francis Crick, who codiscovered the double-helix structure of DNA.[23])

Among the *Crickler* variants is a "newspuzzle" that draws its clues from the daily news. Unlike *Scoop!*, the *Crickler* newspuzzle requires some syn-thetic knowledge about the content of the news, rather than the simple guesswork of missing words in a headline (see figure 5.4). For example, the October 22, 2009 puzzle includes the following clue: "A court in Miami sentenced Colombian drug kingpin Diego Montoya to 45 years in prison following his guilty plea on trafficking, _____ and racketeering charges." The six-letter answer, "murder," isn't immediately obvious for players unfamiliar with the case.

Oddly, *Crickler* puzzles don't include links to relevant articles on the subject of their clues, even though the puzzles have been syndicated to a number of papers including the *Washington Post*.[24] Completing a puzzle requires players to seek out, read, and comprehend current coverage on a variety of topics, but the player must find the sources on his or her own.

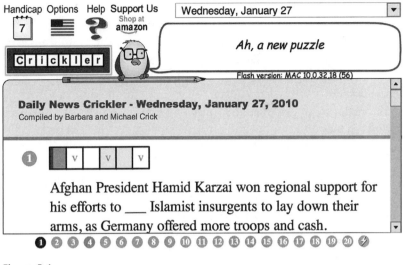

Figure 5.4
Crickler explodes the traditional crossword layout into a numbered list. The owl on top gives clues when clicked, and the bar below highlights player progress, the current clue, and its links to other solutions.

While syndication subscribers like the *Post* might gnash their teeth at the missed opportunity, it's possible that the game benefits by demanding the media literacy skills required to identify the topic, locate additional coverage, and evaluate that coverage for the response in question.

Scoop! and *Crickler* offer a broad perspective on the influence of the crossword. *Scoop!* borrows the crossword's form as a canvas for a low-impact casual game. Its use of the news is primarily a matter of convenience; headlines from RSS feeds offer an easy way to generate an infinite number of puzzles. *Scoop!* takes up the crossword's legacy as a calming exercise, one that can be enjoyed no matter how much of it a player completes. *Crickler* builds on the crossword as an intellectual institution, refining its connection to knowledge and language by adjusting its form to exclude throwaway filler clues. Together, these two digital newsgames suggest that a variety of new puzzle forms might still arise from the humble crossword.

The News Quiz

Though the crossword hasn't always carried deliberately journalistic content, another familiar, traditional form of the puzzle has: the quiz.[25]

The verbal meaning of *quiz*, "to question or interrogate," emerged in the mid-nineteenth century and gave rise to the most common use of the term today, a form of entertainment based on questions and answers. Quizzes seem to have evolved from written examinations, which were first used in collegiate exams in the late eighteenth century. The earliest such use appears in 1867, when William James proposes the quiz as a possible form of educational assessment: "Occasional review articles, etc., perhaps giving 'quizzes' in anatomy and physiology."[26]

In the UK, the United States, Canada, and India, the pub quiz (also known as bar trivia) is a popular way to attract customers on slower weeknights. Individuals or small teams typically compete in these quizzes, vying for mastery of subject matter ranging from general knowledge to current events to trivia about sports, the arts, and entertainment. Games like *Trivial Pursuit* use categorized quiz questions, wherein correct answers allow a player to progress around a game board. Other trivia games require different forms of knowledge, such as lateral thinking and riddle solving. Games like these have proven so popular that the terms *quiz* and *trivia* are often interchangeable, although the former still has a classroom connotation that the latter does not.

Indeed, sometimes the quiz offers a cultural reference familiar enough to provide a productive frame for information. The day before the 2008 U.S. presidential elections, the *New York Times* published a series of small op-ed pieces about the campaign.[27] The quiz format supports the light-hearted, short form of this sort of commentary. One piece reminisces about Obama's victory in Iowa.[28] Another calls attention to John McCain's Viagra gaffe.[29] But to organize and make coherent these news fragments that might otherwise be lost, the *Times* borrowed a familiar form: the *Trivial Pursuit* question card.

The feature presents each bit of commentary as an answer to a *Trivial Pursuit*-style question. For example, "What medicine brought the Straight Talk Express to an end?" becomes the lede for the Viagra piece (figure 5.5). Further embracing the *Trivial Pursuit* structure, each column is matched to the board game's famous categories. Howard Wolfson's editorial about the Clinton campaign's playlist is cast as an Entertainment question ("What did Celine Dion do to Hillary Clinton?"), while Paul Maslin's piece about the Iowa primary falls under Geography.[30]

By framing the op-eds as trivia, the feature turns commentary into a light-hearted guessing game, even if the categories don't match up perfectly. The "Art & Literature" piece, for example, points to how John Edwards's refusal to accept money from lobbyists ended up embarrassing

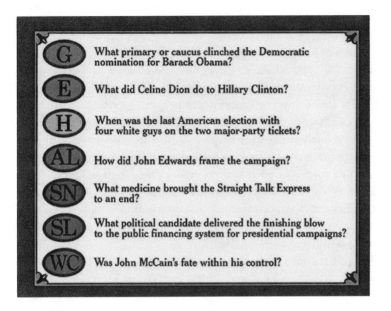

Figure 5.5
The question sheet for the *New York Times* 2008 campaign *Trivial Pursuit* series humorously places an editorial about John McCain fumbling a press question about Viagra under the "science and nature" category.

the Clinton campaign; an interesting observation, but certainly not one directly related to art or to literature. Still, the trivia game card format apologizes for an otherwise random collection of op-eds. And in one case, the quiz-like structure even helps emphasize the message. Michael Kinsley's piece, about the overwhelming whiteness of American politics, is presented as History: "When was the last American election with four white guys on the two major-party tickets?"[31] It turns out to be a trick question. The article suggests that an election with four white male candidates may never again take place, and the reader realizes that "last" in the quiz question means "final" and not "most recent." The history in the op-ed is one being *made*, not remembered.

Other, more familiar quizzes appear in the news regularly. Drawing on the traditions of the quiz show and the bar game, the *New York Times* runs a daily news quiz with scholastic aims: to teach younger readers how to understand and synthesize information in a newspaper article. The *New Yorker* also publishes a news quiz, usually focused on political or pop-cultural topics.[32] For this reason, its quizzes use humor in the style of written pieces in the magazine. Indeed, the publication situates these news quizzes in its humor section, a place where answers and references are otherwise scarce.

Quizzes of a different form appear in popular magazines, particularly in girls' and women's magazines. Of these, the "Cosmo Quiz" in *Cosmopolitan* has become eponymous with the periodical personality test. In this form of the quiz, a set of questions supposedly helps to locate the participant in some social category, such as "What Kind of Sexy Are You?"[33] The form of these tests is familiar not only because of their prevalence in print publications, but also because they bear a similarity to psychological aptitude and personality measures, such as those used to help high school students consider career choices. Unlike news quizzes, these tests offer personal exploration instead of education. Still, this type of quiz has also been used to help readers discover their political or economic leanings (*The Political Compass* is a popular such example).[34]

A hybrid of the above forms can be found on the popular political satire blog *Wonkette*. The quiz, published during the 2008 U.S. presidential election, takes up Rahm Emanuel as its subject.[35] *Wonkette*'s prevailing style is snark; the publication strains political issues through the sieves of satire and Internet humor. Here's how the quiz, entitled "Take Intern Juli's Advanced Emanuel Brothers Personality Test From Hell," begins:

If you're a former ballet dancer with a hot temper and nine and a half fingers, you're probably glad to see that this Rahm Emanuel fellow came along. If he can make it, so can you! Emanuel also has two brothers, Zeke and Ari, with whom you might have more in common than you might think. Take Wonkette's Official Emanuel Brother Diagnostic Personality Test and find out![36]

Snarky veneer aside, the quiz deploys several novel approaches to presenting political news.

First, it borrows the form of the identity quiz, blending the print-style Cosmo Quiz with the Facebook-style "Which [book, film, TV show, or videogame] character are you?" application. This format offers a farcical introduction to Rahm Emanuel, the then-new White House Chief of Staff, as one of three successful brothers in different fields. In so doing, the quiz compactly synthesizes a number of complex facts about the Emanuel bothers, by casting them as cultural icons as much as political operatives.

Second, even though they appear to be off-the-cuff one-liners, possible responses are backed up with source material. Unlike the pedagogical *New York Times* news quiz, the *Wonkette* sources don't offer straightforward answers. Instead, they make general suggestions about the life of each brother. This technique offers a surprising measure of editorial transparency, a virtue all too uncommon in satire.

Finally, *Wonkette*'s over-the-top style absolves it from providing straightforward, objective knowledge. Like viewers of *The Daily Show*, *Wonkette* readers visit the site for gossip and humor as much as for political news. Their expectations are thus different, giving the quiz room to be both funny and informative, a style well-nigh impossible in a traditional article.

As with most character quizzes, the punchline arrives with the answers, in which information blends with offense. Here's one possible result:

Mostly Bs: You're Rahm. You're sassy and petulant and disrespectful—but are grounded by your commitment to Judaism—and now you're working for the Obama White House. You're Aaron's Sorkin's wet dream. Congratulations?

Following the style of the questions, the results also mimic the Cosmo Quiz: they cast the reader as one of the three Emanuel brothers. But in so doing, the quiz exerts its real purpose: to teach readers about Rahm Emanuel, not only his past political work in Chicago and in the U.S. House of Representatives, but also his personality, his family, and his upbringing, information relevant to his life as a public official.

Irreverence in mind, Jellyvision's daily *DisOrDat* offers an example of a digital news quiz. Adapted from the popular 1990s CD-ROM quiz game *You Don't Know Jack*, *DisOrDat* fashions a trivia game around a daily news item, introducing the gamelike elements of a time limit, points, and leaderboards. Much of the personality of *DisOrDat* comes from the biting commentary by the quiz's host. Though the game focuses strictly on trivia only tangentially related the news, it also suggests ways news quizzes can be made more exciting.

Overall, the quiz is an incredibly simple type of game, but one that nevertheless can transmit factual information in a refreshing way. Still, most news quizzes do little more than dress up a list of facts. The *New York Times* quiz, for example, only asks readers to remember facts temporarily. That failing suggests an unexplored opportunity for the news quiz: to inspire players to perform more detailed analysis and synthesis of facts into information that might inform civic decisions.

Reading the Paper for the Puzzles

If Margaret Ferrar, Will Shortz, and Michelle Arnot are right that puzzles and quizzes serve a higher-order need than information, and if newspapers have been a major source of such puzzles—perhaps even the primary source—then a question suggests itself: how many newspaper subscribers buy the paper specifically for the puzzles?

Statistics on the matter are hard to come by, as the question is one that publishers might not want to ask. Rarely do newspapers conduct research asking their readership why they subscribe. But in a 2004 interview, Will Shortz mentioned survey results suggesting that 27 percent of newspaper readers play the crossword occasionally.[37] Shortz added that 1 percent of Americans named crossword-solving as "their favorite activity in the world." Another study by Richard Browne of the *London Times* estimated that 10 percent of their readership (or roughly 75,000 people) did the crossword regularly.[38] Over 7,000 of that group also take part in crossword competitions. Browne conjectures that these percentages (10 percent and 1 percent, respectively) are approximately the same for every major paper. Yet, Browne adds that British culture may possess a unique fervor for crossword puzzles: "many [British] people will take a paper for its crossword even it they don't like that paper's political stance." The endorsement of the crossword by Queens Victoria and Mary, along with the form's disengagement with politics, might partly explain Britain's affinity with the puzzle.

There's also reason to believe that many readers of more "serious" papers would be reluctant to admit that they buy them just for the puzzles. Internet anonymity helps: 54 percent of 3,500 surveyed at About.com's puzzle section buy a newspaper "all the time" just for the puzzles.[39] Archimedes-Lab.org claims a much higher number: only 13 percent of their readers answered "never" to the question "do you buy a newspaper just to do the puzzles?"[40]

People seem to open up about their puzzle practices when talking about their local papers. In 2001, Kristin Tillotson of the *Minneapolis Star Tribune* cited an industry estimate that 25 percent of readers considered the crossword a part of their daily routine.[41] This number didn't surprise Tillotson, as she remembered readers' violent reaction to the *Star Tribune*'s decision to syndicate the *New York Times* crossword instead of the *Los Angeles Times* version of the puzzle. One of the subscriber comments stands out: "This puzzle makes me feel very, very stupid. I am not stupid. I am a physician. . . . You have ruined my morning. You have ruined my ritual."[42]

A 2004 report in the *Bluefield Daily Telegraph* further confirms the importance of the puzzles for local paper subscribers, calling them "a bedrock element."[43] These findings are both encouraging and frightening, because they show that local newspapers—which are more vital to the average citizen than national papers—have more to lose if the population of puzzlers emigrates completely to free puzzles online.

Yet, if many people really are buying newspapers for the puzzles, why haven't puzzle books and Internet sites posed a serious threat? Perhaps it's because people want a crossword *today*, no matter the quality. It's a shared human experience, and one that can be delivered to the door like a pizza. Playing networked games over the Internet offers an implicitly shared experience, but it also robs it of its magic. A newspaper puzzle is unique and specific, in a way that a generic puzzle from a thick collection is not. This in mind, blogger Russell Beattie predicted crosswords would become "the prototypical mobile killer app."[44] Since mobile players are always playing somewhere local, Beattie points out that "fresh, local, and topical content is key."

The human touch also helps explain why Sudoku puzzles have not significantly cut into the player-base of crosswords. Crossword puzzles have to be created by people, even if some use computer authoring tools as an aid. Sudoku puzzles, by contrast, are much more easily generated by computer than by human hand. Part of Sudoku's appeal is its antithetical relationship to the local and temporal qualities of the crossword: numerical in nature, Sudoku transcends language boundaries.[45] So why did they only enjoy a brief flourish of popularity in papers before being quickly replaced by Internet editions and bookstore puzzle compendiums? One of the major reasons is the simplicity of programming a puzzle generator.[46] The ease of Sudoku generation has led to a glut of homogeneous puzzles. Different newspaper crosswords have different character, thanks to the personal touch of particular editors and creators. But any Sudoku book is as good as another, making collections and online puzzles convenient alternatives to undifferentiated puzzles that happen to be printed in newspapers.

Puzzles Are the New Classifieds

All of these factors suggest an important and surprising insight: puzzles might comprise a much larger part of the business of news than newspaper publishers have ever realized. And if it's true that the local and topical qualities of crossword puzzles are their greatest strengths, then there's something additionally special about puzzles shared across the breakfast tables of a community. Moreover, the properties of random access, physical size, and rapid scanning that the print newspaper affords might lead print puzzlers to encounter more articles on more topics than they are likely to encounter reading online. After all, one has to flip through the paper to get to the puzzle page. Interestingly, *Scoop!* and *Crickler* offer precisely this randomization of content, scraping news from syndication and encouraging players to discover what's in the headlines that day.

The unexpected centrality of puzzles suggests a further lesson for news publishers: the news business has ceded the market for daily puzzling to videogames, particularly online, downloadable, and mobile casual games. Descended from tabletop puzzles like the Rubik's Cube and videogames like *Tetris*, the name *casual games* describes simple titles intended for a mass market. Today, entire companies are devoted to the genre, including commercial publishers like PopCap Games, Web portals like Newgrounds.com, and newer social network–oriented tech startups like Kongregate.com and Zynga. According to the International Game Developers Association, the market for casual games weighed in at $2.25 billion in 2007, and grows 20 percent annually;[47] 25 percent of Internet users play casual games, amounting to 200 million users. Mobile phone marketplaces like Apple's App Store, the Blackberry AppWorld, and the Android Market have appeared since this report was issued, and they have underwritten significant additional growth in this sector (2009 iTunes App Store game revenues totaled $500 million alone).[48] Social gaming powerhouse Zynga, which publishes Facebook games exclusively, is reported to have brought in over $200 million in revenue in 2009 alone.[49] According to analysts, the social gaming sector may account for over $1.5 billion in 2010 revenue, with annual growth of up to 40% projected for the coming years. Even if mobile and social game sales were to cannibalize half of casual games' revenues, the total market still exceeds $3 billion.

Hindsight is 20/20, but the news business hasn't even bothered to ask itself if the casual games market represents a missed revenue opportunity akin to the lost classifieds business of eBay and Craigslist. Games are probably seen as trifles, and the nation's publishers would surely not be alone in assuming that dollars spent advertising stuff for sale far eclipses that of little puzzles. The numbers may startle them. eBay's 2008 revenue weighed in at $2.12 billion.[50] Add in an estimated $80 million in revenue from privately held Craigslist and you still haven't reached the size of the casual, mobile, and social games market.[51] These games are a real business, one the news industry hasn't much considered as a partial salve for its financial heartburn.

An exception comes from a surprising place. Despite its conservative political leanings and age, 150-year-old British broadsheet the *Daily*

Telegraph publishes a Web site devoted entirely to puzzles and casual games. The site, called CluedUp, takes a unique approach to the sometimes noisy market of casual games.[52] Instead of competing with the *Bejeweleds* and *Diner Dashes* of the gaming world, CluedUp focuses on versions of popular newspaper puzzles like the crossword, cryptic crossword, knowledge quiz, and number puzzle. These new versions of existing games fit in nicely with the print paper's tendency to run clever, unique traditional puzzles (for example, a crossword-derived numerical puzzle in which correct answers correspond with mobile phone keypad strokes necessary to text message the response).

Also not lost on the *Telegraph* is the revenue opportunity from such puzzles. To play them, subscribers must pony up £4.99 for monthly access or £35.88 for an annual subscription. Given the paper's print circulation of roughly 815,000, even a small adoption could easily add hundreds of thousands of pounds a year to the paper's bottom line; the 10 percent puzzle adoption figure cited by the *London Times* above would offer roughly £3 million in revenue.[53] That's not enough to save the industry, but it might just be enough to keep some at-risk desks operating.

Another, somewhat different example comes from *Parade* magazine, a national Sunday newspaper insert that reaches seventy-two million readers via 470 different papers.[54] While it hardly offers hard news, *Parade* is distributed entirely in newspapers, so its interests overlap considerably with those of more serious journalism. Among *Parade*'s signature features is the "Ask Marilyn" column, in which Marilyn vos Savant poses and answers riddles and puzzles for readers to solve. One of her more recent offerings is a puzzle called *Numbrix*, which *Parade* often publishes in her weekly column. It is a number grid puzzle similar to but easier than Sudoku, in which the player must fill in the center of the grid by assigning numbers contiguously, such that a cell adjoins the next lowest number vertically or horizontally. *Parade* has successfully marketed the puzzle on a number of platforms, including on their own Web site, as a downloadable game, as a Facebook game, and as an iPhone game (figure 5.6). Each method earns money from purchases or advertisements, showing how a well-constructed, unique puzzle can rise above the noise of the traditional casual games marketplace.

There are some questions that remain unanswered about newspaper puzzles. For one, how to avoid the eBay effect: given the global nature of the Internet, one good portal can earn all the business. How can localities cater to the puzzle needs of their constituencies to recreate the benefits of local puzzles? For another, how to lead puzzlers to the hard news:

Figure 5.6
Numbrix rewards veterans of the popular mobile game *Snake* for their adept abilities in compartmentalizing and stringing together a series of numbers. The only way to lose this game is to forget how to count.

the pleasurable routine of the crossword, the criptoquip, the comic—all can provide a surprising welcome mat to the rest of the contents of daily events, so long as one has to traverse that news to get to the puzzles. Once one has the paper in hand, and once the crossword is done or abandoned, heck, "might as well read the rest of the paper." How can a casual games site provide access to the meat and potatoes part of the news? The *Telegraph*'s CluedUp site is strictly separate from its online news, with only small links ferrying the reader from puzzle to headline. In *Scoop!* we find a game that performs something resembling the work of shifting puzzle players to articles, whereas the *Crickler* integrates such content but fails to link to it.

A new investment in digital puzzles might be able to re-create demand, not through the primary product, news, but through the secondary product, puzzles, which publishers may not want to admit have become a primary product for many readers. Such a move will require smart innovation in a surprising area—game design. The crossword offers a striking lesson in this regard. It began as a puzzle that happened to be published in newspapers, rather than as a newspaper feature that happened to be a puzzle.

Dead Rising tells the story of Frank West, a rugged, individualistic reporter who will do anything to get an exclusive. Because the game is set in a shopping mall infested with zombies, doing so can be a chore: it requires beating, shooting, or exploding the living dead with any implement available. *Dead Rising* doesn't bill itself as a journalism simulator, and it is certainly not recognizable as *edutainment*—entertainment software made explicitly for an educational context, like *Math Blaster* or *Oregon Trail*. However, given how its rules structure both gameplay *and* narrative, *Dead Rising* is a work that encourages its players to enter the mindset of a photojournalist embedded in a humanitarian crisis.

Although combat serves as the game's core mechanic, its introduction emphasizes photography. It opens with Frank West flying over the quarantined town of Willamette, Colorado. Hanging off the side of a helicopter, the player is introduced to aiming, zooming, and focusing the camera. Players primarily gain experience points by taking photographs, points which allow the player to "level up" in strength and resilience. An automatic photo scoring system encourages players to straddle different photographic roles; action oscillates uncomfortably between wartime documentarian and tabloid paparazzo (extra points are awarded for sexual, violent, or otherwise emotional imagery—see figure 6.1).

Frank has three days to discover the truth behind the zombie outbreak in Willamette, after which a helicopter will arrive to rescue him and any survivors he finds at the mall. After the photography tutorial, the game begins with a scene establishing Frank's relative helplessness, letting players know that West is a human and not a superhero. A throng of zombies breaks in and slaughters a number of survivors, forcing West to flee to the roof of the building. There he encounters two National Security Agency (NSA) agents and the mall's janitor. The NSA agents propel the game's main story forward by presenting West with "cases," or mandatory

Figure 6.1

A player's photography skills are scored for framing and subject matter in *Dead Rising*. Surviving the zombie attack means nothing to Frank West if he has no way to document it.

story-based missions. The janitor Willy sends the player "scoops," or optional side-missions to rescue survivors, via walkie-talkie.

Cases trigger in precise locations and at particular times. If Frank fails to arrive at the proper place and time to pick up the case, the game simply reports, "The truth has faded into darkness." Though melodramatic, the sensation does reproduce the fleeting nature of journalistic opportunity. Scoops are special, requiring the player either to rescue survivors or combat an uninfected "psychopath" within a slightly broader timeframe. Together, scoops and cases make *Dead Rising* a game more about time management for reporters than about combat for vigilantes. Since it only allows players to save progress at a few key locations, missing a scoop becomes a permanent event. When the player blows a deadline, the game cuts to the survivors being overrun and turned into zombies, putting a face to each failure. Every choice matters.

Simulating film or memory cards, the game limits the number of photos Frank's camera can store. Frank can replenish his supply at two kiosks at either side of the mall, but doing so is an onerous process. The Willamette mall is architecturally accurate down to the dimensions of every store, rest room, and escalator. Trekking from one end to the other to complete tasks is both time-consuming and dangerous. Players learn to prepare carefully before each outing, scrounging for scraps of food and weapons for health and defense, and ascertaining the safest and most effective routes between any two given points. Recalling the path-finding and information-gathering a wartime reporter must perform in a hostile environment, sometimes saving a survivor will unlock secret passages or provide keys for locked doors, allowing faster and safer travel. Journalists can relate, as even an ordinary camera crew needs to learn the nuances of a home city quickly so as to plan a physical approach toward a breaking news story.

One could view *Dead Rising* as escapist fantasy, but truly active engagement requires the player to evaluate the game world, making hypotheses about how to engage with it while testing different methods and strategies. The best games provide both positive and negative feedback for success and failure, something that *Dead Rising* accomplishes through the structuring of missions as journalistic and humanitarian endeavors. But can we rightly call *Dead Rising* a game that teaches players something about journalism? For such a claim to ring true, players would have to become critical of their play process, meditating on how the game constructs a reporter's experience.[1]

Dead Rising offers an interactive version of what is becoming known as "interventionist media," a form that highlights tragedy by embedding a viewer in one.[2] These works claim that outcomes improve when participants declare their intention to help, not just to observe. Usually this is a job entrusted only to experienced journalists who are familiar enough with objective reportage that they can be trusted to editorialize and produce solid opinion work on grave matters like war, terrorism, and political intrigue. *Dead Rising* takes the largely theoretical idea of intervention through reportage and implements it as a single, repeated trade-off: reach the next "case" with time to spare, or run the risk of missing the case by filling that time rescuing survivors. Although the creators of the game surely didn't intend it to educate players about journalism, their assumptions about the profession are embedded in the rules. If a zombie beat-'em-up game can begin to engage complex and morally ambiguous topics at the edge of current journalistic practice, then surely other videogames have the power to teach us something about the daily duties of public watchdogs and sense-makers.

Journalism has to be learned somehow, be it from school or experience in the field. It demands a specialized type of *literacy*. Broadly speaking, literacy describes the learned practice of understanding, creating, and critiquing a particular mode of communication.[3] There are many types of literacies in journalism. News readers know how to access and consume the news, but they don't necessarily understand the values and work methods that lay the foundation for reporting. Likewise, editors engage with news on a different level, stepping back from individual pieces to correct, guide, and contextualize them within the paper, television program, or Web site. Most often, people develop journalism literacies through practice and work experience. Today we read a lot about *citizen journalism*[4] and the *wisdom of crowds*—some of the ways that the Internet has allowed ordinary citizens to participate in reporting.[5] But just because someone can publish opinions, serve as an eyewitness, or dig up dirt doesn't mean he or she is conducting journalistic practice—the process that creates the output is important too.

Can games teach us how to be good news consumers, reporters, or editors? Clearly a person cannot become an expert just by playing a game, but games can teach a mindset, a way of approaching problems through a set of rules, values, and practices. This is what videogame scholar and literacy expert James Paul Gee calls a *semiotic domain*: a realm of knowledge shared by a group of practitioners.[6] *Dead Rising* asks its players to follow the journalistic rule of verification; it embodies the value of the watchdog role of the media; and it models the practices of following leads (scoops), documenting through photography, and navigating physically through a problem space to a source of information.

Some games underscore the rationale and values of the profession, while others teach the fundamentals of its practice. Games that *illustrate the purpose* of journalism develop support for the profession by modeling both the positive and negative aspects of reporting. Like *Dead Rising*, these games might not be explicitly designed for journalism education. Instead, through their status as popular consumer entertainment, they can encourage support for journalism's role in contemporary society. Games that *teach the practice* of reporting range from secondary educational classroom tools to college-level simulations. These works are created explicitly for educational use, helping players learn to create and critique journalistic artifacts. Together, both mainstream and educational games about reporters and reporting can advocate for the profession, supplement a proper journalistic education, and perhaps even spark interest in such a career in the first place.

Illustrating the Purpose

Before *Dead Rising*, there was another "action reporter" videogame: *Beyond Good & Evil*. Unlike *Dead Rising*, *Beyond Good & Evil* isn't particularly effective at emulating the schedule and mindset of a reporter. Instead, the game asserts the value of journalism through plot and theme. The game is set in the twenty-fifth century on the mining planet of Hyllis, where a variety of sentient human and animal species coexist. This once peaceful planet has been invaded by the DomZ, an insect-like alien species who capture and enslave the native Hillians.

A newscast opens the game; Hyllis's most popular newscaster announces an oncoming attack by the DomZ. He transfers control of the broadcast over to the voice of General Kex of the Alpha Sections—an intergalactic military that purportedly protects the people of Hyllis. He begins, "Loyal Hillians, the impending battle will be a difficult one, but thanks to the Alpha Sections..." before being cut off by a fadeout to the game's protagonist, Jade, who meditates on a rock. When the DomZ invasion begins, Jade springs into action, depicted in a series of black-and-white in-game snapshots. These scenes cast Jade as both a contemplative free thinker and a rugged photojournalist, an independent force flying in the face of the Alpha Sections' media hegemony. If, as Finley Peter Dunne asserted, "the business of a newspaper is to comfort the afflicted and afflict the comfortable," then Jade is a newspaperwoman in the truest sense of the word.[7]

Hannah Arendt calls one of the forces of totalitarianism "centripetal"— it monitors and structures public opinion by drawing everyone into the shared space it dominates.[8] Although *Beyond Good & Evil*'s gameplay is a mix of nature photography and third-person action adventure, the game's mise-en-scène and plot weave a story of government control and its eventual resistance by citizen revolt as a result of improved media transparency. From the outset of the game, radios and televisions buzz with the propaganda of the Alpha Sections. Even the children under Jade's care mention that they want to grow up and join the intergalactic military someday.

An oppositional, underground organization called the Iris Network attempts to disrupt the intergalactic information control exerted by the Alpha Sections. Among other things, it strives to offer an independent source of news. Yet, since Iris is a guerrilla operation shrouded in secret, it struggles to overcome its own opacity. Throughout the game, the Iris Network withholds key information from Jade and the player. Through a series of revelations about the nature of the organization and Jade's unknowing relation to it, the player ascertains the importance of transparency by feeling the consequences of its absence.

Beyond Good & Evil simulates the watchdog role of the press by transporting players to a society where citizens enjoy fewer freedoms and experience more government control. Though the game is set in a relatively large

Figure 6.2
In *Beyond Good & Evil*, Jade's ability to navigate the world in her hovercraft is
impeded by robot sentries. Many open-world games use arbitrary environmental
boundaries to block off inaccessible areas, but here they also highlight themes of
government control.

world, exploration is constantly constrained by governmental blockades.
While moving through the city, the player sees Alpha ships flying overhead
and guards at every corner. By blocking access to its physical environments,
the game conveys a tangible feeling of oppressive public control (figure
6.2). As citizens of a *real* world, players can reflect on the game as an alle-
gory for the governmental despotism often depicted in science fiction. But
unlike a novel or film, *Beyond Good & Evil* gets the player to *experience* the
trade-offs between coverage and on-the-ground intervention.

Anticipating the recent crisis in print journalism, Jade's career as a
photojournalist has fallen on hard times. Jade doesn't have sufficient funds
to pay for basic power needs or transportation costs, so she takes on a job
as a nature photographer. The pictures in her studio depict the orphans
she cares for—hardly the album one would expect to see in a professional
reporter's darkroom. The player experiences life within a broken news
system as a journalist with standards and passion. Jade's enduring appeal
lies in her resolve; she takes action to fix the situation and thus affirm the
importance of her profession.

Another game that espouses the need for honest reportage within a
broken journalistic system is *Pictures for Truth*, a game funded by Amnesty
International and developed by a team of French Canadian volunteer game
developers.[9] The player takes the role of an American journalist in China
just prior to the 2008 Beijing Olympics. In this role, the player intends to

meet with a Chinese journalist friend covering poor living conditions at a toxic electronics dump. But upon arriving in the country, the player receives an unexpected phone call: your Chinese friend has been detained by authorities.

As in *Beyond Good & Evil*, the player of *Pictures for Truth* begins in a hostile environment without any reporting tools. Arriving on the scene, a police officer confiscates the player's camera and hauls the Chinese journalist friend off to jail. To succeed, the player must find a new camera, conduct interviews at the dump and outside a jail, and take pictures to accompany the stories generated by the interviews. In the process, the player produces three stories: one about the health issues at the dump, one about the working conditions of those living nearby, and one about China's municipal policy with respect to the death penalty.

Players receive "fame" points for every interview question posed, and for adding pictures relevant to the stories they are composing. Fame unlocks three power-ups: a zoom lens, a handheld computer with more storage, and a hidden camera. Unfortunately, composing an article is a rudimentary process that merely amounts to choosing two lines of conversation culled from investigation, rather than recombining many facts into a cohesive story. Scoring each quote would have provided feedback about the quality of different types of information. That said, the player can also add photos to a story, and the game does respond to images based on their journalistic quality. As in *Dead Rising*, capturing points of interests (represented as nodes or "hot points" once the cameras snaps) awards more fame points; reusing the same subject twice in an article subtracts points.

Amnesty International endorsed *Pictures for Truth* not to teach journalism, but to teach the difficulty of doing journalism in China. Ancillary communication goals cover living, working, and municipal conditions in China, giving the game a modestly documentarian sensibility. The game underscores the importance of an open media environment to Western players, while inviting intervention outside the game via Amnesty International's various programs.

In terms of appearance, *Beyond Good & Evil* and *Pictures for Truth* share little in common. *Beyond Good & Evil* implements the third-person perspective during primary gameplay and only switches to the first person for snapping photographs, whereas *Pictures for Truth* takes place entirely in the first person. The former takes place within a colorful fantasy landscape, whereas the latter puts the player in a black-and-white, hand-sketched abstraction of a real location. What both do share is important: playing the role of a specific character in a real-time 3D environment.

In our discussion of current event games, we explained how Gonzalo Frasca eschews narrative so that players might experience critical distance from the subject. Yet, engagement in a fully realized 3D world and fiction works well in the context of news literacy games like those just discussed. Why? The answer is *situated meaning*—the idea that human learning is enhanced within an embodied context.[10] There's no definitive word on whether a first-person camera or a third-person view of one's avatar within a game world is best for building identification between the player and a virtual identity.[11] But both create the same expressive atmosphere, an embodied experience of a credible world that lacks journalistic freedom. The idea that "freedom of the press" is crucial for ensuring other freedoms is something that most players understand in the abstract, but such concepts remain hard to grasp from the comfortable context of Western democracy. Games like *Beyond Good & Evil* and *Pictures for Truth* allow their players to feel a virtual loss of this freedom along with an opportunity to remedy that loss.

Designers of commercially produced games don't necessarily set out to teach players about journalism as a profession. But journalists still have much to learn from commercial games. These games construct living, breathing virtual worlds in which news is a part of everyday life, rather than isolating journalistic learning from the rest of that world.

Beyond Good & Evil features two newspapers; one is a propaganda paper from the Galaxy News network controlled by the Alpha Sections and the other a counter-propaganda pamphlet distributed by the Iris Network. This written material, comprising reportage on events in the game's storyline from both sides, helps characterize the two organizations. The player can judge them based on how they report events while comparing the articles to what they've actually read in the paper or online. They reinforce the designers' respect for independent watchdog media and their distaste for global news conglomerates' ability to restrict the flow of information to the public. But Jade is something of a covert operative; her exploits aren't widely reported throughout the game, giving the player a sense of the fragile influence of unchecked power. The future success of journalistic practice arises partly from citizens' desire to support it, and videogames have a role to play in culturing that desire.

In-Game News Sources

Dead Rising and *Beyond Good & Evil* simulate the purpose of journalism through its practice, but other games depict the news by incorporating it into the background of a simulated world. One of the earliest examples of generated in-game news can be found in the *Grand Theft Auto* titles. Outside of gaming circles, the series is probably best known for its controversial simulation of criminality, but the games offer a more important innovation: a large, open world with suggested rather than required goals. Cities in *Grand Theft Auto* are enormous, and traversing them by car can be a pleasure (or a chore) in and of itself.

It is here that the need for news emerges: driving can be boring. The first *Grand Theft Auto* features seven music stations and a police band radio. The music stations just play background tunes, but the police station sends out all points bulletins (APBs), which air chatter about various crimes throughout the city. Committing criminal acts in the sight of witnesses raises the player's "wanted level," which triggers the APB notices to cover the player's most recent crime. Hearing about one's exploits on the APB provides a satisfying burst of positive feedback to the player, not to mention a measure of strategic advantage.

Grand Theft Auto III added a number of news stations and talk radio channels to the airwaves. These simulated sources broadcast news about the player's misdeeds from the perspective of the citizenry rather than the enforcers. Although players might still be inclined to congratulate themselves for criminal acts, the perspectival shift sets the act in relief. The news stations mix stories about events outside the player's control, breaking reports tied to player actions, and retrospective reportage about past havoc wreaked during the game's missions. In so doing, the player's crimes become socially contextualized.

Infamous, a game about a bike messenger who develops electrical superpowers after an enormous explosion, features network news broadcasts that parrot propagandist government press releases as well as a rogue signal from "The Voice of Survival." *Infamous* depicts a fictional U.S. city that suffers a massive cataclysm and then isolation following a government blockade, a theme that prompted critic Evan Narcisse to call the title "the first true post-Katrina videogame."[12] The government drops food and supplies into the city by plane as a public show of support for the populace, but the television broadcasts don't communicate that the same government is actively slaughtering the citizenry in order to root out bioterrorists. Both the official broadcast and the rogue Voice of Survival paint the player character as a terrorist, effectively cornering him. Like *Beyond Good & Evil*, *Infamous* uses biased news to convey the importance of independent media (while nevertheless admitting that it's not an assured panacea).

In-game news broadcasts reach their technical peak in Bethesda's *Fallout 3*, a role-playing game about a nuclear-war-devastated Washington, D.C., of the twenty-third century. Players carry a PDA that holds equipment data, maps, and a radio tuner. Signals are broadcast both globally and locally, coming from major stations and isolated radio towers across the ruins of D.C., Maryland, and Virginia. A guerilla radio personality named Three Dog runs a station called Galaxy News Radio, which offers an alternative to the government propaganda station Enclave Radio. While Enclave Radio always broadcasts the same cycle of "fireside chat" speeches by President John Henry Eden (the game's primary antagonist), Three Dog constitutes what game designer Nels Anderson calls a "procedural skald," who describes the impact of the player's choices by "providing disc jockey poetics of the player's decisions."[13] Three Dog creates a context for the player by means of a fictional rationale to explain why the game's characters recognize the player and, more importantly, by clarifying the effects of government propaganda on the populace.

These examples of in-game news show that designers have evolved more sophisticated models of the media in their works. The earliest examples from the *Grand Theft Auto* series operate as passive commentary on the actions of the player, providing an aesthetic texture that makes actions more meaningful. In *Fallout 3*, radio reports offer synthetic evaluation and critique of the player's choices and their impact on the broader society. In each case, these games highlight the temptations and dangers of media bias. Players listen to these reports and compare them with their understanding of the "truth" of their own actions. They gain a contextualized understanding of the difference between accurate and biased reporting by finding themselves implicated in media bias or collusion.

Finally, radio has enjoyed a long history in another popular genre: the virtual worlds of text MUDs (multi-user dungeons) and graphical MMORPGs (massively multiplayer online role-playing games). Because these games feature large numbers of highly active human players, individuals sometimes establish Web radio stations where they invite players to create programming, including music broadcasts and regularly scheduled talk shows, to be broadcast while playing.[14] Common topics of discussion include the progress of player groups, discussions of strategy, news of recent exploits among the best-ranked teams, and commentary on the direction of the game world as carried out by its operators. Talk radio may not represent the apotheosis of journalistic productivity, but the members of these online communities do take pride in sharing knowledge about the microcosm of the game.

These broadcasters serve as the watchdogs of a virtual citizenry, holding the game designers accountable for changes within the game. Can this

phenomenon rightly be called part of the game proper? In an early eth-
nographic study of the virtual world *EverQuest*, T. L. Taylor argues that it
must: virtual worlds extend beyond the out-of-the-box experience crafted
by the game designers, incorporating the labor of the players.[15] Simply
creating an *opportunity* for journalistic projects by players is an important
cultural contribution by virtual world designers. If journalism helps people
make decisions, then "Radio MMO" might fit the bill.

Teaching the Practice

The commercial games discussed above teach the purpose of journalism
to citizens: what it is, the service it provides, and what might happen if it
disappeared tomorrow. Such efforts hold promise, especially since many
citizens do not share, or even recognize, the ideals journalism sets for itself.
Indeed, journalism remains a curiously secretive practice, its values and
principles locked up inside professional vaults. In light of the continued
consolidation and disappearance of news outlets of all kinds, embedding
these lessons in a popular medium like videogames offers a provocative
way to communicate the differences between journalism and raw information, and why the former needs to be preserved even in light of a changing
media ecology.

A more familiar kind of journalism literacy has also found a place in
videogames—that of professional training. For years, organizations of all
sorts have deployed educational simulations when real environments
become too expensive or dangerous for training. The most familiar examples come from the military, where complex simulations of equipment and
procedure have been common for decades. Private industries like airlines
and shipping companies followed suit.

At first blush, journalism may seem to have little in common with heavy
equipment. But more recently, corporations have begun to use games to
help employees become familiar with rules and best practices.[16] These
games simulate business processes like customer service. Some, such as *Cold
Stone Creamery: Stone City* (which simulates both portion sizing and fran-
chise economics) also contextualize those processes within the larger goals
of the organization to help the player/employee understand the consequences and purpose of individual actions. It is here that journalism connects with educational videogames.

High school and college newspapers allow journalism students to learn
about the workflow of a news desk, how to write concisely, how to take
photojournalistic pictures, how to do archive research, and how to operate

within an editorial hierarchy. But apart from practice, there is no way to prepare students to interview a subject in a tense or grave situation. Finding stories can also be challenging; the student of journalism can't necessarily be expected to cover a beat or hound sources on the telephone for a scoop. By simulating these situations, and by offering many variations of them, videogames can give students an opportunity they simply cannot train for in the classroom.

At the Newseum in Washington, D.C., two game installations allow children to experience a simplified form of the interview experience.[17] The first is a simple interview simulation featuring attractive computer-animated characters. In a corner of the screen, a virtual editor accompanies the user as they interview a number of protestors on the streets. The game offers a few talking points for approaching interview subjects, and the editor offers feedback on how to interpret the resulting statements (figure 6.3). At the end, the game generates a story based on the kids' choices.

While perhaps too linear, the guided hand technique employed here seems particularly effective at introducing the basic concepts of how to ask concise questions and handle editorial oversight. And the generated article

Figure 6.3
This game exhibit at the Newseum in Washington, D.C., puts children in the role of journalists, teaching them how to ask questions, collect facts, and create a news story using animated figures and humorous subject matter.

connects the actions the players take to demonstrate how a story gets produced. Nearby in the Newseum facilities, one finds an interactive table-top game, which asks players to judge the quality and origin of different opinions. Players are asked whether they think a given statement is fit for print, and the game explains to them why or why not their answer was correct.

Children often talk about wanting "to be a (something) when I grow up," without actually knowing what the profession is all about. But one of the reasons why choices like "fireman" or "garbage collector" are so appealing to kids is that they understand what such occupations entail. By clarifying the reporting experience, the Newseum games introduce the basics of *what a reporter does*. While all games inculcate what literacy scholar James Paul Gee calls a "projective identity"—the persona that lies somewhere between who the player is in real life and the role he or she enacts inside a game—games for early childhood education take the development of this in-between identity as their primary goal.[18] The projective identity allows players to test their own desires and strengths against the situation simulated within the game. Whereas games for adults or otherwise advanced gamers may seek out challenge simply for the fun derived from frustration and eventual mastery, games such as those offered by the Newseum serve to reinforce the validity of professional dreams by providing a low cost of access and risk.

Older kids and adults alike can take advantage of the educational games on the online journalism education hub NewsU.[19] The project, run by the Poynter Institute, collects and organizes specialized lessons and exercises about print and multimedia journalism. One of these is a game called *Be a Reporter*.[20] The player, cast as a green reporter, learns about an outbreak of food poisoning at a school in the town of Medina. After a brief introduction by the fictional editor of the local paper, the player traverses a cartoon map of the city, clicking on buildings containing possible interview subjects (figure 6.4). Although simple, the game provides clear cues to help the student determine the credibility and quality of each account collected. Each interview is summarized in a virtual notebook, and the player can stop at any time to submit these notes to be synthesized into an article. The resulting story varies in quality based on how thoroughly the player posed questions to the interview subjects. The editor also offers a final evaluation of the player's performance. Whereas the Newseum's interactive tabletop game gives the younger player instant feedback on their decisions, *Be a Reporter* withholds this information to demonstrate the choices a journalist must make independently.

Figure 6.4

In NewsU's *Be a Reporter*, an editor sometimes appears in the top right of the screen to suggest places where key information might be gained. On the map of the city, the Hospital and Valley Elementary School are shown to be points of interest. Along the toolbar below, the player can review notes from previous interviews or file the story.

The University of Minnesota Institute for New Media Studies has created a similar reporting education tool, called *Disaster at Harperville*. The game teaches players to conduct interviews and synthesize the information gathered in low-trust environments. In the game's scenario, a tanker truck accident has caused poison to leak into a downtown neighborhood; the player must cross-reference a number of accounts in order to arrive at a suitable level of objectivity. The game factors in the player's attitude (through dialogue choices), the reliability and demeanor of the interviewee, and the player's initiative to double-check and compare claims.

All of the reporter training games just discussed have something in common: they present a single assignment as a paradigm. For the young kids at the Newseum, the resulting concreteness does its job: to explain that "reporter" is a viable career choice and to demonstrate what it involves. But for adults, such an approach is too simplistic. It overlooks the connections between different investigations, the development of journalistic reputation, and the effects of time and experience on the working dynamics of a newsroom.

The *Global Conflicts* series by Danish developer Serious Games Interactive attempts such a feat, underscoring the processes of reporting rather than its end product. *Global Conflicts* is a much larger effort than the others, offering 3D-rendered worlds more like *Beyond Good & Evil* than the basic top-down map of *Be a Reporter*. It is delivered as a retail game and comes packaged with teaching guides for in-class play and discussion.[21] One of these games, *Global Conflicts: Latin America*, is aimed at middle-schoolers, while the other, *Global Conflicts: Palestine*, was created with high school students in mind.

Global Conflicts: Palestine focuses primarily on target audience and bias. After choosing a character, the player must choose to write for an Israeli or a Palestinian newspaper. This initial decision affects available choices for the rest of the game. The point is clear: writing a good story is not about revealing a simple, ultimate truth, but instead involves understanding and clarifying contextually relevant information.

During the game's missions, the player interviews soldiers, detainees, civilians, and politicians via relatively complex dialogue trees (figure 6.5). These statements reveal a spectrum of political opinions, and the player must learn how journalists can alter their attitudes and interactions to get information from their sources. For example, a pro-Palestinian reporter can act as a sympathizer of Israel so that an Israeli official might let his guard down to reveal information. Rather than encouraging manipulation, the game demonstrates the complexities of human interaction and the difficulty of extracting information from uncooperative sources.

Unlike the Newseum titles, *Pictures for Truth*, and *Disaster at Harperville*, *Global Conflicts: Palestine* complicates the assembly of stories after raw source accounts have been acquired. When it comes time to file a story, the player must choose from the gathered quotes to construct a newspaper article, including a headline, body text, a pull quote, and a photo. After submitting the newspaper page the player is scored based on the quality of the story and how well it matches the political alignment of the chosen publication.

In *Global Conflicts: Latin America*, the developers add more ambiguity to the information-gathering process. The game separates interviewee responses into arguments and statements. In addition to serving as raw material for a story, the player can also deploy these responses as facts in other contexts. At the end of a mission comes a "final interview," in which the player confronts the interview subject using arguments collected

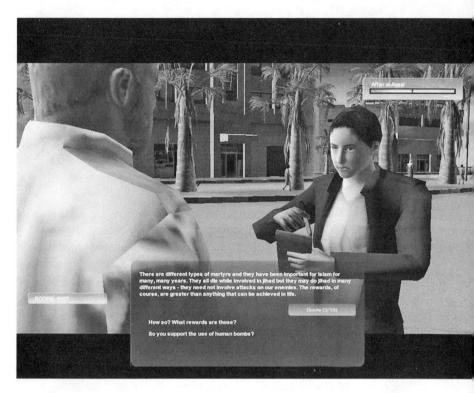

There are different types of martyrs and they have been important for Islam for many, many years. They all die while involved in jihad but they may do jihad in many different ways - they need not involve attacks on our enemies. The rewards, of course, are greater than anything that can be achieved in life.

How so? What rewards are those?

So you support the use of human bombs?

Figure 6.5

In this dialogue choice from *Global Conflicts: Palestine*, the player can choose either to ask a neutral question that progresses the interview about suicide bombing or to press the subject about his personal beliefs. A bar on the top right of the screen displays the subject's "anxiety" level. In this case, it's neutral: he neither trusts nor fears the player.

earlier. Depending on the quality of his or her reporting, the player may or may not have enough evidence to accomplish this final task.

The game exercises an important skill: a journalist does not simply report reality from existing knowledge, but re-creates reality based on bits and pieces collected from different sources. When a journalist uses the arguments to influence a dialogue with an interviewee, the plain facts serve as a catalyst to find more pieces of the puzzle and to confirm or invalidate previously collected information. In this way, *Global Conflicts: Latin America* improves upon the unquestioned facts of interview subjects in the Palestine edition of the game. The *Latin America* episodes also add time limits, an essential constraint to master in the practice of journalism.

These game scenarios are effective teaching tools not only because they provide situations that journalism students don't often have access to, but also because they facilitate what Gee calls a "psychosocial moratorium": a space where one is free to experiment because of the reduction or removal of real-world consequences.[22] Building interview skills requires practice. In the real world, missing an interview or pushing an interview subject to rage or timidity can blow a story. Videogames allow players to experience the consequences of such missteps without any real-world risk—they are free to learn safely inside the "magic circle" of the game.[23]

There are some things that reporting literacy newsgames do not teach. In particular, *writing* is notably absent in all these games. Instead, stories are either generated from interview materials or interpolated from chunks of evidence. Technical challenges are partly to blame; computational language processing is still unable to understand and assess arbitrary prose. Still, it might be possible to apply rudimentary linguistic analysis to player-authored text to determine if key words and facts have found their way into a draft.[24] Or perhaps the game might turn the tables, asking the player to assess the logical validity, bias, or tone of a story from the editor's desk.

Without exception, literacy newsgames intended for pedagogical use focus on the editorial side of the profession. The publisher's view of the business represents an unexplored opportunity. One inroad to such a perspective might come from the "tycoon" genre. These titles borrow conventions from industrial simulations like *Railroad Tycoon*, in which players make strategic choices to build and grow a business. Since the release of *Railroad Tycoon* in 1990, innumerable variants have covered almost every industry, from restaurants to zoos to prisons. At least one tycoon game has taken up the business of news, although not in the most earnest fashion. *Tabloid Tycoon* challenges players to build a media empire by publishing timely stories in a scandalous rag. The description on its box colors the game yellow: "The aim is to sabotage your rivals, settle lawsuits, give would-be paparazzi jobs and take pictures of the most scandalous things." *Tabloid Tycoon* might not make its way onto journalism school curricula, but there is no reason why someone couldn't take up the tycoon formula to produce a more legitimate experience of running a news organization in a changing media environment.

In fact, Bryan Murley, a professor at Eastern Illinois University, pitched just such a concept for consideration in J-Lab's 2009 Knight-Batten awards:

Imagine being offered the chance to purchase family-owned newspapers, and trying to juggle the debt created by such purchases, and figuring out how to survive the Internet cuts in your classified income. Trying to come up with new ways to boost circulation, dealing with labor strife, advertiser complaints over negative coverage, etc.[25]

Although Murley's design treatment does not plumb the depths of the models and mechanics needed to flesh out the simulation, it does successfully identify the challenges a good newspaper tycoon game would have to address. Murley's intentions are more speculative than pedagogical; his concept casts the game as method for "crowdsourcing," mining player data to solve the economic woes of the newspaper business. The scenario might be possible in the context of what we will call *community newsgames* in the next chapter, but it seems an unlikely outcome for a rigidly defined simulation.

Transparency

We have offered some ways to apply game design to teach journalism literacy. But we can also turn the tables and ask what journalists can learn from game design. When building a simulation or game of any kind, on any subject, journalists might hone occupational skills indirectly. Among those skills overlapping game design and journalism, we find the discipline of verification, the practice of revealing bias through transparency, and the interrogation of complex systems of facts and conflicting reports.

Transparency is a value in journalism, but it is also of key interest in software usability and game design. Certain elements of games are designed to be completely transparent, because they are the functions players must learn in order to play a game in the first place. These usually come in the form of a tutorial, the way games quickly familiarize players with the controls, interface, and most common actions allowable in the game. More complex forms of transparency are required to communicate the operation of a game system through feedback. Just as journalists build trust in readers, game designers build trust in players through transparency.

In fact, the two fields share concerns about at least three forms of transparency: influence, construction, and reference.[26] *Influence transparency* addresses ideological or political bias in a creator, including the disclosure of conflicts of interest. *Construction transparency* deals with forthrightness in revealing how a work has been constructed from research and investigation. And *reference transparency* deals with the collection, presentation, and citation of sources in a work. These modes of transparency operate in a complementary way in both game design and journalism.

Simulation games are perhaps the best models we have for explaining transparency in videogames. In the popular *Civilization* series, the simulation grants specific statistical attributes to civilizations and combat units through the culture and technology the player chooses to develop over time. Sometimes these are mutually exclusive, as in the choice of a democratic or totalitarian government. In other cases, such attributes affect gameplay more ambiguously. The *Civilization* games feature a "technology tree" that houses different advancements a player can research (metallurgy, religion, democracy, and so forth). Each one leads to different abilities but also closes down other competing options in a compromise of risk and reward. This compromise also creates intrigue, as players must make educated guesses about the evolution of competing civilizations.

Assumptions about the source and consequences of technological advancement are clearly presented in *Civilization IV*; for example, the game tells the player that developing environmentalism will grant six health points in all cities, two extra commerce points from windmills and forest preserves, and an increase of 25 percent in maintenance costs from corporations. The game appears to be making persuasive, systematic claims about history and the benefits of certain advancements, but its designers have bracketed any ideological bias by carrying out a transparency of influence that reveals the connections between technical and social ideas.

Game artist Jason Rohrer's game *Crude Oil*, about the consequences of oil drilling in the Arctic National Wildlife Refuge (ANWR), exemplifies transparency of construction.[27] In the game, two players compete against each other for virgin oil fields and their potential profits. Players take turns bidding for oil plots and drilling to release supply into the market. Moves are made in private, then revealed publicly when both players have finished a turn. The dynamics of the game are affected by two simple equations:

$$\text{Change in Demand} = \frac{(\text{Supply} - \text{Demand})}{2}$$

Price = 2 + 8 × (Demand − Supply)

The first formula dictates that demand only increases when supply outstrips demand. The second insures that the price of oil increases the more demand outstrips supply. The complexity of the game lies in the fact that these two dynamics conflict.[28] Players quickly realize that it is often beneficial *not* to sell ANWR oil at current prices, precisely the reverse of common opinion on the matter: if allowed to drill, oil companies wouldn't necessarily find the profit motive to raise supply in the United States, the very premise of justifications to drill in the first place.[29]

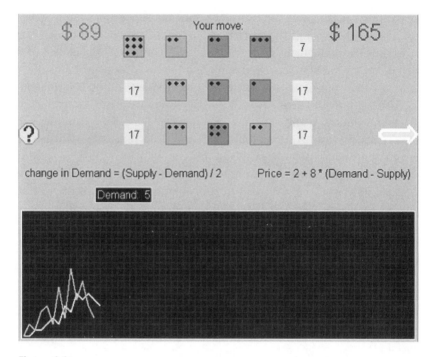

Figure 6.6
The interface of *Crude Oil* shows the oil fields where prospecting takes place, each player's current cash reserves, a graph mapping change in supply and demand over time, and the two formulas that drive the game's economic model. The last element offers an example of an algorithmic transparency of construction.

Even though Rohrer is attempting to question a prominent political opinion, he doesn't mislead his players by hiding the math on which he bases his critique. The game's single, spartan screen prominently features the two equations above, which encapsulate its author's assumptions about the nature of oil prices, supply, and demand (figure 6.6). By being transparent about the simplicity of his formulas, he is in fact elucidating that it is possible for oil companies to operate on similarly simplistic models for their own business operations.

Transparency of reference is perhaps the hardest to accomplish in video-games, because there is no clear way to cite a particular unit of geography, character, or mathematical modeling within the game itself. While there may be real-world evidence behind designer Sid Meier's decision to make organized religion lead to cities constructing buildings 25 percent faster in *Civilization IV*, the actual citation of such materials via in-game messages would defy convention. Additional references and explanations might be provided in the game documentation, but retail games rarely come with manuals anymore, to reduce costs. Usually it is up to communities of players to interpret and elucidate such influences.

Compare *Civilization IV*'s situation to the political simulation game *Democracy 2*, which ships with a set of spreadsheets defining its political logic, data that any player can view or edit. Designer Cliff Harris actively solicits the opinions of his players about any changes they think he should make to the official data.[30] The game is meant to be as politically neutral as possible, and Harris often engages in discussion about the political assumptions and implications of the numbers he uses to drive his model.

Citation in print or broadcast usually takes the form of quotes from interviews. But *Democracy 2* exemplifies a different kind of citation, one that resembles a journalist opening his notebook of interviews and research instead of cherry picking a convenient quote.[31] This kind of reference transparency may seem more extensive than more traditional methods of citation, but it also risks occlusion. Just as infographics sometimes cite data openness as a rhetorical device to avoid synthesis, so simulations can make their references onerous to find or understand. Indeed, understanding the data used in *Democracy 2* will overwhelm all but the most committed players.

Procedural Literacy

The ability to operate a computer adeptly is sometimes called *computer literacy*, and it has become an important part of vocational education. There is another type of computer literacy that goes beyond the ability to use databases and spreadsheets: a literacy for *creating* software artifacts themselves.

MIT computer scientist A. J. Perlis first advocated for a "first course in programming" in 1961. But Perlis intended programming to serve a much broader purpose than mere software development. As he explains, "the purpose of my proposed first course in programming ... is not to teach people how to program a specific computer, nor is it to teach some new languages. The purpose of a course in programming is to teach people how to construct and analyze processes."[32] By *processes*, Perlis means the general behavior of systems, whether they be mathematical, physical, logical, or cultural in nature. Extensions of Perlis's original proposal have taken the name *procedural literacy*, the reading, writing, and critiquing of systems of rules. Although the concept has enjoyed wider adoption in computer science,[33] it finds equal relevance in any field that relies on systems-based thinking and problem solving.[34]

Journalism is no exception. For each preparation of an article, a journalist must examine an event that took place in a particular geographical location, cultural situation, and historical context. Participants, witnesses, and affected parties operate under sometimes conflicting motivations. A journalist must evaluate the scope and impact of an event, the stakeholders, what information is available and by what means, along with myriad other factors. This practice *demands* procedural literacy, even if it doesn't involve computers at all. Journalists look for the underlying situations that produce particular events, tracing their connection to larger social, political, or economic situations.

When seen in this light, journalism shares much in common with game design. Processing is the way computers express ideas. Videogames benefit from this computational heritage by mustering computational processes to represent worldly processes—*Civilization* depicts the cultural logic of an expanding empire; *Dead Rising* depicts the political logic of journalistic intervention. All professions involve processes of some kind, but journalism has a unique relationship with it: at its best, the sense-making responsibility of journalism takes the journalistic mantra (who, what, when, where, why, how?) and extracts broader implications about public and private life in general.

But typically, the form of journalistic expression does not afford sophisticated depictions of cultural logics. Newspaper columns, blog posts, or video segments can only tell a story, a single instance of a larger system: the Goldrick family foreclosure, rather than the dynamics of the local housing market;[35] a batch of salmonella-tainted peanut butter, rather than the spotty operation of industrial food conglomerates.[36] In many cases, reporters do connect local stories to the general logics from which they arise. But the hook of a lede can erode the visibility of underlying processes. Specific examples win out over system dynamics. By contrast, game design puts system dynamics first, allowing specific examples to emerge from repeated plays. If the sense-making work of journalism lies primarily in developing accounts of cultural processes, then it is possible that game design itself might prove the best method for developing literacy as a journalist.

7 Community

In a blog report from May 2007, an unemployed woman named Rainey talks about the feasibility of reintroducing coal-fired locomotives for regional passenger and freight transport in the United States.[1] Given the efficiencies of steam, she reasons, and the local availability of both coal and steel in the United States, it might be possible to counteract the high price of diesel fuel, which, at $5 per gallon, still looks like a bargain compared to ordinary gasoline's price of nearly $7 per gallon.

The problem, it turns out, is not one of material but industrial feasibility. Steel mills long closed would have to be reopened, as would erection shops on rail lines still servicing major destinations. Worse, those qualified to manufacture and service steam locomotives have nearly vanished. Even though some violence had already flared up around the country in response to the high cost of oil, truly widespread civil unrest would need to erupt before the governmental support required to revive the steam railroad might become a reality. In the meantime, the idea would remain a dead end.

Of course, gasoline never hit $7 per gallon in 2007, nor did any civil unrest erupt, nor did anyone consider reviving the steam rail as a salve to a collapse in logistics. But the blog post just described was real, one of many incredibly detailed scenarios proposed over the thirty-two days of *World Without Oil*, an alternate reality game (ARG) organized by writer Ken Eklund and collaborators, and funded by the Corporation for Public Broadcasting's Independent Television Service (ITVS) (figure 7.1).

The game poses a make-believe scenario, a hypothetical global oil shortage of the kind often described by "peak oil" advocates.[2] As with most alternate reality games, play took place not just on a game board or a computer screen, but in the world, on streets and in gardens, and through a variety of online media channels like blogs and YouTube. Rainey was a fictional character, played by one of many real human "puppetmasters"

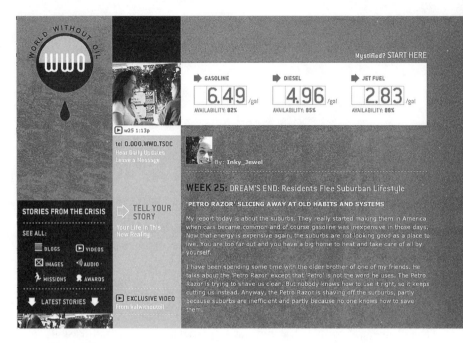

Figure 7.1
Weekly updates to the *World Without Oil* Web site include fictional news stories, data about the rising cost of oil, and links out to player blogs, where individuals describe how the fictional crisis affects them.

who pull the proverbial strings of the game, seeding scenarios and problems for its players to solve. Each day in the game represented a week in the fiction, with new geopolitical problems and consequences arising regularly.

Players (numbering 1,800 from twelve countries, according to the game's Web site) recorded their responses to the global crisis, real and hypothetical. Some documented the changes they might make in their own lives, such as starting community gardens when oil shortages prevented freight shipments to supermarkets, or defending those gardens against less collaboratively minded citizens.

In some cases, player documentation involved the construction of fictions, blog posts about what one might do when faced with unaffordable gasoline, or staged videos of a hypothetical riot at a grocery store whose supplies had not yet been expended. But in other cases, players actually enacted the solutions they submitted as plays to the game, from creating the community gardens just mentioned to walking or bicycling to their real workplaces for the duration of the game. According to their own reports, some players continued these practices after the game concluded, incorporating them into their routines as a way of combating less exigent versions of the energy crisis the game presented.[3]

World Without Oil is unlike other games in many ways. But perhaps its most important feature is that its gameplay focuses on producing new discourse about a global energy crisis, extending that discourse toward real action.

Discourse in Games

News is social because it affects groups of people. It results in a desire for new facts, ideas, and opinions. As Kovach and Rosenstiel observe, discourse not only promotes informative dialogue between citizens, it also acts as a way for people to talk to the newsmakers about their news.[4] One of the goals of journalism is to help citizens make decisions in a democracy.[5] But most games, like most writing, film, photography, and other media through which news is delivered, do not produce *direct* action in the world. We read the paper, watch the evening news, look at a magazine war photograph, and then presumably we think, converse, and make decisions about how we live. Those decisions might take the form of votes, purchases, dissent, or additional discourse in the form of conversations, letters, and other media artifacts.

When we think of discourse in this context, we are prompted to think about socially based discussions. Of course, the outlets for conversation in traditional news media aren't as democratizing as we might hope; a newspaper can only print so many letters to the editor. Common opinion holds that online news outlets counter such exclusivity by providing easier methods of feedback and unlimited space for participation, though a quick glance at the comments section of any news story prompts questions of the quality of this feedback. News radio often allows listeners to call in to argue (or perhaps more commonly, to agree) with the host. Cultural critic David Golumbia rightly wonders if most of this "discourse" amounts to censure and skewering.[6]

Though the Internet has been lauded for giving power to the people—providing outlets for feedback or turning consumers into creators by providing a distribution channel for various forms of citizen-created media—Golumbia notes that it still often replicates existing structures rather than creating new forms of discourse. It is not our newly found ability to talk back that makes digital media powerful; after all, we've had feedback outlets long before the Internet. Instead, we should look to digital media for new forms of discourse that do not have a place in the current structure.

When we think of the social structure present in games already, two candidates emerge. One is the external discussion a single-player game can prompt, a kind of discourse no different from the kind that other forms of media inspire. There is already a long history of discourse occurring around games (e.g., reviews, discussion forums, academic and enthusiast criticism) and this discourse is largely governed by the conventions of nongaming media (e.g., print, blog posts and comments, video).

Another sort of single-player discourse can be imagined too: one that takes place internally between the player and the game. Games, after all, do create systems of feedback that can reinforce or negate the actions of their players. If procedural rhetoric is based on the authoring of arguments through processes, and one of the tenets of journalism is to strive to represent the many angles of a story, then designer-journalists can create forms of play that reveal these issues by forcing the player to see them on multiple sides. Such a game would build in opposing viewpoints, discouraging a single solution. Single-player discourse systems in games are based on dynamics that allow a possibility space within which the player can convince the software that their points are valid. It is about finding different results that can be juxtaposed to reveal what might have been concealed. The act of playing these games simulates the kind of social conversations we most commonly think of as discourse based around news.

The system is by no means perfect, however. One of the important elements of discourse is that it introduces new ideas. Can a game designer take into account every possibility? Of course not. Our current news structures don't attempt such a thing either, but we can imagine a game able to take external inputs into account. We can imagine games explicitly created for counterargument.[7] In these cases, social inputs make solitary activities public.

World Without Oil includes the seeds of such a system. Players are invited to pursue approaches to a (fictional) oil crisis, suggesting whatever method they wish. The aggregate result is a myriad of different "moves," which other players can also view and consider. Of course, this perspective also illuminates a problem with the game: any perspective is counted as "just as good" as any other, like the comments on a blog. There is no simulation that detects or judges the viability of a solution. We'll return to this problem shortly.

The other type of discourse comes from multiplayer games, games in which multiple players are conversing about and around the game as a part of play itself. We can imagine playing a newsgame in which two opponents take opposite sides and hurl information back and forth. Or envision tackling a single-player game and then talking about it on a Web forum or comment thread. Useful, for sure, but far less so than a game in which all the players collaborate toward a common goal.

eRepublik is an massively multiplayer online strategy game. Its creators intend to design strategy games for adults to pursue when professional and family demands make playing traditional strategy games like *Civilization*, too challenging or time-consuming. The approach is a browser-based environment, which facilitates low-bandwidth worldwide cooperative and competitive play. The company bills the game as a casual strategy game, to be played over several months but for only fifteen minutes per day.

You start as a "citizen" and can choose among four careers: politics, the corporate world, journalism, and the military. There are 13,000 newspapers in the game, intended as "self-expression tools" for citizens. Players cover events in *eRepublik*, either at the level of the game (political ideas) or the metagame (cheating, strategy, administration, etc.). Some use the papers for advertising and promoting their companies. One Swedish newspaper has over 2,500 readers and generates a hundred comments per article, about the same as a reasonably popular blog.[8]

Yet, more familiar journalistic practices also take place in *eRepublik*. The developers report that many players in the role of president steal from their country's treasury, and in-game impeachments have occurred when these events are reported in the in-game press. In one related example, a Spanish bank housed most of the funds collected from state taxation. When the political climate changed, a new group was poised to take power. As his last move in office, the player running the bank embezzled all of the tax money before relinquishing power. The press, driven by popular interests and against the rogue government, supported the act. Eighteen hundred comments were posted on a single article during the upheaval.[9]

The result is a rough-round-the-edges yet tangible example of a game in which players seem to do something like journalism as a part of play itself. And unlike games such as *Beyond Good & Evil* or *Global Conflicts: Palestine*, *eRepublik* does so by encouraging players to write about in-game and metagame events.

From Discourse to Action

As meaningfully discursive as *eRepublik* is, its consequences exist primarily within the game's fiction. By contrast, alternate reality games like *World Without Oil* may be producing "real" multiplayer discourse and action already.

The idea of "collective intelligence" or "the hive mind" has been a common one in endorsements of Internet communication in general.[10] Projects like Wikipedia suggest that a large number of people making small, even incremental contributions to an ongoing project can result in outcomes far greater than the sum of their parts. Consider a less familiar but more specific example of collective digital effort. The presidential inauguration of Barack Obama was commemorated in many different ways, from top ten lists to official swag.[11] One new digital form that captured the moment of President Obama's inauguration was Photosynth, a tool created by Microsoft that stitches together 2D photographs to form a navigable 3D space. This kind of technology is reliant on mass contributions—the more viewpoints the better the image. Photographers were told to "Take one photo of the moment when Obama takes the oath ... [and] take three [other] photos (wide-angle, mid-zoom, full-zoom)" and email them to a specified address. Microsoft's software stitched these photos together, and the resulting product, "The Moment," was displayed on CNN.com.[12]

Unlike Wikipedia, creators of "The Moment" had to balance and combine multiple goals: their own interest in creating a meaningful photographic documentation of the inauguration for personal memory, and their collective interest in contributing to a larger project. "The Moment" thus offers a good example of the individual and the crowd working together—the individual photos need to be visually engaging on their own while serving the collage in full. The area closest to the president was the most heavily covered and thus makes for the most dynamic view of the oath. When moving through the photos, it is apparent that professional photographers did a lot of the work (a necessity of emerging technology, perhaps). In other cases, singular photographs stand as keyframes, awaiting new image submissions from inauguration attendees returning home, learning about the Photosynth collage, and uploading their images.

Contributors to "The Moment" certainly aren't making a game, but they are also not merely making a slideshow. Their input data is being used to construct something new—something that could not exist without them. Perhaps in the future, something like the Photosynth software could also stitch together navigable 3D models of a place in time, created from 2D photographs. The resulting environment could then be explored using the kinds of interfaces we are accustomed to in games and virtual worlds. A 2010 Independent Games Festival grand prize finalist, *Trauma*, shows the gamelike potential of the technology. Although not a collaborative work, this game stitches together images of Cologne and allows players to explore the space by constantly shifting perspectives. Through clicks and a Wii-inspired gesture system, players unlock the latent spatial memories of *Trauma*'s protagonist.

Many players and designers of alternate reality games take advantage of collective intelligence, adopting challenges like the one "The Moment" issued to photographers and situating them at the heart of a game in the form of distributed puzzles, storylines, or collectibles across widely geographically and conceptually disparate areas. Such games assume that players will self-organize to solve them. For example, the alternate reality game *I Love Bees*, designed to promote the release of the commercial video-game *Halo 2*, split a science fiction story into minute-long segments and distributed them across the world to payphones that would ring in specific locations at specified times to deliver a segment of the narrative (figure 7.2).[13] The locations and call times provided a secondary puzzle, and the players of the game were expected to coordinate to insure that someone would be present in the right place at the right time to take the call, and then to report the new content back to other players through an equally decentralized network of Web sites, message boards, and chatrooms.

In *World Without Oil*, player-to-player contact was made more explicit, the game's Web site offering a directory of blogs, videos, images, audio, and other resources players had created as proposed solutions to the crisis as it evolved during each day of play. In these games, something unique and unusual is going on: players' actions serve a dual role. On the one hand, they have implications for the game itself. In *I Love Bees*, one of the most engaging forms of player involvement entails collecting, assembling, and interpreting payphone-delivered narrative elements. In both *I Love Bees* and *World Without Oil*, progress and competition is realized in free-form Web-based responses to the situations presented by the games. But on the other hand, these same player actions have an actual, material effect on the world itself.

For example, players of *I Love Bees* payphone missions were forced to find and use payphones in their local communities, artifacts that are quickly disappearing as mobile telephony becomes ubiquitous. As *I Love Bees* and *World Without Oil* designer Jane McGonigal notes, such acts bear

Figure 7.2
Players of *I Love Bees* take a call from the game at one of many payphones scattered throughout the United States and abroad. The "alternate reality game" (or ARG) uses these phones to deliver fragments of a radio play. Photo by Andrew Sorcini.

similarity to world sports and leisure activities like geocaching and letterboxing, which invite participants to explore new spaces—ones they might not otherwise find, let alone scrutinize.[14] As cultural interventions go, finding one's local payphones hardly counts as a monumental act of community involvement, although it may act to train that sort of cultural literacy, as McGonigal herself has argued.[15] A more immediate social benefit comes from another ARG, *Last Call Poker*. Like *I Love Bees*, the game was initiated as part of a marketing campaign for a commercial videogame, this time Activision's wild west shooter *Gun*. And like its predecessor, *Last Call Poker* presented a distributed narrative about the history of American violence as vignettes connected to a specific gun throughout history (much like François Girard's film *The Red Violin* did for an instrument). But in addition to its Web-based narrative, *Last Call Poker* offered a real-world element, a game McGonigal designed for real graveyards around the United States called *Tombstone Hold'em*.

The game itself was a variation of Texas Hold'em poker, the same game players of *Last Call Poker* were enjoying on a special Web site created for the game. Instead of the "hole" cards used in Texas Hold'em, players complete their hands by assembling card values out of tombstones, using a simple algorithm by which the last digit of the death date and the shape of the stone itself are converted into the suit and face value of the card. A pair of players must be able to touch both tombstones that represent the cards, as well as each other, in order to play them as a part of their hand (figure 7.3).

While some might recoil at the idea of throngs of people contorting themselves across the hallowed ground of graves to complete a poker hand, one of the game's intentions was to reactivate cemeteries as the public and social spaces they had been in the nineteenth century. Far from being revered, most graveyards are now considered hallowed through disuse, a

Figure 7.3
Two players at the Atlanta session of *Tombstone Hold'em* stretch across a walkway in order to play a hand. Flat stones are diamonds, pointy ones spades; a cross on top means the stone is a club. Rounded tombstones, which one player can be seen touching, represent hearts. Photo by Mirjam Palosari Eladhari.

fact that has caused many of the nation's cemeteries, often located on prime real estate, to be dug up and relocated in the interests of commercial development.[16] By getting players into these spaces to begin with, the game initiates a relationship between citizens and their local cemeteries, one that will likely result in future visits and, perhaps, civic action in the event that such spaces become threatened. At the very least, playing the game requires a single visit to a local cemetery, which is more action than most citizens take with respect to their historical dead.

Alternating Realities

Players of games like *Tombstone Hold'em* and *World Without Oil* literally alter their world through play. But they do so in an unusual way, not through appeals to logic, through persuasion, or through the simple presentation of a variety of facts and opinions for a reader or viewer to reflect on. Instead, alternate reality games are imaginary worlds, more like the fantasy of make-believe than the reality of hard-hitting news. But don't take the label of "make-believe" as a criticism. The core feature of alternate reality games is their ability to inspire players to compare their current, lived reality with an alternative one—a potential future reality that players can have a hand in creating.

In discussions of the genre, many incorrectly substitute "alternative" for "alternate" reality games, a title that would suggest ARGs offer an escape from the real world—much like the fantasy role-playing game *Dungeons & Dragons* or even live action role-playing games (LARPs), in which stereotypically geeky players pretend to be mages or vampires for an evening. McGonigal makes an important theoretical distinction between alternate and alternative realities. *Alternate* realities, she argues, are "real worlds that use games as a metaphor."[17] She contrasts this notion with *alternative* realities, realities one chooses between. McGonigal further connects the concept of "alternate reality" to science fiction, where the term refers to depictions of a world of changed history and, consequently, of changed dynamics. This idea of *alternation*, then, is central to McGonigal's claims that ARGs allow players to actively change the nature of their lived reality by participating in these alternate ones. Far from escaping reality, players of ARGs are instead trying out different realities. Such experimentation bears much in common with the goals of good journalism.

McGonigal's games are technology enabled, although not deeply computational. As with many ARGs, they take advantage of many media to deliver a distributed narrative through computational or broadcast formats.

But the same sort of "reality alternation" can be found in computer games, as well.

Videogames are good at representing the behavior of systems.[18] When we create videogames, we start with some system in the world—traffic, football, whatever. We can call this the "source system." To create the game, developers build a model of that source system. Videogames are software, so the model is constructed by authoring code that simulates the behavior of interest. Writing code is different from writing prose, taking photographs, or shooting video; code models a set of potential outcomes, all of which conform to the same general rules. As we have discussed on numerous occasions, *procedurality* is a name for this type of representation, for computers' ability to execute rule-based behaviors.[19]

Consider some examples: *Madden Football* is a procedural model of the sport of American football. It models the physical mechanics of human movement, the strategy of different sets of plays, and even the performance properties of specific professional athletes. *SimCity* is a procedural model of urban dynamics. It models the social behavior of residents and workers, as well as the economy, crime rate, pollution level, and other environmental dynamics.

A videogame thus boasts a source system and a procedural model of that source system with which the player needs to interact, providing input to make the procedural model work. When the player plays, he forms some idea about the modeled system, and about the source system it models. He forms these ideas based on the way the source system is simulated, which varies based on why it was chosen. One designer might build a football game about the strategy of coaching, while another might build one about the duties of a particular field position, such as a defensive lineman. Likewise, one designer might build a city simulator that focuses on public services and new urbanism, while another might focus on Robert Moses–style suburban planning.[20]

This is not just a speculative observation: it highlights the fact that the source system never really exists as such. One person's idea of football or a city or any other subject for a representation of any kind is always subjective. The same is true of the subjects of ARGs, like peak oil in the case of *World Without Oil*.

The inherent subjectivity of videogames creates dissonances, the gaps between the designer's procedural model of a source system and a player's subjectivity, his preconceptions and existing understanding of that simulation. This is where videogames become expressive: they encourage players to interrogate and reconcile their own models of the world with the models presented in a game. While videogames are often considered playthings, this charge toward reconciliation can also make games challenging or disturbing.

As mentioned in the context of editorial games, Bogost has called this chasm the "simulation gap," a structure that creates a condition of crisis in the player.[21] The simulation gap can also describe the space that sits between actual reality and the alternate reality an ARG sets atop real environments. In *Last Call Poker* and *World Without Oil*, that alternating reality is constructed by a fiction delivered via Web-based media. But there is another way of accomplishing the same feat, while also invoking the alternating realities of alternate reality games: mobile phones and computers.

Often, we treat mobile devices as tiny microcomputers, more convenient, pocketable versions of laptops. But a notable property of mobile devices is precisely their *mobility*, our ability to use them fluidly out in the world. The values we associate with this kind of mobility often have to do with the ubiquity of access and control; values like seamlessness and immediacy pervade such notions. But if we recall the gap between the procedural representation in a videogame and the source system that game models, we might take another approach: using mobile devices' properties of presence and location to *amplify difference and incongruity* rather than to remove them. This technique recalls the artistic technique of *defamiliarization*, most commonly associated with Russian formalism of the mid-twentieth century.

As an example of this kind of mobile persuasive game design, consider a game Bogost created at Persuasive Games. *Airport Insecurity* is a mobile game about the Transportation Security Administration (TSA). In the game, the player takes the role of a passenger at any of the 138 most trafficked airports in the United States. The gameplay is simple: the player must progress through the security line in an orderly and dignified fashion, taking care not to lag behind when space opens up, as well as to avoid direct contact with other passengers. Upon reaching the X-ray check, the player must place luggage and personal items on the belt. The game randomly assigns such items to the player, including "questionable" items like lighters and scissors, as well as legitimately dangerous items like knives and guns (figure 7.4).

For each airport, Persuasive Games gathered traffic and wait time data to model the flow of the queues, and they also gathered as much as they could find in the public record on TSA performance. General Accountability Office (GAO) analysis of TSA performance was once reported publicly, but the agency started classifying the information after it became clear that it might pose a national security risk. The upshot of such tactics is that the

Figure 7.4
A player of *Airport Insecurity* decides whether to discard a pair of scissors and a lighter at the TSA checkpoint, unaware of exactly how strict the security procedures are at this specific location.

average citizen has no concept of what level of security he or she receives in exchange for the rights he or she forgoes. Though the U.S. government wants its citizens to believe that increased protection and reduced rights are necessary to protect us from terrorism, the effectiveness of airport security practices is ultimately uncertain. The game makes claims about this uncertainty by modeling it procedurally: players can choose to dispose of their dangerous items in a trash can near the X-ray belt, or test the limits of the screening process by trying to carry them through.

Nothing mentioned so far about *Airport Insecurity* couldn't have been done on a non-mobile platform. But the mobile phone was chosen precisely so the game could be played *while in line at airport security*. When in queue for travel, many of us file blindly through without asking ourselves how well or justly security actually operates. By inviting players to explore a videogame-based model of the very experience they are taking part in, the game amplifies their estrangement by collapsing the source system and the modeled system on top of one another. Mobile devices help make this possible.

Consider another example, this one a live-action game played via text messaging on mobile phones in a real-world environment. *Cruel 2 B Kind*, a ubiquitous game McGonigal and Bogost created, is a modification of the popular social game *Assassin*, wherein players attempt to surreptitiously eliminate each other with predetermined "weapons" like water pistols. But in *Cruel 2 B Kind*, players "kill with kindness"—each player is assigned a "weapon" and "weakness" that corresponds with a common, even ordinary pleasantry (figure 7.5). For example, players might have to compliment someone's shoes, or serenade them. While *Assassin* is usually played in closed environments like college dorms, *Cruel 2 B Kind* is played in public, on the streets of New York City or San Francisco or anywhere else.

Players not only remain in the dark about their target, they also don't know who is playing. In these situations, players are forced to use guesswork or deduction to figure out who they might approach. As a result, players often "attack" the wrong groups of people, or people who are not playing at all. The reactions to such encounters are startling for all concerned; after all, exchanging anonymous pleasantries is not something commonly done on the streets of New York. *Cruel 2 B Kind* asks the player to layer an alternative set of social practices atop the world they normally occupy. Instead of ignoring their fellow citizens, the game demands that players interact with them. This juxtaposition of game rules and social rules draws attention to the way people do (or more properly, don't) interact with one another in everyday life.

Mobile devices thus offer a particular opportunity to produce player deliberation—not by making those arguments seamless and comfortable, but by making them disruptive and strange. When alternate realities go mobile, they hold power not only because mobile devices can easily insert aspects of the real world into daily life, but also because they can insert aspects of imaginary worlds into daily life.

Serious ARGs

As *Cruel 2 B Kind* and *Airport Insecurity* demonstrate, there are many genre variants of games that take place fully or partly in the real world. Many names for such games exist too: Frank Lantz and his New York studio Area/Code have suggested the title "big games" to draw attention to the large-scale nature of such work. A classic example of a big game is *Pac Manhattan*, a fanciful adaptation of the classic coin-op arcade game *Pac-Man* played in

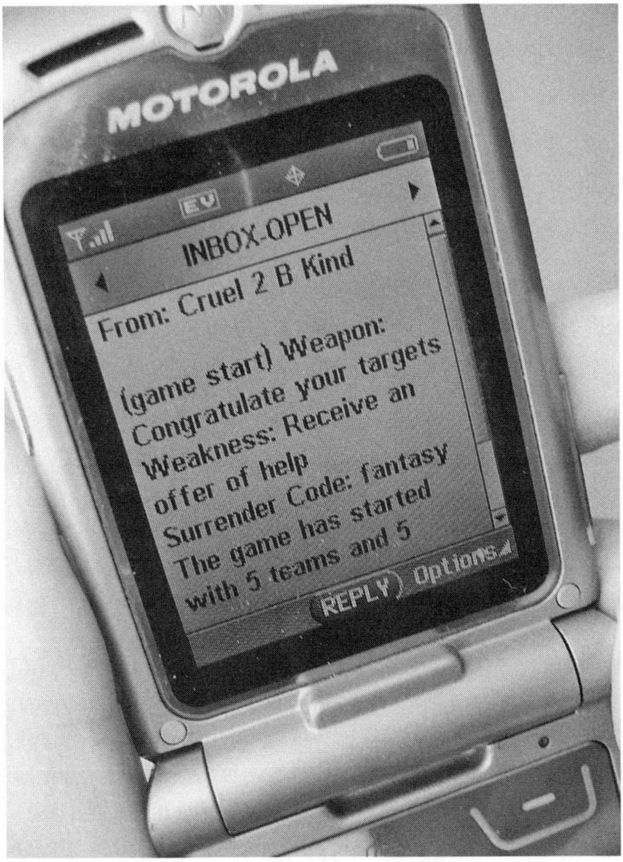

Figure 7.5
One of many roving warriors receives instructions for assaulting the passing citizenry with flowers, song, and compliments during a round of *Cruel 2 B Kind*. The game forces players to assess everyone as potential predator and prey, leading to sometimes-hilarious but always-polite impromptu interactions. Photo by Kiyash Monsef.

the streets of New York. To play, players dressed up like the game's hero and enemies chase each other throughout the mazelike streets of the city.[22] Such games bear much in common with avant-garde performance art movements, especially Situationism and Fluxus, with their focus on reclaiming public spaces.

Though definitions are loose and rapidly changing, alternate reality games have typically included certain common features, most prominent among them an ongoing, distributed narrative, a set of independent puzzles to be solved, and, perhaps most important, a deliberate blurring of the fictional nature of the game itself—a feature often shorthanded with the catch-phrase "this is not a game," after a tagline used in the early ARG *The Beast*. Such games usually involve a "rabbit hole" or a "trailhead"—a subtle, hidden clue that the game has begun. For *I Love Bees*, the rabbit hole took the form of a URL (www.ilovebees.com), which flashed for only a few frames at the end of a trailer for the *Halo 2* game it promoted. The Web site was purportedly the homepage of a humble Napa Valley beekeeper that had been hacked by aliens. The beekeeper became an actor in the fiction, asking players to help her figure out what was going on.

But as the ARG has slowly transitioned from a complex publicity stunt funded by advertisers to a legitimate genre in its own right, these games have rejected the rabbit hole in favor of more deliberate announcements and invitations to participate, a feature probably necessary to make the genre more widely accessible. And, perhaps counterintuitively, *World Without Oil*'s real world theme might have made it more appealing than the unusual fictional fantasy worlds depicted in previous ARGs like *The Beast* and *I Love Bees*.

The fact that *World Without Oil* also tackled a serious issue, and appeared to present viable potential solutions in some cases at least, was a fact not lost on others. *World Without Oil* codesigner Jane McGonigal happens also to be a researcher at the Institute for the Future (IFTF), a future forecasting research institute in Palo Alto. McGonigal and IFTF realized that one of the powerful features of *World Without Oil* wasn't just its ability to train or persuade players to adopt a particular reaction to an oil crisis. Just as promising was the game's ability to reveal what people might do when faced with such a crisis, even a fictional one of their own imagining. Since IFTF deals in predicting the future, the opportunity seemed obvious. IFTF adapted the ARG into the "forecasting game," a way of predicting what people might do in future scenarios by allowing them to role-play those scenarios in advance.

Their first effort was *Superstruct*, a game that takes the *World Without Oil* concept—a challenge from the near future—and expands it beyond the concerns of energy shortages. *Superstruct* presents a variety of problems from the year 2019, including insufficient food supplies, global pandemics, communication network attacks, alternative energy demands, and massive refugee migrations. As in *World Without Oil*, *Superstruct* is played by making and posting media to the Internet. From the game's FAQ:

Superstruct is played on forums, blogs, videos, wikis, and other familiar online spaces. We show you the world as it might look in 2019. You show us what it's like to live there. Bring what you know and who you know, and we'll all figure out how to make 2019 a world we want to live in.[23]

But unlike *World Without Oil*, *Superstruct* adds an explicit score, both personal and collective (figure 7.6). This design revision makes the act of creating media more gamelike, at least in a basic way. Players can earn individual

Figure 7.6
The *Superstruct* Web site updates regularly with new scenarios in a myriad of global "Superthreats," pictured at left. "Quarantine" suggests global health threats, "Ravenous" involves the dwindling food supply, "Power Struggle" signals international political conflict, "Outlaw Planet" represents technology in society, and "Generation Exile" deals with mass population migration.

points by recruiting other players, and they can earn badges by meeting certain requirements or "powers." For example, the "Longbroading" badge requires the player to "see a much bigger picture; thinking in terms of higher level systems, bigger networks, longer cycles," and the "Influency" badge requires "knowing how to be persuasive and tell compelling stories in multiple social media spaces." Badges are awarded by the "Superthreat Guides," IFTF agents who run the game.

At least one game of *Superstruct*'s future predicting ilk has been mustered explicitly as a journalistic endeavor. In 2009, ABC released *Earth 2100*, a television series about the potential calamities of the next century.[24] As ABC's marketing describes the project, "the 'perfect storm' of population growth, resource depletion and climate change could converge with catastrophic results." Borrowing more than a few pages from the IFTF's crowdsourcing and future forecasting project, *Earth 2100* included a game in which players view video summaries about the state of the world in 2015, 2050, and 2100 before making their own videos based on the possible conditions presented by those scenarios. The best submissions were promised airtime during a two-hour prime-time special on ABC.

Whereas *Superstruct* considers all of its different disaster scenarios as individual, encapsulated alternate futures that don't interrelate, *Earth 2100* takes a holistic approach. It asks players to imagine what would happen if multiple such conditions converge over time; therefore, *Superstruct* tends to have many well-developed storylines for each possible future, whereas *Earth 2100* details the complex yet undefined soup of a traumatic future.

The *Earth 2100* timeline proceeds as follows. In 2015, the world continues to suffer increased numbers of floods, droughts, and wildfires. Humanity fails to adequately confront the global climate crisis in this short period and coastal regions suffer increasingly severe hurricanes and flooding as glaciers melt. Provocative video clips show an African exodus and a Mexican mass border crossing. Food shortages become a mounting problem in the less industrialized countries.

By 2050, food production cannot meet consumption levels as populations in Africa and Asia balloon. Water runs dry as the climate heats up. Major urban centers risk ocean floods, and major reservoirs like the Colorado River dry up, making it impossible to live in vast stretches of North America. By this time the country is nearly out of gasoline, and brown-outs or complete electricity loss is common. Scientists urge citizens to prepare for the possibility of nuclear war, as desperate countries with nothing left to lose grow irritable.

Finally, in 2100, potable water has completely run out. The world resembles a second Middle Ages; meager pockets of affluence are surrounded on all sides by subsistence living. Accompanying video clips show subsistence living in African villages. One is left to imagine the political and religious consequences of these conditions.

In the early weeks of the game, submissions came in two forms: typical talking head video logs and meticulously constructed vignettes with actual acting and pyrotechnics. The TV producers encouraged more of the amateur talking head content to elicit a greater number of submissions and to capture the low-fi aesthetic of the viral vlog genre. Despite a confusing map interface to view submissions, entries trickled in from literally all around the world.

For example, under the "Solutions" category, Jason Mann of the University of Georgia's Agroecology Lab and Full Moon Farm gives a basic explanation of the changing politics of farming in the United States. His rundown explains how agriculture has become a niche in formerly rural states such as Georgia, and he encourages everyone to understand the scary future of uncertain food supplies. Mann also gives an explanation of his work to correct public ignorance about food production: students from around the state can come visit his farm to spend half their time working the field and the other half learning textbook ecology and biology in a synergistic setting.

Many entries simply reflect on the conditions presented by the introductory video: water shortages, rising prices on groceries, and climate change. One impressive video (in the shaky handheld style of the 2009 J. J. Abrams film *Cloverfield*) depicts the "next big attack" on Manhattan through flashback. Just as in *Cloverfield*, the cameraperson documents smiling New Yorkers chatting with each other and having a good time before running outside to view a noxious cloud of poisonous gas exploding over the city.

At the beginning of her vlog entry, Dionne Figgins of Los Angeles mentions that although Obama's presidency raised spirits in 2009, few people heeded his call to reduce our environmental impact. Now widespread water rationing efforts crisscross the United States. She details her disgust at an emerging divide between the rich and poor (one can pay $300 to bypass the ration for a week). Figgins offers one of the only "series" of videos submitted. Although most users put specific dates on their videos, she explicitly establishes a rough timeline for the two pieces she created for 2015. Her second entry takes place on July 4 and highlights the irony of America's growing dependence on other countries, a dependence that the world regards with disdain on account of our former unwillingness to cooperate with them or to successfully decelerate the tragedy in Africa. An African American woman, Ms. Figgins clearly understands that by politicizing her submissions she engages the current power structures leading to the convergence of escalating disasters in the 2015 scenario.

In the sole example of a video from 2100, two Chinese men run through a dusty, destroyed village while avoiding gunfire from invading Russians. The scenario doesn't mesh well with the introductory material provided by the producers, who predict events such as this occurring in 2050 as opposed to this late date, but the submission was approved anyway. Since it reflects a fear of Russian imperialism among Chinese citizens, players might learn something about a current condition that mainstream news media ignores. In America one only hears about climatological and political crises in China.

If *Superstruct*'s status as a game is limited to just a scoring system, *Earth 2100*'s is practically nonexistent. Whereas the former game rewards players for specific contributions to the game community, the latter offers no such affordances for player achievement. The "winners" of the contest were supposed to receive airtime on ABC, a political nod to television culture's ongoing obsession with reality television fame. Moreover, the creators of *Superstruct* released content regularly in order to drive the narrative of their game—that is, they did actual design work—whereas *Earth 2100* users only get the introductory footage that would have been used in the television programming anyway. A lack of a community feel and ludic structure results from all of these shortcomings.

By the time the *Earth 2100* program aired in June 2009, the producers realized that the game had played only a minor part in the overall cross-media production, and the Web site reflected this marginalization. Player submissions were now simply called "video submissions," and the game, relegated to a sidebar below the fold, now used scare quotes to describe itself: *Earth 2100 "Game."* In fact, following the link loaded an entirely different game, an "international climate change 'war game'" from the Center for a New American Security, a centrist beltway think tank, run in July 2008. The Center's report indicates that "45 scientists, national security strategists, and members of the business and policy communities from Asia, South Asia, Europe, and North America" played, although, alas, "the Climate Change War Game did not result in a fictitious international agreement."[25]

Earth 2100 is not a game, but a future-predicting video contest. Without the well-designed structures of goal, challenge, and reward, the "players" of *Earth 2100* struggle to understand exactly how they're supposed to construe their narratives, and the benefits of doing so, either for themselves or for any broader social purpose. *Superstruct* is a research game created for the benefit of the Institute for the Future. In fact, critics might point out that the project is little more than a massive, uncompensated outsourcing project, since IFTF sells its services privately to large corporations like Intel and Johnson & Johnson. But even such a critic could not deny that the game's goals and eventual use were far more journalistic than those of ABC's effort, which amount to little more than a clever marketing effort for the television show.

From Alternate Reality Games to Community Games

As *Earth 2100*'s silent withdrawal attests, numerous problems face games of this sort. Practically, they are collaborative, public, and difficult to manage, requiring careful attention both in initial conception and during play by experienced puppetmasters. They are also open ended, with no guarantee of success, if indeed success is even a valid way to measure an experience like *I Love Bees* or *World Without Oil*.

Journalistically, one might issue another charge against alternate reality games: they have questionable veracity. In a fictional context, one can say anything about a fantasy world. But in the context of a plausible future, as in *Superstruct* or *World Without Oil*, the accuracy of the game's claims is hard to demonstrate and defend. Shouldn't a journalistic ARG at least have the responsibility to present verified, factual underpinnings to problems before it throws them out to players for possible solutions? It is good to see discourse take place on these topics, but how much must they be based in an immediate reality to perform a journalistic function?

A solution might come from a reframing of the genre itself. Despite the intrigue of alternating realities, perhaps the journalistic power of this genre lies not in the alternation itself, but in the choice of the actual reality that the game attempts to provide an alternative for.

In a world of complex global issues, getting people to think seriously about future scenarios like those presented in *World Without Oil* or *Earth 2100* is undoubtedly important. But one of the most interesting *outcomes* of the former game was not a set of overarching global solutions but a number of specific, local ones: players who started carpools with their colleagues, or found and documented the best bike routes in their areas, or started and then maintained real community gardens, or developed real disaster plans for their families in the event of a more humble cataclysm. There are a number of lessons worth drawing out of such a perspective.

First, in such cases it is not the "alternate reality" part of the game that is the most meaningful, but the community—the *specific* community—in which the realities alternate. Even if a problem is regional or global, its causes and effects are always rooted in specific places and situations. Given the fact that newspapers are inherently local (or at least, they used to be), *community games* is perhaps a better name than *alternate reality games*, particularly in a journalistic context.

Second, good community games produce meaningful discourse through trial and error rather than through opinion. Such discourse does not amount to the interpretive work that one might perform on a film, book, or play. Nor is it the conversation one has with friends or strangers to discover how to solve a puzzle or beat a videogame boss. Instead, the discourse of community games involves movement toward the solution to some specific problem. Furthermore, that discourse can be tested and measured for its value as a potential solution through action, rather than as a measure of a specific number of comments, subscribers, or links.

And third, exerting effort means expressing interest. As game scholar Espen Aarseth has observed, all games require "non-trivial effort" to play, as player interaction is required for a game to operate at all.[26] But community games require a different kind of labor, one that involves even greater personal effort and investment, one that goes beyond manipulating tokens on a board or characters onscreen. In addition, these games ask players to put themselves on the line, in public, often in front of strangers. This is a type of community involvement that community activism, let alone the local news, rarely accomplishes.

So far, just one example of this kind of community game exists. *Picture the Impossible*, developed jointly by the Lab for Social Computing at the Rochester Institute of Technology and the *Rochester Democrat and Chronicle*, is a game situated in a specific geographic location. The Web site describes the game's mission:

The game engages members of the community in exploration of the City of Rochester, and encourages both creativity and charitable giving in the community. Players participate in a range of activities, including casual web-based games, games that bring players out to events and locations throughout the city, and games that involve the tangible aspects of the *Democrat and Chronicle* newspaper itself.[27]

The name "Picture the Impossible" is meant to play on the city's history in the field of optics: Kodak, Xerox, Bausch & Lomb, and Pictometry were all founded in Rochester.[28] The game began September 12, 2009, and ended a month and a half later, on Halloween. Players were organized into factions (The Tree, Forge, and Watch), which competed for points to earn prizes. The faction dynamic created competitive drama in the game, though it seems like a holdover trope from ARGs rather than an integral design choice.

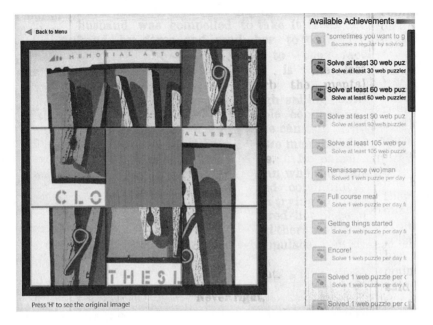

Figure 7.7
This sliding tile puzzle from week one of Rochester's *Picture the Impossible* ties in with a gallery showing at a local museum. These Webgames made use the talents of local game design students from the Rochester Institute of Technology, including Joe Pietruch, who designed and coded all twenty-one of the ARG's sliding puzzles.

The game separated activities into online and off-line tasks. Online, the game offered tile-sliding puzzles of local photographs, map quizzes to test Rochester trivia, as well as jigsaw puzzles and video quizzes (figure 7.7). Off-line, players would extract passwords for online sites from the paper's crossword puzzle, go geocaching and do scavenger hunts in the community, create videos, take photographs, and do charity work. These activities portray the cultural heritage of Rochester while forming a sense of local community. Secondarily, the game's creators hoped they might help boost tourism, newspaper sales, and the local economy.

Though the game's online discussion board did not boast huge numbers, it showed a tight-knit group who became invested in the project. One player by the name of Tazwalker posted a lengthy entry on the *Picture the Impossible* forums discussing how the game had improved his community involvement. "I find myself to be a better person from it," he wrote, "and I feel accomplished for helping and getting to know others while I've used the city as my playground."[29] Though isolated, these responses suggest a viable example for future community games.

Given the state of the news industry, especially the local paper industry, the *Democrat and Chronicle* and RIT accomplished something important in *Picture the Impossible*. They developed a model for a platform that involves a variety of organizations, drawing together the local community and advancing the role of the local paper.

The game also coalesced the local community through its very underwriting. *Picture the Impossible* would have remained impossible without the collaboration of community sponsors and partners.[30] Microsoft Bing provided much of the technical implementation, local charities underwrote some of the cost, local media company WXXI provided the multimedia support, Rochester-founded Kodak donated prizes, and Boston-based SCVNGR created the platform for the local scavenger hunts and geocaching. The Rochester Institute of Technology's Student Innovation Center and its Department of Interactive Games and Media developed the game's structure, mechanics, and implementation, while the *Democrat and Chronicle* supplied material and puzzles created by its reporters, artists, photographers, and editors. The *Democrat and Chronicle*, facing the hardships of the print media industry, chose to try something fresh and inventive. "Picture the Impossible" could just as easily describe the undertaking itself: in a time of economic hardship, get local companies to team up with a newspaper and a university to develop a game.

Picture the Impossible suggests a final reason to prefer the name *community games* over *alternate reality games* (or even designer Frank Lantz's name *big games*): people can understand the idea of engaging in play in their own communities as a means to better both themselves and their community, far more easily than they are likely to grasp the idea of becoming citizens of some hypothetical fantasy or science fiction world told through distributed media. Community games are, at their hearts, immensely nostalgic: they invite a kind of wholesome return to a time when communities were local, when people knew their neighbors and their shopkeepers, when someone's problem was everyone's. Is this too retrograde a promise to deliver on realistically? Perhaps. But at a time when the local newspaper is almost as much a memory as the milkman, maybe there's no harm in trying.

8   Platforms

Think about how today's citizens engage with the news. We flip rhyth-
mically between cable news channels until something strikes us. We
click hastily through a multitude of Web sites with little regard for brand
or authority. We comment shamelessly. We spread links for argument
or social status as much as or more than for debate. News comes and
goes quickly. It is no longer sufficient to count on the morning train
or the evening recliner as a surefire context for engagement with the
news. Information runs rampant, mixed up among the hundreds of television channels, the thousands of specialty news sources, the millions of
blogs.

News organizations did not create the tidal wave of content delivery
systems that have overtaken newspapers, periodicals, and television broadcasts. The World Wide Web, blogs, online video, status updates, social
networks, even videogames—all of the infrastructures into which journalism is emigrating—were created with other primary purposes in mind.
Journalists have been trying to understand and exploit these digital media
for their purposes, but they have infrequently attempted to intervene at
the level of the *platform* itself.[1] Instead of asking how journalists can *use*
platforms like the Web or Facebook to deliver news, what if we asked a
different question: how might journalists *create new* platforms for news?
Such systems might alter our foundational notions of what news looks like
and how it behaves.

Playing the News

After the modest success of their political simulation and documentary
game *PeaceMaker*, about the Israeli–Palestinian conflict, ImpactGames
cofounders Eric Brown and Asi Burak came to a realization. Even though
they had sunk years of development and hundreds of thousands of dollars

of investment into the creation and release of *PeaceMaker*, they would have to go back to the drawing board for their studio's next game.

It's not that unusual: most media, from articles to books to software, have to be created afresh, designed for specific content and contexts. With a subject like conflict in the Middle East, Brown and Burak placed a safe bet: it was unlikely that political and social resolution would come about during the game's two-year development cycle. Many documentary games share *PeaceMaker*'s relative timelessness. Even though they were created years after the fact, there is still much to learn from *9-11 Survivor* and *Kuma\War*.

But as the other genres of newsgames suggest, not all newsworthy subjects justify lengthy investments of time and money. For example, though *PeaceMaker* successfully characterized the overall shape of the crisis in Palestine, it was unable to adapt itself to specific events as they happened. The game traded robust dynamics for a focus on specific events. Current event games address particular events as they arise, documentary games after they have taken place. Both require some degree of lengthy, custom development. Brown and Burak wondered if there might be a way to expedite the process.

The result was *Play the News*, an unusual newsgame that gives players the opportunity to play with news coverage itself, rather than playing out events within the news.[2] The *Play the News* Web site presents visitors with a handful of events taken from current news stories—for example, the late December 2008 Israeli attack on the Gaza Strip, code-named Operation Cast Lead; a July 2009 Los Angeles City Council moratorium on the construction of fast-food establishments in the city's poorest areas; and a celebrity sleaze story about the exploits of Britney Spears. The player chooses an event, and the game presents background information and context for the story, some of its underlying causes and issues, and key stakeholders. Such presentation can include text, audio, photographs, video, and infographics.

After gathering enough knowledge through exploration, the player chooses a role as one of the event's stakeholders. In the case of the Los Angeles burger ban, stakeholders include city residents, community activists, the state government, consumers, fast-food franchisees, independent restauranteurs, mobile vendors, and health experts.[3] The game first explains the exact interests of the selected stakeholder role, and then it prompts the player to make one decision and one prediction: what should be done in the presented situation, and what will actually happen (see figure 8.1 for an example).

Figure 8.1
In the "Operation Cast Lead" episode of *Play the News*, players learn about the events leading up to a conflict between Israel and Palestine. ImpactGames layers a static image with location- and time-based nodes that can be clicked for more information. The toolbar below tells the player about major political forces at work in the area, past actions, and stakes in the issue.

After submitting a decision, the player waits for the event to play out in the real world, at which point the game's operators update statistics and player scores. *Play the News* judges predictions for accuracy, publishing scores to the Web site under the player's profile. ImpactGames hopes these public scores create an incentive to play the game regularly, overcoming some of the challenges of infrequently updated current event games. But the system also offers another benefit: a community-based prediction market allows the game to recast stories about events in the recent past as cause-and-effect scenarios in the near future. A discussion board for each scenario allows players to debate the relative merits of different choices in order to clarify their predictions, rather than just to argue about ideology.

ImpactGames faced unique challenges as it attempted to reframe news reading as a game. What kinds of stories make for the best games? How do you ensure the possible outcomes are accounted for? How do you foster community involvement and discourse? What kind of business model is needed to keep such a game running? And, perhaps most critically, what does this kind of game offer that is lacking in traditional news media outlets? According to Eric Brown, the game was meant to inspire citizens to explore different news stories so as to develop both a broad view and a deep comprehension.[4]

In order to cover many different scenarios, from politics to health to entertainment, ImpactGames attempted to standardize a structure for each story. Inspired by their work on *PeaceMaker*, Brown and Burak concluded that conflicts made for the best playable stories. An event like a bombing in the West Bank, for example, could be cast as a contextualized act rather than a reported event. Whether or not it would cause reciprocation, it might highlight the dense issues that lead to the climax, cueing players to synthesize a more detailed understanding of those issues as they moved from fact to prediction.

The scenario about the Los Angeles City Council fast-food moratorium offers a more detailed example. On the surface, the story seems like a simple statement of fact, but details underlying the situation highlight issues of public health and government regulation. In an era when news stories are often one-sided (or no-sided), the community participation and discussion surrounding the game sparked many-sided debates. In the Burger Ban discussion thread, one player wondered if preventing the establishment of new restaurants, rather than enforcing new regulations on existing ones, would reach a desirable result. Another agreed, highlighting the importance of suppressing specific ingredients, like trans fats in cooking oils. Another suggested that education, not regulation, offered the best path to long-term health.[5]

In order to construct these scenarios, ImpactGames formed a kind of videogame newsroom. They hired a small team of writers, artists, programmers, and community managers. Brown and Burak served as editors.[6] In the newsroom, creators could pitch ideas for stories or decide on events from the daily news. Once the team chose a story, they would break it down into issues and possible follow-ups. The group would then evaluate these issues to extract underlying causes, parties involved, similar or preceding events, and any oppositional positions. The editorial team would condense all this material into roles and actions, paying special attention to perspectives that offered players a chance to understand the issue in a new and unobvious way.

Play the News asked its users to experience both information and gameplay uncomfortably. World events might play out in hours or days, but they could just as easily draw out for weeks or months. Unlike fantasy football, in which a prediction round will always be completed by the end of the next week's game, *Play the News* operated on an irregular schedule. ImpactGames communicates with players by email when stories realize their outcomes. Brown reports that around half of the players who had completed a game clicked back to the Web site to check their results, many of whom also took the opportunity to review a new story.[7] Though promising, this figure describes a small group of dedicated players recruited for the game's late 2008 beta test.

Ultimately, *Play the News* failed for financial reasons. ImpactGames was never able to develop a successful business model for the game, even though Brown used the beta as a proving ground for a number of possible business models. First, he tried to run advertising on the site to capitalize on Web traffic, but the small company wasn't able immediately to draw an audience that would generate significant advertising revenue. Next, Brown considered reducing costs by replacing staff-created games with contributions from the player community, as so many Web 2.0 contemporaries had done. But such an effort would have been difficult or impossible, since ImpactGames had essentially developed a small, professional newsroom to create journalistically meaningful games. Such professionalism could not be guaranteed in user-submitted scenarios. Finally, ImpactGames attempted to license its software to news organizations who would publish it on their own Web sites using their own newsrooms to create content. A game scenario written by the news organization would be integrated into their normal distribution models, offering a novel interactive experience for their readers. Brown reports that potential licensees were ready to commit to this option, but the global economic crisis of autumn 2008 clobbered all their remaining leads.[8]

What Is a Platform for News?

News publishers liked the idea behind *Play the News*. Yet even though the product offered supplementary material to encourage reader engagement, none were willing to put it into use. During meetings with ImpactGames, these publishers asked how they could sell advertising against a niche offering that needed to be cultivated over time.

The misunderstanding is instructive. A sensationalist story, image, video, or current event game might attract many visitors to a Web site in the near term, but it would be a one-off affair. *Play the News* offers something different: not just a new way to package news in the form of a game, but a novel form of the news itself. *Play the News* is a *platform* for turning stories into prediction games—games that in turn encourage potentially sophisticated discussion about the possible outcomes of an event or situation.

In the most basic terms, a platform is a system that simplifies the development of other things built atop it.[9] Platforms can be abstractions, like a standard or specification, or they can have material form, like an architecture or infrastructure. Individual creators can use a platform as a basis for constructing something. For example, the Gutenberg printing press is a technology that enables the mechanical reproduction of text with movable type, enabling easy, rapid copying of textual materials. Improvements on this platform during the industrial revolution led to the ability to print pamphlets and newspapers, which in turn created another new platform— the newspaper industry—for the dissemination of information and ideas. Soon after, the newspaper industry invented and evolved a network of reporters, editors, advertisers, printers, distributors, and retailers to create the daily news as it existed throughout the twentieth century.

Once the printing press, newsroom, and distribution system existed, newspapers didn't have to reinvent infrastructure every time they wanted to publish. They could focus on reporting instead. And the inverted pyramid of the typical news story provides a formula or platform for writing that offers a standard for acceptable results. Other media platforms like broadcast television or the World Wide Web also provide infrastructures for creating and disseminating content, including news. For example, the Web browser's ability to download and render linked multimedia documents served by a remote server means that online stories can include streaming video and photo galleries.

Creators benefit most from platforms when they choose them deliberately. Such volition has been uncommon on the Web, as media publishers have adopted it as a distribution platform without sufficient concern for what the Web does well and poorly. To cite but one case, the layout of the print newspaper doesn't fit well on a computer screen, which is better served by hyperlinked ideas that allow readers to dig deeper. Yet, most newspaper Web sites remediate the general form of the newspaper, with masthead, headlines, and jumps. Understanding how platforms work, where they excel, where they falter, and how people engage with them is a critical part of understanding the adoption of new media forms based on existing media types.

When platforms work well, they disappear into the background. Newspaper journalists don't think about the newsroom or presses that facilitate the construction of their paper. Likewise, readers don't think about the wire services and trucking companies that facilitate their delivery. We don't dwell on the format of the evening news, or the operation of a Web server that delivers the bits that comprise a blog post. When platforms don't work, they advance into the foreground, where we can question, revise, or abandon them.

Such a moment has arrived in journalism. Thanks to a confluence of factors, the familiar platforms for news production, consumption, and dissemination have been called into question. In some cases, current computing platforms need further adaptation to the news. In other cases, perhaps, new platforms must be developed. In some cases, however, those new platforms might already be sitting right under our noses.

Fantasy Sports

ESPN. Yahoo! Sports. CBS Sportsline. Not only are these three companies traditional sports news organizations, they are three of the biggest providers of a wildly successful newsgame platform: fantasy sports. Sports deals in detailed information. Fans memorize yardage and turnovers from the previous night's football game. Athletes look to their statistics to find areas of improvement. Ordinarily, that information just determines who won or lost a game, although sports fans pay careful attention to statistics as they dig into the details of their favorite teams and competitors. Like *Play the News*, fantasy sports takes data and information from real-world events, in this case athlete performance, and turns them into points in a prediction game. The raw materials for fantasy sports are statistics, data created from the exhaust of professional athletics.

A fantasy sports competitor assembles a team of real-life athletes who earn points based on their performance during competition. In a real game, athletes compete for a particular team, like the Washington Redskins or New Orleans Saints, which can win, lose, or draw. But the players themselves accrue more specific statistics that represent their individual performances. For example, the "owner" of a fantasy football team builds a lineup of quarterbacks, running backs, receivers, tight ends, kickers, and defenses. Players usually join a fantasy league with friends or colleagues. Two owners' teams compete head-to-head each week, and when Sunday rolls around, the sum of the individual performances of one owner's athletes are compared to those of his or her opponent. These two players comprise one match-up in a league that parallels that of the NFL.

Like the crossword, fantasy sports are among the old-timers of news-games.[10] In the 1950s, Wilfred Winkenbach invented fantasy golf, in which players select several golfers in a tournament, and the player with the lowest number of combined strokes wins.[11] Fantasy versions of more popular sports like baseball and football arrived by the end of World War II, although the practice did not become a popular hobby until the 1980s.[12] In 1962, Winkenbach, who was then part-owner of the Oakland Raiders, brought the form to football, expanding its features more thoroughly.[13] He called his group the Greater Oakland Professional Pigskin Prognosticators League (GOPPPL), and its first members were either Raiders' staff or sports reporters for the *Oakland Tribune*.[14] They used the GOPPPL as a way to actively track league statistics, examining the competition to see how the Raiders measured up. In 1980, sports writer Daniel Okrent established the "Rotisserie League" variety of fantasy baseball (the name was derived from a New York restaurant where Okrent and friends sometimes met, La Rôtisserie Française).[15] Instead of using statistical information from past seasons, the league would draft players at the beginning of a season, and players would make predictions and adjustments based on athlete perfor-mance, injury, and other circumstances that might befall a real baseball manager.

Sports journalists covered the fantasy version of the game extensively during the 1981 season, largely because the baseball strike of that year hadn't left them with much else to write about.[16] Okrent credits Rotisserie league baseball with much of *USA Today*'s early success, since the paper published much more detailed box scores than its competitors. Eventually the paper even created a special edition, *Baseball Weekly*, just for statistics.[17] While this issue wasn't used exclusively for fantasy sports, it's clear that baseball fans' fascination with stats helped fuel the growth of the form.

By the late 1980s, fantasy football had caught up with the national pastime. The year 1987 saw the introduction of the Fantasy Football Index, although USA Today didn't add the NFL to its *Sports Weekly* magazine until the early 2000s. The rise of the World Wide Web in the mid- to late 1990s also provided a new home for fantasy sports, offering both simplified dis-tribution and automated computer statistical tracking for online leagues.

Today, most newspaper sports sections devote a portion of their ink to fantasy sports, as do television broadcasts like ESPN's SportsCenter. ESPN.com even offers both "Regular" and "Fantasy" tabs that allows users to quickly switch from sports reporting to fantasy-related news (figure 8.2).[18] Furthermore, fantasy sports have expanded beyond the traditional domain of baseball and football to include cricket and soccer, among

Figure 8.2

The fourth tab at the top of ESPN's Web site loads a Fantasy version of its coverage, one just as feature-rich as the site devoted to actual sports news. Readers can access relevant videos, commentary, and stats about sports ranging from football to stock car racing.

others. In 2004, a trade association even emerged, the Fantasy Sports Writers Association, to represent the growing numbers of journalists covering fantasy sports exclusively.[19]

In the 2007 season, running back Adrien Peterson enjoyed not only a stellar performance on the field, but also increased values in fantasy leagues and rising stock in the following year's fantasy draft. Fantasy sports have thus exerted a strong influence on sports reporting—football news affects fantasy decisions, and fantasy participation affects the focus of football news. Because much of sports news involves the dramatic framing of data and statistics (scores, records, team and individual performances, predictions of match-ups based on the comparison of data), it's easy to see how fantasy reporting integrates with the news. The results are significant: some twenty-seven million Americans generate $800 million to $1 billion in revenue each year playing fantasy football and baseball.[20]

Fantasy sports offer a perspective on the role of platforms in newsgames. Though news companies are not the only organizations with access to sports statistics—anybody can pay for a statistics service—it is something they already possess and use regularly. Fantasy sports rely heavily on the infrastructure of the sports news, which performs the drudgery of collecting the massive amounts of data produced each week by sports events around the country. A lesson emerges: creating a new format for news does not necessarily mean starting from scratch. Rather, it requires carefully assessing and exploiting existing assets to enable new forms.

Fantasies Off the Field

If sports statistics begat the platform that created fantasy sports, then fantasy sports inspired another, more general platform: the "fantasy market." Even though sports are replete with instrumented data collection, the idea of assigning scores to predictions applies to many other areas.

The Hollywood Stock Exchange (HSX), for example, has created an entire valuation ecosystem for all things film and television.[21] Unlike fantasy sports, the structure of which resembles its source material (teams, owners, tournaments), HSX models itself after a financial exchange, using words like MovieStocks and StarBonds, offering IPOs, trades, and options, and describing a player's lineup not as a cast but as a portfolio. The service takes the idea of remixing the individual performance data of actors, directors, and films and uses these market dynamics to predict films' box office revenue and award pickup.

Yet not all fantasy games need to arise from traditional numerical data. The now defunct game *Fantasy Congress* combined objective and subjective data to rate members of U.S. Congress: how many bills they cosponsored, their attendance record, how often they deviated from the party line, and how often their bills passed.[22] Player feedback suggested that legislation and voting records amounted to a boring way to keep track of politicians, so the site's creators implemented a system to track the frequency of mentions of politicians in the media. More noteworthy coverage of a congressperson scored more points. Creator Andrew Lee viewed the game not only as a means of raising awareness for the daily proceedings of Congress, but also as a way to hold politicians numerically accountable for their actions.[23]

Play the News and fantasy sports offer two different examples of newsgame platforms that sit atop existing news infrastructures. Both are structured as prediction markets, both offer community-based competition, and both frame existing news in new ways. Differences in the types of information mustered for play make for palpably different experiences, both in terms of their play value and their journalistic value. On the one hand, fantasy football deals with discrete outcomes that require no journalistic intervention, whereas *Play the News* requires a staff of researchers, writers, and editors to determine likely outcomes for each story. But on the other hand—and with all due respect to the world's many sports fans—*Play the News* extends the prediction platform to more urgent domains of journalistic coverage. Future efforts might take this idea even further, drawing from the lessons of experiments in fantasy games. Though the service didn't last long enough to test Lee's hopes for its journalistic accountability, *Fantasy Congress* suggests the potential of such an application.

Videogame Platforms

Prediction and fantasy markets offer lessons in repurposing extant approaches to the news as platforms for newsgames. But other sorts of platforms also exist: the computer platforms that software developers and game creators use to create the tools and media we use at work and at home.

Creating effective software is hard, and it requires specialized training. Creating effective videogames is even harder, since games are subjective, expressive artifacts that rely on artistic merit as much as they do on craft. Furthermore, computer platforms evolve rapidly, introducing new features much more quickly than has ever been the case in the publishing or broadcasting industries. From a journalist's perspective, mastering hardware and software platforms for the construction of newsgames can seem like an impossible task. In the future, the news will benefit from the general adoption of computational literacy, as more new journalists develop proficiencies with software as a part of their professional training. These *computational journalists* might wield computer science and engineering backgrounds, but they also might draw from software development experiences in their ordinary lives.

In recent years, more tools have appeared that make complex computer programming accessible to much larger populations. The most familiar software development tool for journalists is probably Adobe Flash, an authoring and programming environment that began as a simple Web animation tool but became a general-purpose, Web-page-embeddable multimedia scripting environment. Because it uses Web browsers, Flash is cross-platform by default, avoiding the trouble of developing for multiple operating systems. But more importantly, Flash abstracts the more complex aspects of real-time computer graphics, sound, and input, shortening the development times for newsgames. Current event games like *So You Think*

You Can Drive, Mel? and *Madrid* were produced and distributed quickly thanks to Flash and the Web. Even though Flash has traditionally not been able to offer the realistic 3D games familiar to players of commercial games, improvements to the format appear rapidly. Other in-browser platforms are also available, including Unity, which runs real-time 3D games but requires users to download and install a special plug-in. And other Web-based venues for games have emerged, particularly on social networks like Facebook, which offer accessibility along with an existing community of players connected to one another for collaboration or competition.

Although the Web might offer the most familiar venue for computer journalism, videogames are often played on personal computers or specialized hardware. At first blush, downloadable games might seem to reduce the potential audience for a newsgame undesirably, but they also afford certain benefits, not the least of which is their ability to take greater advantage of modern computer hardware. Downloadable games might also change the context of play for a newsgame. Unlike *Madrid*, which takes only a few minutes to play, *Pictures for Truth* is a longer-form documentary-style game, so it justifies the additional time commitment and focus of download and install. And when a player runs the game, it takes over the whole screen, averting the low switching cost of the Web.

PC games don't always have to be created from scratch, either. Many games are derived from the level editors and authoring tools that ship with retail entertainment games—new games built on game engines like Source or Unreal. When one builds a modification or "mod" in these engines, the result can usually be distributed for free to anyone who owns the retail game. In one case, the Lindart Center in Tiranë, Albania, worked with survivors of that nation's widespread "blood feuds" to create *Medieval Unreality*, a mod built atop the popular commercial game *Unreal Tournament*.[24] The documentary game *9-11 Survivor*, discussed in chapter 4, is also an *Unreal Tournament* mod. Though it might seem unintuitive to repurpose shooter games for journalism and documentary, mods built atop such platforms have the strengths of being able to create a first- or third-person perspective within a 3D environment with relative ease and minimal expense.

Shooter platforms are not the only creation tools available for aspiring designers. The genre of role-playing games (RPGs) emphasizes dialogue, exploration, and resource management over action. In chapter 6, we discussed the University of Minnesota's Institute for New Media Studies' newspaper reporting simulator, *Disaster at Harperville*. This literacy newsgame was created using the authoring tools provided with the popular medieval RPG *Neverwinter Nights*. Other accessible development platforms for RPGs include *RPGMaker*, which independent developer and filmmaker Danny Ledonne used to create his controversial documentary game about the Columbine massacre, *Super Columbine Massacre RPG!*, discussed in chapter 4.

A videogame console is a dedicated piece of hardware for playing games, usually with a controller for an input device rather than mouse and keyboard. Consoles like the Microsoft Xbox, the Sony PlayStation, and the Nintendo Wii currently dominate the commercial market for videogames, earning some 80 percent of videogame sales.[25] Game consoles cost much less than computers, and they allow players to enjoy audiovisual benefits like large high-definition displays and surround sound—features much more associated with the couch than the office chair.

Until recently, however, it has been difficult for small developers to get games published on these major consoles, owing to a unique and complex software licensing system. Unlike books, CDs, DVDs, computer software, and other manufactured media, console videogames require special approval and manufacturing by the companies that make the consoles themselves. This process is expensive and time-consuming, effectively closing off the consoles from all but the largest and most entrenched game publishers.

Over time, all three major manufacturers have begun offering channels for digital distribution of smaller, more specialized games for videogame consoles. Xbox Live Arcade (XBLA), PlayStation Network (PSN), and Nintendo WiiWare have become home to games produced either independently or by small companies. Mobile platforms like Google Android and Apple iPhone offer similarly viable console platforms for newsgames. These services are more likely to support unusual games with niche markets, titles like *Braid* on XBLA and *World of Goo* on WiiWare. *Pictures for Truth*, the literacy newsgame about an American journalist in China just prior to the Beijing Olympics, was created using Microsoft's XNA software development kit, a free environment that can compile games for Windows and the Xbox 360 console. Although this platform can help developers produce a professional-looking game, it limits possible players to those with sufficient 3D hardware and software updates to run the game. Players must also take the time to download and install the game, as they would with any software package.

Microsoft has expanded Xbox distribution even further, offering an open channel called Xbox Live Indie Games for games created with the XNA toolkit. In May of 2009, Arrogancy Games released *Angry Barry*, an

Xbox Live Indie Game that dabbles in the news.[26] The game purports to offer political satire in the form of beat-'em-up. The cartoonish rendition of Barack Obama, renamed "Barry," beats up enemies as he fights his way to electoral victory. Though the journalistic merits of the game are debatable, it proves that political newsgames are already for sale on the videogame consoles in living rooms worldwide.

Developing for videogame console platforms is still not an easy task even with toolkits like XNA, partly because of the complexities of the development process itself, and partly because of players' expectations of these services. But the fact that it is now possible for individuals and organizations to distribute such games makes the consoles a viable option for newsgames that warrant them. Unfortunately, as the console platforms have opened up their doors to any creation, a profusion of games has flooded these channels, increasing both noise and competition. Nowhere is this more visible than on Apple's iTunes App Store, which swelled from zero to 65,000 offerings in its first year of service.[27] Such competition makes it hard for individuals to stand out, but news organizations enjoy the benefit of large audiences elsewhere. Since many console platforms, including Xbox Live and the iTunes App Store, allow for direct linking to videogame purchases, news organizations might find it easier to rise above the din.

Still other opportunities for pursuing newsgames on consoles might exist for those who don't want to take on the cost and complexity of custom development. Media Molecule, the company behind the successful PlayStation 3 title *Little Big Planet*, released a "history kit" add-on for the game, available to download for $3.99. *Little Big Planet* has been praised for its sophisticated user-creation tools, and the add-on allows players to create historically themed levels comprised of special objects and characters, including Genghis Khan and Ada Lovelace (figure 8.3). Although Media Molecule does not claim that the kit serves as an educational tool, it offers a possible model for news organizations to follow: partnerships to embed current or historical events into successful commercial games with built-in audiences.

Episodic content also offers platform opportunities, as traditional boxed software meets the serialization of print or television. *Kuma\War*, the company discussed in chapter 4 in the context of the John Kerry Silver Star game, designed its product around episodes, even using the framing of a television news anchor to introduce them. After launching the Kuma application, players are shown a list of recently released episodes and current multiplayer games. Choosing an episode brings up a download

Figure 8.3
Sackboy, the ubiquitous hero of Media Molecule's *Little Big Planet*, is dressed as Ghengis Khan. A time machine has taken him back to ancient Egypt in search of historically themed stickers and architectural pieces to bring back to his spaceship.

progress bar window. Because Kuma's titles are ad-supported, the long installation times are filled with animated and video advertisements supplied by an advertising platform network.

Possible Platforms

Play the News didn't succeed as a newsgame platform, but it also never really had a chance to prove its salt. Fantasy sports took decades to reach the cultural and financial mainstream, and the prediction game format is just beginning to expand into broader topics. In these cases, platform development is unintuitive and risky, but it offers significant rewards if done effectively and supported over time. The most promising newsgame platforms, then, may not bear any resemblance to earlier efforts. Instead, they might represent entirely new ways to apply investigative and beat reporting to playable media.

It's easy to enjoin journalists to "be creative" or to "reinvent" their field. But concrete examples of platform creativity really do require journalism to bend itself into new shapes. In the following pages, we offer some starting ideas for both new newsgame platforms and approaches to exploiting existing platforms. They range from the familiar to the bizarre, the serious to the silly. A few already exist in rudimentary form, while others are mere fancies. Some of our suggestions might seem downright absurd, but so did rotisserie baseball when it began thirty years ago.

Visualizing Local News

Modern videogame hardware has become more open thanks to production frameworks like Microsoft's XNA and distribution networks like Nintendo WiiWare. In addition to this digital distribution channel, Nintendo has explicitly integrated news into its videogame hardware. Once booted up, Nintendo's popular Wii console offers different "channels," most of which aren't related to videogames at all. These serve as dedicated portals for different media formats. The Photo Channel encourages Wii owners to use the device to share photos with friends and family. The Forecast Channel suggests that the designers at Nintendo thought the Wii might be the kind of device people would turn on in the morning for quick information. Expanding on this idea, Nintendo released the News Channel shortly after the Wii's 2006 launch.[28] The News Channel distinguishes itself from a televisual media hub like the video- and audio-streaming Xbox 360 and PlayStation 3. Instead, it offers a straightforward integration of information into players' daily habits.

The result is a quite pleasurable experience that differs from today's common methods of news delivery. It isn't plastered with overlays, scrolling graphics, and ads like television and Web site news. Instead, it uses large fonts, minimal colors, and soothing ambient music. The opening screen offers a menu of "sections" as seen in print and print-emulating Web sites. Selecting a section brings up a list of headlines, and clicking on a headline brings up an AP story that occupies most of the screen along with a satellite image of the globe flashing a related location. The user can increase or decrease the font size, go back to the list of headlines, or choose to use the globe as an interface for browsing stories by location.

The News Channel's Globe View offers a different experience of world news, situated somewhere between exploration and information-gathering. In this mode, users can grab a part of a 3D-rendered Earth and pull the planet around as if it were a desktop globe (figure 8.4). A pleasant tactile sensation arises from this action, offering a more deliberate, slower experience than rapid zooming and scrolling online. News events show up on the map as either little newspaper icons or as photos pulled from the stories. Clicking on them brings up a list of regional headlines. The user can also zoom in and out on the globe to access more detailed information. When zoomed out, stories will lump into a single stack represented by

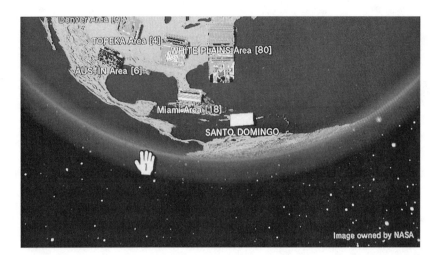

Figure 8.4
The Wii News Channel converts the pointer into a cartoon representation of the player's hand, which can grab and spin the globe to focus on new areas or select a stack of localized news stories to peruse. Playing with the globe becomes an amusing part of news reading.

whatever major city is closest to the center of the screen. For example, all the United States stories might get lumped into "Chicago Area," but rotating it a bit causes "Chicago" stories to be populated in a U.S. city closer to the center of the television display.

This seemingly minor sorting method illustrates an obvious but unscrutinized way to experience traditional news. News is always local, and most people have a personal investment in multiple regions (my home and my hometown) or with one region at multiple scales (Atlanta, North Georgia, the Southeast United States). But we rarely experience news as a *visit* to different locations. Though its current incarnation offers little more than a browser for news content, the spatial exploration of the Wii news globe invites a new way to think about the geographical exploration of news.

Newsgame Middleware

Scoop!, discussed in chapter 5, is a crossword game that generates puzzles based on keywords pulled from news article headlines through an RSS feed. The game excels at raising awareness of news stories because it forces the player to read headlines he or she might not normally encounter. But this strength is also its greatest weakness, as awareness is really the extent of the game's influence. Though it is possible to access the stories for additional information, who wants to pause in the middle of a fast-paced casual game to do research? Using RSS feeds is a great way to take advantage of an existing information structure, but too often it is only used to regurgitate that information in a new format. The real question becomes: "What do we do with this information once we have it?" The answer is that we need to *process* that information into synthetic behaviors.

Middleware is a name for software subsystems that abstract common tasks so that developers don't have to write code from scratch. Middleware can be used to handle graphics, artificial intelligence, sound, lighting, physics, character behavior—anything whatsoever that can be encapsulated into a set of software libraries. Developers license middleware in order to avoid the time and risk associated with reinventing the wheel. A physics engine, like the popular Havok engine, handles realistic movement and collision between 3D objects, allowing game designers to think about how they might use physics, not how they will build it.

Even though they are treated like tools, middleware systems exert a normative force on game design. Once a particular tool is available, its features become easier and less risky to integrate into new titles. Some games may not require complex object physics to service their expressive intent, but the fact that Havok has been integrated into most game engines makes it easy to add realistic physical movement to objects, whether it's needed or not.

What if such a thing could be said about synthesized journalistic analysis? What if game developers felt compelled to integrate local politics or economics into their games, thanks to middleware systems that made such a thing easy to do?

"The Lost and Damned" is a downloadable episode for the popular console game *Grand Theft Auto IV* (GTA IV). Released almost a year after the original, "The Lost and Damned" focuses on a new character but exists within the same timeline as the original. When *GTA IV* was originally in production, the full force of the global economic crash of 2008–2009 was not yet in full swing. But by the time the game appeared on store shelves, the United States found itself plunged into a deep recession. The original *GTA IV* made no mention of the economic climate of Liberty City (a fictionalized New York), but "The Lost and Damned" updates the *Grand Theft Auto* universe to coincide with the current economic recession. Characters make reference to the financial health of the United States and, in part, blame the city's troubles on recession. Though it required a new episode of the game to add this information, it is not unreasonable to imagine a middleware system that could handle updating current event data to fit any game world.

Such a middleware system might manage all kinds of data. At the most basic level, a news organization's weather service could feed information into a game that affects the real-time game weather; if it's raining in New York City, it's raining in Liberty City (something already done in a rudimentary way by individual games). Games that have news outlets built into them, like the radio in *Grand Theft Auto*, or billboards or news tickers, could easily integrate updated news information.

Still, these examples merely change surface effects in a game. More journalistically meaningful newsgame middleware might simulate the economic and social *dynamics* of current states of affairs. Instead of just making mention to the economic recession, what if Liberty City itself were affected by the economy in real time? Increasing or decreasing joblessness might affect population flows, crime rates, and the overall operation of the criminal rackets the player encounters in the game. A mayoral scandal might drive one mayor from office, bringing in a new mayor with new policies on the crime and corruption that lie at the heart of the game's action.

The *Grand Theft Auto* series depicts realistic versions of major cities—New York, Los Angeles, Miami. But a game need not be true to life to deploy a socioeconomics middleware system. *Final Fantasy XII* for the PlayStation 2 contains an entirely fictional world, one more like Middle Earth than Midtown Manhattan. But situations in the game take up the political dynamics of different state factions within this imagined universe. If the proper middleware existed, the game could represent relationships between neighboring states in conflict, applying an allegorical representation of current events to a fantasy world. Playing the game would not necessarily teach someone about the conflict directly, but it might offer a more fundamental experience of the dynamics of world politics by representing the processes of a particular conflict.

Besides convention and inertia, what prevents popular game characters from experiencing the reality of political and economic conditions? Once the playthings of children, characters like *The Legend of Zelda*'s Link and *Super Mario Bros.*' Mario are now blank canvases ready to accept adult scenarios like political scandal, insurance fraud, dysfunctional health coverage, spousal abuse, and more. Middleware offers different leverage than individual titles: rather than influencing player belief directly through specifics, it might influence developer uptake of newsworthy topics.

News Discovery

Budget Hero, the infographics game discussed in chapter 3, does more than just teach the complex process of arranging the United States' financial future. It also gives its creators a means to understand public opinion by mining the data players create during play.

Kovach and Rosenstiel argue that journalism provides "a forum for public criticism and compromise."[29] Ordinarily, this process happens through back-and-forth discussions. Journalists report issues to the citizenry, who render judgments in response. The outlets for these judgments are many: letters to the editor in the newspaper, radio call-in shows, man-on-the-street interviews, comments on Web stories, or responses on blogs, podcasts, and social media Web sites. These conventions don't just promote informative dialogue between citizens; they also allow people to talk back to newsmakers about their news, clearly communicating their beliefs and concerns.

Videogames do not have to be one-way transmissions; they can facilitate discourse in at least two ways. First, games can partake of the usual methods of eliciting feedback through comments or reactions. American Public Media sought such feedback for *Budget Hero*, conducting a survey with players who had completed the game. One wrote, "The complexity of the issues was much more apparent. I realized that the decision-making process is a lot more extensive than plain black-and-white values. With a record of the cards I played, I listen to [public radio] with a new interest in fiscal policy."[30] These surveys help the creators gauge their own success and justify future investments in games. It's a soft discourse, but it's just as useful as soliciting reader or viewer feedback from print or television news sources.

To gather more scientific data, American Public Media turned to a second means of game-based discovery: instrumentation. As networked software, videogames can keep track of the actions players perform, transmitting that information to a server for storage and later analysis. *Budget Hero* includes such digital meters to collect information about player choices during play, such as chosen goal badges or taxation policies.

American Public Media recognizes that data gathered this way can't accurately represent public opinion. The game encourages multiple plays, which means players can choose alternative goals and experiment; they do not necessarily play based only on their own values, if indeed they do so at all. As such, it's not possible to draw accurate conclusions about "what Americans think" about budget priorities from *Budget Hero* gameplay alone. But by mining correlations among player choices, *Budget Hero*'s creators might discover trends worth investigating. For example, do players who self-select health care as a goal make or avoid certain foreign policy decisions? Are those correlations accidental, or might they be grounded in real opinion? By mining play data, American Public Media can develop ideas for new stories, ones they might pursue in traditional formats.

American Public Media is also experimenting with a variation on instrumented research with the game, a closed version that they may employ "as a policy sounding board."[31] They hope to test the game with statistically selected players to crowdsource budget proposals, some of which they might present to Congress. As opposed to a written survey in which a person can indicate that he or she would like to increase the funding of programs supporting those in need, players are faced with the reality of balancing a budget that demands many compromises. We might call the result a *procedural poll*.

The results of a news quiz could be used in a similar way. When a professor gives an exam and finds that most of the students could not correctly answer a question, the result recommends another, more effective way to teach that material. Through a game, a news organization might discover that an audience does not fully grasp a particular topic. Mining this material, the organization could alter future publications or broadcasts to include new material on the dynamics of the issue. The quiz would become a feedback loop, informing both the media and the public—an instrument rather than a unit of content. Our voices are transmitted on radio programs, our faces are broadcast on television news, and our letters are printed in the newspaper. Newsmakers can also create platforms allowing the public to respond to games, through games.[32]

Not Stories, but Systems

In early 2009, Positech Software emailed registered users of its political simulation game *Democracy 2* to describe the additions and changes contained in the version 1.23 software patch for the game. The patch included changes to numerous simulation variables intended not only to improve game balance, but also to address changes in the global economic climate. The additions read as follows:

Increased probability of prison riot event
Reduced positive effects of legal aid policy
Creationism policy now affects technological backwater and technological advantage situations
Oil prices now affect the chances of the petrol protests situation
Reduced effectiveness of free bus passes for retired people

New Pirates Attacking Oil tanker event
Liberals are now angered slightly by citizenship tests
Stem cell research now boosts lifespan[33]

These dynamics correspond directly with headlines of the moment, but *Democracy 2* interprets these events as new social dynamics, not just as isolated events. The game simulates public response to policy changes in a society, showing how events can sway belief, opinion, and support. Play involves changing policies and watching the public's reaction to those changes (figure 8.5). The 1.23 patch added both policy options and public responses. These additions are possible because *Democracy 2* operates at a high level of abstraction—it is a game about the bidirectional causal connections between general types of policies and public interests.

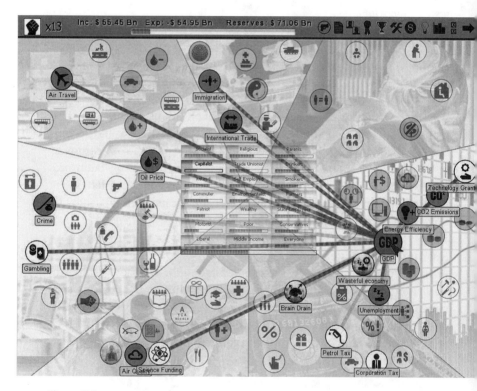

Figure 8.5
Democracy 2's main display shows the direct positive and negative influences of separate sectors of the economy on gross domestic product. Players use this information to inform policy decisions, which are made in turn using political capital derived from the support of cabinet members.

When we think about the possible uses of games in journalism, issues of feasibility quickly come to the fore. As we discussed in chapter 2, it often seems logistically impossible to create videogames fast enough to cover breaking news—or even longer-term news. Starting from scratch is hard. But a game like *Democracy 2* doesn't have to start from scratch; elements can be added to the game over time with relative ease, because concrete additions like the "citizenship tests dilemma" are translated into mathematical behaviors. It is a platform for simulating democracy.

Instead of creating many games with short life spans, or larger games whose relevance might not outlast the time required to develop them, journalists might consider creating larger, ongoing platforms into which current events could be funneled as settings, scenarios, or variables. Creative accessibility also benefits from platform play: *Democracy 2* ships with a folder full of spreadsheet files that its players can access and update. The same could be true for newspaper readers or for journalists and editors themselves.

Even if a platform like *Democracy 2* shows promise, it also raises doubts. For one, it is unclear if a social platform gives citizens a satisfactory perspective to make decisions in their own lives. Like many games, *Democracy 2* is about power and control; it offers a view of a society from the role of its leader—and a leader with impressive, godlike power. Ordinary people need the opposite view, that of the ordinary, yet empowered citizen. Second, platforms necessarily rise to a level of abstraction not normally found in public media. *Democracy 2* abstracts governance to public polling and slider-based policymaking. The relationships between decisions are depicted via screens of abstract line-connecters, rather than told through stories of specific experiences. The result may be difficult for many people to understand or enjoy.

But these challenges also suggest unmet opportunities in journalism at large. A story about Joe Average's foreclosure woes might personalize a problem, but it doesn't explain the complex dynamics that produce that result. Perhaps one of the future roles of journalism involves analyzing and explaining the world at a much higher level than the event or the story. In short, newsgame platforms might be modeled not on *news stories*, but on the *systems* from which news stories arise.

9 Journalism at Play

In 2006, Persuasive Games created a series of editorial current event games, which Web portal Shockwave.com published under the series name The Arcade Wire. The games were more like opinion columns than cartoons, taking nuanced positions on then-current events like the airport security liquid ban that September (*Airport Security*), an outbreak of E. coli in domestic spinach and tomato crops that autumn (*Bacteria Salad*), the dynamics of global conflict and natural disaster that contributed to high oil prices that summer and fall (*Oil God*), and the frenzy of holiday shoppers struggling to capture scarce toys that holiday season (*Xtreme Xmas Shopping*).

The games use simulation to express opinion. In *Airport Security*, players take the role of a Transportation Security Administration (TSA) agent trying to keep up with rapidly changing security rules. In *Oil God*, players apply civil unrest and natural disaster in order to manipulate oil futures such that fuel costs in a target nation reach a target price. And in *Bacteria Salad*, players face the difficulty of tracing contaminations back to farm networks managed by big agribusiness. They are well crafted and unusual, and they take their editorial positions seriously—factors that may have contributed to some tens of millions of plays since the first title's release. They are profitable, too: players pay nothing, but Shockwave.com sells rich-media advertising that runs before the games start. Though the cost per impression (CPI) for such ads have fallen from highs of $30–$50[1] when the series was originally released, these units still commanded $15–20 in the sour economy of spring 2009.[2] Atom Entertainment, which owns the sites on which the Arcade Wire games appear, does not release gross revenue figures to developers, but based on these figures it is reasonable to conclude that the games may have brought in several hundred thousand dollars of revenue even if inventory wasn't always fully sold.

The following spring, Persuasive Games inked a deal with the *New York Times* to create editorial games for the op-ed section of their Web site. The feat was brought about partly by high-profile publicity The Arcade Wire series had earned, including features in the *New York Times* itself,[3] *Wired*,[4] *USA Today*,[5] ABC News,[6] and *Playboy*.[7] Game news Web site GamePolitics.com called it a "cultural milestone."[8] Persuasive Games had high hopes too, both journalistically and commercially. From an editorial perspective, what venue could be better than the Gray Lady? And from a commercial perspective, the series offered a chance to establish a system to support editorial games on an ongoing basis. Concerned about finances but eager to bring newsgames to the paper, Persuasive Games agreed to a trial run of editorial games, one a month for six months. They accepted the *Times'* offer of "columnist pay," $1,500 per month.

The first title, *Food Import Folly*, addresses the difficulty the Federal Drug Administration (FDA) import inspectors face when inspecting ever-increasing volumes of foreign food at America's ports. The second, *Points of Entry*, operationalizes the complex calculus of the merit-based evaluation system proposed for green card awards in the Kennedy–McCain immigration reform bill under debate in mid-2007. We offered both as examples of reportage games in chapter 2.

Soon after *Points of Entry*, progress ground to a halt. The editorial desk editor began rejecting the studio's treatments, including a game about gun laws and state lines following the April 2007 Virginia Tech massacre, and a game about the cult of Apple in anticipation of the release of the iPhone in June of that year. Persuasive Games had completed a third game, *Steroid Slugger*, about the social and business dynamics of steroid use in baseball. Despite the fact that the game was ready to be released just as Barry Bonds passed Hank Aaron's home run record that August, the *Times* editorial desk had stopped responding to contact from the studio. The game was never released, and none of the remaining games were created. The newspaper quietly paid out the remaining, modest monthly checks, although the payments were assuredly a result of corporate automation more than shame. Shockwave.com had paid the company a small advance for games in the Arcade Wire series, but they had also paid a royalty based on advertising sales. Even though the *Times* sells video ads on their Web site, the editorial desk responsible for publishing the newsgames wasn't able (or willing) to determine how to run such ads.[9]

In retrospect, Bogost is convinced that the *New York Times* meant no harm in dropping their arrangement with his studio so suddenly. Rather than wickedness or deceit, organizational politics are likely to blame. As budgets tightened and staff reduced, who could blame an editor for making compromises? Certainly nobody would notice if a videogame didn't make it onto the Web site. No horseman was deployed to the front of the charge of the newsgames brigade at the *New York Times*, so the cavalry retired to their desks.

Battered but still determined, Persuasive Games engaged in many further conversations with other news organizations. The *Washington Post* and National Public Radio both expressed considerable interest, and the studio engaged in extensive discussions with editorial, publication, and business development personnel at those organizations, among many others. At the end of the day, the prospect of changing existing practices to accommodate games proved too difficult a burden to overcome, even when the small game studio bore the burden of the risk, as it had done for the *New York Times*. In response to one of Bogost's proposals for a series that would require no up-front investment from the publisher, an editor responded without irony, "Budgets and staff are so tight right now. The interest is there, but any extras are a tough sell right now, as you can imagine."

We tell these stories not to seek empathy or to assign blame, but to characterize the organizational circumstances under which particular newsgames have been proposed and developed. It's a matter worth putting in context. There is a concern today that the news business is dying. Local papers are shuttering, while larger ones are making cuts just to stay afloat. The social value of print news, which has taken up residence on the Web, has been undermined by bloggers and commenters. Its economic viability has been threatened by falling advertising revenue and competing services. Figuring out how videogames fit into the world of news is even more difficult than building the games themselves: in addition to determining how to tackle newsworthy topics in game form, journalists must also fit games into news media and news organizations more broadly.

Andrew DeVigal, multimedia editor for the *New York Times* online, discussed the evolution of that paper's newsroom structure at the 2008 Society for News Design conference.[10] The multimedia section of the *Times*, DeVigal explained, had been converted into a "transverse" endeavor, with new, overlapping roles replacing the once separate areas of graphics, photography, design, and multimedia. At that year's Online News Association Conference, *Las Vegas Sun* New Media Projects Editor Josh Williams revealed a similar approach.[11] As a part of a wholesale redesign, the paper had added new jobs, including database developer, software developer, Flash journalist, and design technologist. These moves toward integrated work environments demonstrate real progress in adapting the newsroom to a different media landscape. Today it is more common to see Web sites that unfold news stories progressively, as new information arrives, and efforts that were once entirely independent are now more tightly integrated. For example, since the multimedia department at the *Times* now works more closely with photography, a Flash journalist can update news packages online as soon as the latter department releases new material. These cases suggest two important realizations: news products cannot be created in silos, and new principles are required to create new types of news media.

Journalism is not only becoming digital, it is also becoming playful. As journalists and news organizations consider this charge, they must adopt new ideas to regulate the interaction between games and journalism. We conclude with a few such principles for a journalism at play.

Culture Computation

When we learn to read, to write, to do mathematics, to repair motorcycles, to design bridges, or to architect software, we tend to start with first principles. We learn the basic knowledge in a domain so that we can master its exercise in a variety of ways, ways that are usually not obvious at the time of our training. We've already suggested that both journalism and game design bear similar principles of construction: both seek to understand and represent the behavior of systems in comprehensible ways. But another fundamental area of knowledge must be added to that of game design for newsgames to flourish: the *computational* expertise required to construct them.

Despite advances exemplified by the *New York Times* and *Las Vegas Sun*, these organizational solutions might be too instrumental and overly connected to technological roots to signal enduring change. Although the multimedia department of papers like the *Times* has become more comprehensive, roles themselves still rely on specifics of implementation for the present moment. Duties are separated, and novelty is arrested. Newsrooms are still struggling with digital multimedia (video, audio, interactive applications, and so forth), the pursuit of which amounts to playing catchup. Rarely do news organizations inspire and reward new approaches that haven't already been beaten into the ground by creators outside the newsroom.

Rather than focusing on the instrumental skills of tool-use, journalists must develop a first-principles expertise in computation. These future *computational journalists* will spin code the way yesterday's journalists rattled off prose, and they will do so as if by second nature, in the service of journalistic goals.

Choose Systems Over Stories

Journalists write, shoot, produce, edit, and publish stories. They think of their work in terms of people, events, locations, moments, motivations. They craft ledes and choose images to draw readers or viewers into a specific individual's plight, and then they move from the particular to the general.

But as we have shown, games are better at depicting the general than they are at the particular. *Cutthroat Capitalism* addresses the economics of Somali piracy, not the tale of a particular pirate or freight captain. *September 12th* offers an opinion on the inevitable outcome of surgical missile strikes, not a perspective on one such attack. *PeaceMaker* depicts the political dynamics of the Israeli–Palestinian conflict, not the run-up to a particular period of hostility. The crossword offers a calming feeling of mastery in a world of uncertainty, not a test of the meaning and usage of particular words.

Games can and do include characters, settings, and events. But even when they do, they work best when those features are rallied in the service of system rather than a story (just think of *Freedom Fighter '56*, which uses real events and fictionalized characters to relate the overall experience of the Hungarian Revolution). Games offer journalists an opportunity to stop short of the final rendering of a typical news story, and instead to share the raw behaviors and dynamics that describe a situation as the journalistic content. It's a paradigm shift, to be sure. Those who create newsgames don't "get the story," they "get the system" instead.

Specialize

Just as there are different forms and genres of print and broadcast journalism, from the investigative report to the editorial cartoon, so there are different forms of newsgames. Each one serves a different purpose, and knowing when to use one over another proves as important as—if not more important than—executing well within a particular form. As we've shown in this book, different types of games can do different things for journalism, from characterizing the operation of an economic system to offering a light mental exercise between the front page and the sports page.

Newsgames are not monolithic. Their different genres, from current event games to newsgame platforms, serve unique purposes. As a creator, choose a purpose and develop an expertise in it. And as an editor, identify opportunities for newsgames as you would do for any type of coverage.

Furthermore, expand those horizons, creating new forms of newsgames by translating old forms, combining existing ones, or inventing new ones.

Scale Up

As *Play the News* and the Arcade Wire series suggest, successful newsgames might need to be created at scale, with frequency, to enjoy long-term success. Imagine if the new form were the televised newscast instead of the videogame. No one would imagine that a single broadcast would offer a satisfactory sign of long-term potential. Hiring a Flash journalist or a database developer won't inspire the op-ed editor to change his priorities about editorial games. It won't invent new ways of integrating news puzzles to recapture the value lost to casual games. It won't devise new ways to synthesize current events into computer behaviors that might be licensed for use in tomorrow's blockbuster entertainment videogames.

Deeper structural barriers must disappear before news organizations will be able to set the stage for success with computational media. For newsgames to become successful, their creators must expect to fail often, to learn from those failures, and to translate them into more frequent successes. That will take time.

Make Something

At its core, news is comprised of ideas. It is not made of folded newsprint, broadcast studios, or Web pages. It is not run by television anchors, radio talk show hosts, newspaper editors, beat reporters, or bloggers. And journalism is not an industry, nor is it a profession. It is a practice in which research combines with a devotion to the public interest, producing materials that help citizens make choices about their private lives and their communities. There is nothing medium-specific about journalism, no reason that its output must take the familiar form of text, image, or video. This book has offered numerous perspectives on the use of one new medium for journalism, from adaptations of familiar forms like editorial cartoons to resurrections of forgotten forms like puzzles to the creation of entirely new forms like middleware platforms. But none of these opportunities will ever be realized if no one is willing to see them through.

The best way to advance the practice is to make something—and not just as an exercise, but in earnest, as a part of a breaking story, or a local exposé, or a documentary retrospective. What newsgames need most from journalism is its legacy of scrappiness, its heritage of feisty, unstoppable sleuths probing for information, piecing together dynamics of an unseen system, giving voice to an unheard flock. But instead of sitting down at a typewriter, tapping out prose as dusk gives way to night, this new newsgame reporter will crank out code. Compile times, not plate-etching processes, will put a deadline at risk. Perhaps this is the most important lesson would-be newsgame creators must learn: ultimately, whether or not newsgames become an important part of the future of journalism is a question of will rather than a problem of technology.

Notes

1 Newsgames

1. AFP, "New Somalia piracy resolution adopted at UN," October 7, 2008, http://afp.google.com/article/ALeqM5jxzBM8B5jScl8Wirb9gP7aMZ-A0g. The resolution itself can be found at http://www.undemocracy.com/S-RES-1838(2008).pdf, and the passage cited here is found on page 2 of that document.

2. Stephen Foley, "Clinton Vows Somali Pirates Will Have Hostage Money Frozen," *New Independent*, April 16, 2009, http://www.independent.co.uk/news/world/americas/clinton-vows-somali-pirates-will-have-hostage-money-frozen-1669389.html. For example, U.S. Secretary of State Hillary Clinton vowed to freeze Somali funds used to bankroll "banditry on the Indian Ocean," and to "push for diplomatic efforts" in Somalia.

3. "At the Mercy of Somali Pirates," *Spiegel Online*, August 11, 2009, http://www.spiegel.de/international/world/0,1518,641752,00.html.

4. Scott Carney, Siggi Eggertsson, and Michael Doret, "Cutthroat Capitalism: An Economic Analysis of the Somali Pirate Business Model," *Wired* 17.7 (July 2009): 110–117.

5. Ibid., 110.

6. Smallbore Webworks and Dennis Crowther, *Cutthroat Capitalism*, *Wired* 17.7 online addendum (July 20, 2009), http://www.wired.com/special_multimedia/2009/cutthroatCapitalismTheGame.

7. Carney, Eggertson, and Doret, "Cutthroat Capitalism," 114.

8. Ibid., 112.

9. Ibid., 113.

10. Ryan Chittum, "Newspaper Industry Ad Revenue at 1965 Levels," *Columbia Journalism Review*, August 19, 2009, http://www.cjr.org/the_audit/newspaper_industry_ad_revenue.php.

11. For more on this subject, see Ian Bogost, *Persuasive Games: The Expressive Power of Videogames* (Cambridge, Mass.: MIT Press, 2007), particularly chapter 1.

12. Powerful Robot Games, *September 12th* (Newsgaming.com, 2003), http://www.newsgaming.com/games/index12.htm.

13. Michelle Arnot, *What's Gnu? A History of the Crossword Puzzle* (New York: Vintage Books, 1981), 28.

14. James Paul Gee, *What Video Games Have to Teach Us about Learning and Literacy* (New York: Palgrave Macmillan, 2003), 17.

15. Nick Montfort and Ian Bogost, *Racing the Beam: The Atari Video Computer System* (Cambridge, Mass.: MIT Press, 2009), 2–6.

16. Some might object that *Wired* magazine isn't the best example of independent journalism, but the fact that the magazine successfully conceived of and executed the "Cutthroat Capitalism" feature might also suggest that progress and innovation are more likely to be found outside the journalistic elite.

17. Edward Tufte, *The Visual Display of Quantitative Information* (Cheshire, Conn.: Graphic Press, 1983), 13.

2   Current Events

1. See Clive Thompson, "Saving the World, One Video Game at a Time," *New York Times*, July 23, 2006; and Jim McClellan, "The Role of Play," *Guardian*, May 13, 2004.

2. Ian Bogost, *Persuasive Games: The Expressive Power of Videogames* (Cambridge, Mass.: MIT Press, 2007), 84–89.

3. Miguel Sicart, *The Ethics of Computer Games* (Cambridge, Mass.: MIT Press, 2008), 43.

4. Jessica Goldfin, "Knight News Game Awards," *Knight Foundation*, May 29, 2009, http://www.knightblog.org/knight-news-game-awards/.

5. Edward McClelland, "All in the Game," *Chicago Magazine*, May 2009, http://www.chicagomag.com/Chicago-Magazine/May-2009/All-in-the-Game/.

6. See http://www.newsgaming.com.

7. See Frasca's artist statement about *Kabul Kaboom*, at http://www.ludology.org/my_games.html.

8. As of September 2009, Flash was installed on 99 percent of computers worldwide. See http://www.adobe.com/products/player_census/flashplayer/version_penetration.html.

9. Ian Bogost, "Roll Your Own Zidane Headbutt Game," *Water Cooler Games*, http://www.bogost.com/watercoolergames/archives/roll_your_own_z.shtml.

10. For example, 2DPlay, *Rooney on the Rampage* (Addicting Games, 2009), http://www.addictinggames.com/rooneyontherampage.html.

11. Alexei Barrionuevo, "Food Imports Often Escape Scrutiny," *New York Times*, May 1, 2007, http://www.nytimes.com/2007/05/01/business/01food.html.

12. Robert Pear, "A Point System for Immigrants Incites Passions," *New York Times*, June 5, 2007, http://query.nytimes.com/gst/fullpage.html?res=9503E4D91130F936A35755C0A9619C8B63.

13. Ed Halter, *From Sun Tzu to Xbox: War and Video Games* (New York: Thunder's Mouth Press, 2006), 301–303.

14. Gonzalo Frasca, "Videogames of the Oppressed: Critical Thinking, Education, Tolerance, and Other Trivial Issues," in *First Person: New Media as Story, Performance, and Game*, ed. Noah Wardrip-Fruin and Pat Harrigan (Cambridge, Mass.: MIT Press, 2004), 87.

15. For a well-known example, see Janet Murray, *Hamlet on the Holodeck: The Future of Narrative in Cyberspace* (Cambridge, Mass.: MIT Press, 1997), 97–125.

16. See IGDA Quality of Life Special Interest Group, "Quality of Life in the Game Industry: Challenges and Best Practices," *International Game Developers Association* (2004).

17. Zoltan Dezsö et al., "Dynamics of Information Access on the Web," *Physics Review E* 73, 066132 (2006): 1–6.

18. Gonzalo Frasca, "This Just In: Playing the News," *Vodafone Receiver* 17 (2006): 3.

19. Frasca, "This Just In," 1–2.

20. Bill Kovach and Tom Rosenstiel, *The Elements of Journalism* (New York: Three Rivers Press, 2001), 187.

21. Mike Treanor and Michael Mateas, "Newsgames: Procedural Rhetoric Meets Political Cartoons," in *Breaking New Ground: Innovation in Games, Play, Practice and Theory* (Proceedings of the Digital Games Research Association Conference, Brunel University, September 2009), 2.

22. Ibid., 2–3.

23. Raph Koster, *A Theory of Fun for Game Design* (Scottsdale: Paraglyph Press, 2005), 166–169.

24. Frasca, "Videogames of the Oppressed," 85.

25. Ian Bogost, *Unit Operations* (Cambridge, Mass.: MIT Press, 2006), 107.

26. Miguel Sicart, "Newsgames: Theory and Design" (paper presented at the International Conference on Entertainment Computing, Pittsburgh, 2008), 31.

27. Sergei Eisenstein, *The Strike* (Boris Mikhin, 1951).

28. Paulo Pedercini, comment on "Molleindustria's McDonald's Game," *News Games*, comment posted January 14, 2009, http://jag.lcc.gatech.edu/blog/2009/01/molleindustrias-mcdo-fails-to-deliver.html#comment-93 (accessed November 14, 2009).

29. Treanor and Mateas, "Newsgames," 2; Bogost, *Persuasive Games*, 88–89.

30. Treanor and Mateas, "Newsgames," 7.

31. Paolo Pedercini, *Faith Fighter* (Molleindustria, 2008), http://www.molleindustria.org/faith-fighter.

32. Assyrian International News Agency, "Cartoons of Muhammed Published by the Danish newspaper *Jyllands-Posten*," *AINA.org*, February 1, 2006, http://www.aina.org/releases/20060201143237.htm.

33. See http://www.molleindustria.org/faith-fighter-old.

34. Chris Lamb, *Drawn to Extremes: The Use and Abuse of Editorial Cartoons* (New York: Columbia University Press, 2004), 155.

35. Ibid., 181.

36. Ibid., 18.

37. In one libel case, *Russell vs. McMullen*, a disputed editorial cartoon was declared to be "a symbolic expression of the opinion espoused in the accompanying article." See Lamb, *Drawn to Extremes*, 204.

38. Margaret Hartmann, "Octuplets' Grandmother Adds to Criticism of Her Daughter," *Jezebel*, February 9, 2009, http://jezebel.com/5149489/octuplets-grandmother-adds-to-criticism-of-her-daughter.

39. See http://www.imnotobsessed.com/files/imagecache/main_pic/files/images/Nadya%20Suleman%20wants%20to%20get%20paid.jpg.

40. See http://2.bp.blogspot.com/_nWpwm6lhWUs/SZZ_KcCgxAI/AAAAAAAAHVQ/awbuJR6_ooA/s1600-h/Cartoon+Octuplets.jpg, http://www.nypost.com/delonas/2009/02/02052009.jpg.

3 Infographics

1. American Public Media, "Behind the Numbers," http://budgethero.publicradio.org/widget/numbers/#11.

2. Edward Tufte, *The Visual Display of Quantitative Information* (Cheshire, Conn.: Graphic Press, 1983), 9.

3. Eric K. Meyer, *Designing Infographics* (Indianapolis: Hayden Books, 1997) 18.

4. Anne R. Carey and Keith Simmons, "Radio Rebounding with iPod Generation," *USA Today* (Snapshots, digital scan), November 24, 2008, http://www.paragonmediastrategies.com/pdfs/usatoday112408.jpg.

5. Tufte, *Visual Display of Quantitative Information*, 9, 53.

6. Alberto Cairo, *Sailing to the Future: Infographics in the Internet Era*, (University of North Carolina: Produced for Multimedia Bootcamp, 2005) 15, http://www.albertocairo.com/index/index_english.html.

7. Edward Tufte, *Visual and Statistical Thinking: Displays of Evidence for Making Decisions* (Cheshire, Conn.: Graphic Press, 1997), 7.

8. Bill Kovach and Tom Rosenstiel, *The Elements of Journalism: What Newspeople Should Know and the Public Should Expect* (New York: Three Rivers Press, 2001), 39–40.

9. Paul J. Lewi, "Playfair and Lineal Arithmetics," in *Speaking of Graphics* (self-published, 2006), http://www.datascope.be/sog.htm, chapter 4, 2. Note that the book is paginated independently by chapter.

10. Playfair's atlas was originally published in 1789 as *The Commercial and Political Atlas: Representing, by Means of Stained Copper-Plate Charts, the Progress of the Commerce, Revenues, Expenditure and Debts of England during the Whole of the Eighteenth Century*. A contemporary edition exists as *Playfair's Commercial and Political Atlas and Statistical Breviary* (Cambridge: Cambridge University Press, 2005).

11. Tufte, *The Visual Display of Quantitative Information*, 40.

12. Ellen Lupton and Abbott Miller, *Design Writing Research: Writing on Graphic Design* (New York: Phaidon, 1999), 41.

13. Ibid., 149.

14. "Map Showing How the States Voted," *New York Times*, November 3, 1920. Reprinted in Eric K. Meyer, *Designing Infographics* (Indianapolis: Hayden Books, 1997), 19.

15. Meyer, *Designing Infographics*, 17.

16. "Labor Unions," *Fortune*, 1939. Reprinted in Meyer, *Designing Infographics*, 19.

17. See Nigel Holmes, *Designer's Guide to Creating Charts and Diagrams* (New York: Watson-Guptill Publications, 1984).

18. Lupton and Miller, *Design Writing Research*, 145.

19. Joan Gorham, *Mass Media 98/99* (New York: McGraw Hill, 1998), 68.

20. Lupton and Miller, *Design Writing Research*, 143–155.

21. Meyer, *Designing Infographics*, 23.

22. Ibid., 30.

23. Many of Cairo's writings are available on his Web site: see http://www
.albertocairo.com/index/index_english.html.

24. Maish Nichani and Venkat Rajamanickam, "Interactive Visual Explainers—A
Simple Classification," *eLearningPost*, September 1, 2003, http://www.elearningpost.
com/articles/archives/interactive_visual_explainers_a_simple_classification/. Note
the difference between Nichani and Rajamanickam's use of the term and that of the
advertising industry. The latter uses "interactive" to refer to any sort of digital
information, even if the operation is trivial.

25. Ibid.

26. Meyer, *Designing Infographics*, 27.

27. Jen Itzenson and Jacky Myint, "All Together Now," Portfolio.com, http://www
.portfolio.com/interactive-features/2008/05/Boeing-Dreamliner/.

28. Robert Spence, *Information Visualization* (New York: ACM Press, 2001), 57.

29. Joshua Hatch and Juan Thomassie, "Delegate Tracker," *USA Today*, February 11,
2008, http://www.usatoday.com/news/politics/election2008/delegate-tracker.htm.

30. Lupton and Miller, *Design Writing Research*, 142.

31. Tom Jackson and Archie Tse, "Is It Better to Buy or Rent?" *New York Times*, June
2, 2008, http://www.nytimes.com/2007/04/10/business/2007_BUYRENT_GRAPHIC
.html.

32. Stuart K. Card, Jock D. Mackinlay, and Ben Shneiderman, *Readings in Information
Visualization* (San Diego: Academic Press, 1999), 6.

33. Ibid., 5.

34. Zachary Pousman, John Stasko, and Michael Mateas, "Casual Information
Visualization: Depictions of Data in Everyday Life," *Proceedings of IEEE InfoVis 2007*,
http://www.cc.gatech.edu/gvu/ii/infovis/, 2.

35. Nathan Yau, "5 Best Data Visualization Projects of the Year," *Flowing Data*,
December 19, 2008, http://flowingdata.com/2008/12/19/5-best-data-visualization
-projects-of-the-year/.

36. Johan Huizinga, *Homo Ludens* (Boston: Beacon Press, 1955), 13.

37. Roger Caillois, *Man, Play, and Games*, trans. Meyer Barash (Champaign, Ill.:
University of Illinois Press, 2001), 9–10.

38. Katie Salen and Eric Zimmerman, *Rules of Play: Game Design Fundamentals*
(Cambridge, Mass.: MIT Press, 2003), 304.

39. Meyer, *Designing Infographics*, 177, 247, 213, 231, respectively.

40. Laura Wattenberg, *The Baby Name Wizard: A Magical Method for Finding the Perfect Name for Your Baby* (New York: Broadway Press, 2005); Martin Wattenberg, NameVoyager (Generation Grownup, LLC: 2005), http://www.babynamewizard.com/voyager.

41. Martin Wattenberg, "Baby Names, Visualization, and Social Data Analysis," in *Proceedings of the 2005 IEEE Symposium on Information Visualization* (Washington, D.C.: IEEE Computer Society, 2005), 1.

42. Ibid.

43. Richard Bartle, *Designing Virtual Worlds* (New York: New Riders, 2003), 130.

44. "Make Your Own Hurricane," *SunSentinel.com*, http://www.sun-sentinel.com/broadband/theedge/sfl-edge-t-canemaker,0,4142989.flash.

45. Douglas Wilson, "Game-Like Infovis: Hurricane vs. Asteroid," *News Games*, January, 15, 2009, http://jag.lcc.gatech.edu/blog/2009/01/game-like-infovis-hurricane-vs-asteroid.html.

46. Robert Marcus, H. Jay Melosh, and Gareth Collins, "Earth Impact Effects Program," 2005, http://www.lpl.arizona.edu/impacteffects/.

47. Salen and Zimmerman, *Rules of Play*, 340.

48. Jon Huang et al., "Hurricane Gustav Sweeps Across the Region," *New York Times*, September 2, 2008, http://www.nytimes.com/interactive/2008/09/01/us/20080901-gustav-map.html; Rhonda Prast et al., "13 Seconds in August," *Minneapolis–St. Paul Star Tribune*, December 5, 2007, http://www.startribune.com/local/12166286.html.

49. deeplocal, "Pittsburgh Bike Map," 2007, http://www.bike-pgh.org/onlinemap2/.

50. Don Wittekind and R. Scott Horner, "2000 Butterfly Ballot: See How the Palm Beach County Ballot Confused Voters," SunSentinel.com, November 10, 2000, http://www.sun-sentinel.com/broadband/theedge/sfl-edge-n-butterflyballot,0,4467323.flash.

51. Jiggman and Greg Wohlwend, *Effing Hail* (self-published, 2009), http://www.intuitiongames.com/effing-hail/.

52. Kovach and Rosenstiel, *The Elements of Journalism*, 48.

53. Ibid., 49.

54. Amanda Cox, Shan Carter, Kevin Quealy, and Amy Schoenfeld, "How Different Groups Spend Their Day," *New York Times*, July 31, 2009, http://www.nytimes.com/interactive/2009/07/31/business/20080801-metrics-graphic.html.

55. http://twitter.com/raphkoster/status/3238299803.

56. A quick Google search illustrates the vast number of references to the graphic on Twitter: http://www.google.com/search?q=site%3Atwitter.com+how+people +spend+their+day.

57. Amanda Cox, Shan Carter, Kevin Quealy, and Amy Schoenfeld, "For the Unemployed, the Day Stacks Up Differently," *New York Times,* July 31, 2009, http:// www.nytimes.com/2009/08/02/business/02metrics.html.

58. Paul Farhi, "CNN Hits the Wall for the Election," *Washington Post,* February 5, 2008, http://www.washingtonpost.com/wp-dyn/content/article/2008/02/04/ AR2008020402796.html.

59. Sergio Goldenberg and Bobby Schweizer, "Less Magic in the CNN Wall," *News Games,* March, 16, 2009, http://jag.lcc.gatech.edu/blog/2009/03/less-magic-in-the -cnn-wall.html.

60. See http://infosthetics.com/archives/2008/10/cnn_magic_wall_versus_the _megamap.html.

61. See http://manyeyes.alphaworks.ibm.com/manyeyes/page/About.html.

62. Marc Frons, "The New York Times Data Visualization Lab," NYTimes.com, October 27, 2008, http://open.blogs.nytimes.com/2008/10/27/the-new-york-times -data-visualization-lab/.

63. "About Visualization Lab," http://vizlab.nytimes.com/page/About.html.

64. Searching for "inauguration" on the Visualization Lab Web site produces nearly 100 results. See http://assets1.manyeyes.nytimes.com/visualizations?q=inauguration.

65. Tufte, *The Visual Display of Quantitative Information,* 53.

4   Documentary

1. Jason Tuohey, *"JFK Reloaded* Game Causes Controversy," *PC World,* http://www .pcworld.com/article/118717/jfk_reloaded_game_causes_controversy.html.

2. Stephen Totilo, "Walden: The Game Is in Development," *Kotaku,* May 29, 2009, http://kotaku.com/5272278/walden-the-game-is-in-development.

3. Tracy Fullerton, "Documentary Games: Putting the Player in the Path of History," in *Playing the Past: History and Nostalgia in Video Games,* ed. Zach Whalen and Laurie N. Taylor (Nashville: Vanderbilt University Press, 2008), 215–238.

4. Alexander Galloway, *Gaming: Essays on Algorithmic Culture* (Minneapolis: University of Minnesota Press: 2006), 73.

5. Ibid., 74.

6. Ibid., 78.

7. *The Lumière Brothers' First Films*, DVD. Narrated by Bertrand Tavernier (New York: Kino Video, 1996).

8. Joost Raessens, "Reality Play: Documentary Computer Games beyond Fact and Fiction," *Popular Communication* 4, no. 3 (2006): 213–224.

9. Dayna Galloway, Kenneth B. McAlpine, and Paul Harris, "From Michael Moore to *JFK Reloaded*: Towards a Working Model of Interactive Documentary," *Journal of Media Practice* 8, no. 3 (2007): 325–339.

10. Upton Sinclair, *The Jungle* (New York: Bantam, 1981).

11. Bill Kovach and Tom Rosenstiel, *Elements of Journalism* (New York: Three Rivers Press, 2007), 113–161.

12. *Schindler's List*, DVD. Directed by Steven Spielberg (Los Angeles: Universal Pictures, 2003); *Night and Fog*, DVD. Directed by Alain Resnais (New York: The Criterion Collection, 2003).

13. André Bazin and Hugh Gray, *What Is Cinema?* volume 1 (Berkeley: University of California Press, 2005), 23–40.

14. Janet Murray, *Hamlet on the Holodeck: The Future of Narrative in Cyberspace* (Cambridge, Mass.: MIT Press, 1997), 62.

15. Stene, *Berlin Wall* (Team Garry, 2008), http://www.garrysmod.org/downloads/?a=view&id=49861. The game is actually a modification (or "mod") of the popular commercial title *Half-Life 2*, created with the tool Garry's Mod, which developer Valve distributes. See http://www.garrysmod.com/news/.

16. Raph Koster, "(Un)dressing a Game," *Raph Koster's Website*, http://www.raphkoster.com/2006/01/06/undressing-a-game/.

17. Alberto Cairo, "The Ethics Issue: What Should You Show in a Graphic?" *Design Journal*, no. 99 (2006): 30–33.

18. Jeff Cole, Mike Caloud, and John Brennon, *9-11 Survivor* (self-published, 2003), http://www.selectparks.net/911survivor/.

19. Kuma Games, *John Kerry's Silver Star* (self-published, 2005), http://www.kumawar.com/Kerry/description.php.

20. Miguel Sicart, *The Ethics of Computer Games* (Cambridge, Mass.: MIT Press, 2008), 22.

21. For more on the ways procedural documentary can also express perspective and opinion, see Ian Bogost and Cindy Poremba, "Can Games Get Real? A Closer Look at 'Documentary' Digital Games," in *Computer Games as a Sociocultural Phenomenon: Games without Frontiers, war Without Tears*, ed. Andreas Jahn-Sudmann and Ralf Stockmann (London: Palgrave Macmillan, 2008), 18.

22. Michael Schudson, *Discovering the News: A Social History of American Newspapers* (New York: Basic Books, 1978), 187–188.

23. Ibid., 189.

24. Gene Goltz, "Personal Profits Gathered by Mayor and Other Notables," in *The Pulitzer Prize Archive*, ed. Heinz-Dietrich Fischer (Berlin: Walter de Gruyter, 1990), 105.

25. Maurine Possley, "Missteps Delayed Recall of Deadly Cribs," *Chicago Tribune*, September 24, 2007. *The Pulitzer Prizes* archive, http://www.pulitzer.org/archives/7767.

26. Eric Schlosser, *Fast Food Nation: What the All-American Meal Is Doing to the World* (New York: Harper, 2001); John Pilger, *Tell Me No Lies: Investigative Journalism That Changed the World* (New York: Basic Books, 2005).

27. Pilger, *Tell Me No Lies*, 482.

28. Murray, *Hamlet on the Holodeck*, 71.

29. "Report by Soviet Deputy Interior Minister M. N. Holodkov to Interior Minister N. P. Dudorov," in *The 1956 Hungarian Revolution: A History in Documents* (Washington, D.C.: The National Security Archive).

30. This assumption is made very clear in the game and its marketing materials, so the player never need guess. See http://www.peacemakergame.com/game.php.

31. Ernest Adams, "Asymmetric Peacefare," *Gamasutra*, January 31, 2007, http://www.gamasutra.com/features/20070131/adams_01.shtml.

32. See, e.g., South Asia News, "Chronology Until 1400 GMT: Mumbai Terrorist Attack," *Deutsche Press-Argentur*, November 27, 2008, http://www.monstersandcritics.com/news/southasia/news/article_1445378.php/CHRONOLOGY_UNTIL_1400_GMT_Mumbai_terrorist_attack_.

33. Jason Rohrer, "A note about *Gravitation*," *Source Forge*, http://hcsoftware.sourceforge.net/gravitation/statement.html.

34. Mary Flanagan, *[domestic]* (self-published, 2003).

35. Nina Czegledy and Maia Engell, *Medieval Unreality* (self-published, 2003), http://maia.enge.li/gamezone/lindart/.

36. Fullerton, "Documentary Games"; Raessans, "Reality Play."

37. "JFK Shooting Game Provokes Anger," *BBC News*, November 22, 2004, http://news.bbc.co.uk/2/hi/uk_news/scotland/4031571.stm.

38. Fullerton, "Documentary Games," 232.

39. Emru Townsend, "The 10 Worst Games of All Time," *PC World*, October 23, 2006, http://www.pcworld.com/article/127579/the_10_worst_games_of_all_time .html.

40. Kyle Orland, "Columbine Game Blocked from Receiving Slamdance Special Jury Prize," *Joystiq*, January 31, 2007, http://www.joystiq.com/2007/01/31/columbine -game-blocked-from-receiving-slamdance-special-jury-pri/.

41. For example, *Battlefield: Bad Company* and *Call of Duty 4* had both featured desert war settings.

42. Luke Plunkett, "Konami Pulls Controversial Iraqi War Game," *Kotaku*, http:// kotaku.com/5229129/konami-pulls-controversial-iraqi-war-game.

43. Brian Ashcraft, "Konami's Iraq War Game Brouhaha," *Kotaku*, http://kotaku .com/5204550/konamis-iraq-war-game-brouhaha.

44. Dennis McCauley, "Gamer War Vet Fears That *Six Days in Fallujah* Will Dishonor Those Who Served in Iraq," *Game Politics*, http://www.gamepolitics.com/2009/04/08/ gamer-war-vet-fears-six-days-fallujah-will-dishonor-those-who-served-iraq.

45. Sid Shuman, "*Six Days in Fallujah* Preview," *GamePro*, http://www.gamepro .com/article/previews/209611/six-days-in-fallujah-revealed/.

46. Mike Fahey, "Making a Game Out of Today's War," *Kotaku*, http://kotaku .com/5252157/making-a-game-out-of-todays-war.

47. James Brightman, "Atomic Games at Death's Door?" *Industry Gamers*, http:// www.industrygamers.com/news/rumor-atomic-games-at-deaths-door/.

5   Puzzles

1. Michelle Arnot, *What's Gnu? A History of the Crossword Puzzle* (New York: Vintage, 1981).

2. Ibid., 3.

3. Ibid., 14.

4. Ibid., 24.

5. Ibid., 25.

6. Ibid., 27.

7. Ibid., 30.

8. Ibid.

9. Ibid., 53.

10. *New York Times* staff, "Topics of the Times," *New York Times*, November 17, 1924, 18.

11. Arnot, *What's Gnu?*, 55, 56, 59, 63.

12. Ibid., 109.

13. Ibid., 113.

14. Farrar's legacy at the *Times* continues into the present, and the tradition of the crossword editor has become a permanent fixture at the paper. The current editor, Will Shortz, was perhaps the first to make puzzling a career. He designed his own degree in "enigmatology" at Indiana University and worked at *Games* magazine for fifteen years, including serving as its editor from 1989 until he became the *New York Times* crossword editor in 1993. See Emily Shur, "The Puzzle Master," *Wired* 11:11 (November 2003), http://www.wired.com/wired/archive/11.11/start.html?pg=20.

15. Arnot, *What's Gnu?*, 51.

16. Ibid., 176.

17. Jon Zilber, "Living on the Grid: Merl Reagle on His New Role as Movie Subject and the Ultimate Test of Wordplay," *San Francisco Chronicle*, June 25, 2006, http://www.sfgate.info/cgi-bin/article.cgi?f=/c/a/2006/06/25/CMG1QJ740C1.DTL&hw=challengers&sn=451&sc=322.

18. Portions of this section have been adapted from Ray Vichot, "The Crossword as a Platform for Journalism," *News Games*, November 10, 2008, http://jag.lcc.gatech.edu/blog/2008/11/the-crossword-as-platform-for-opinioneditorial-discourse.html.

19. Robert Leighton, Amy Goldstein, and Mike Shenk, "Patriot Games," *New York Times*, July 5, 2003, http://www.nytimes.com/2003/07/05/opinion/05PUZZ.html; Leighton, Goldstein, and Shenk, "Puzzles: Country Club," *New York Times*, October 22, 2007, http://www.nytimes.com/2007/10/22/opinion/22puzzle.html.

20. Ray Vichot, "Professionalism in the New York Times Op-Ed Puzzle," *News Games*, November 3, 2008, http://jag.lcc.gatech.edu/blog/2008/11/professionalism-in-the-new-york-times-op-ed-puzzle.html. This part of this section has been adapted from Vichot's article.

21. Email interview with Amy Goldstein, conducted by Ray Vichot, October 2008. All quotes from Goldstein in this section are taken from this interview.

22. See http://www.crickler.com.

23. John Cook, "Master of the Game," *Eastside Journal*, April 8, 1998. Crick has reprinted the article on his Web site, at http://crick.com/gamemaster.html.

24. See http://www.washingtonpost.com/wp-srv/style/crosswords/crickler/crickler.html.

25. This section is adapted from Ray Vichot, "History of the Quiz," *News Games*, December 15, 2008, http://jag.lcc.gatech.edu/blog/2008/12/history-of-the-quiz .html.

26. William James, letter to a friend, Dec. 26, 1867. Cited in *The American Heritage Dictionary of the English Language*, fourth edition, under the entry for "quiz."

27. This section is adapted from Douglas Wilson, "Digital Media and Unfinish," *News Games*, December 8, 2008, http://jag.lcc.gatech.edu/blog/2008/12/ digital-media-and-unfinish-part-2.html.

28. Paul Maslin, "The Clincher," *New York Times*, November 3, 2008, http://www .nytimes.com/2008/11/04/opinion/04maslin.html.

29. Ana Marie Cox, "Viva Viagra?" *New York Times*, November 3, 2008, http://www .nytimes.com/2008/11/04/opinion/04cox.html.

30. Howard Wolfson, "Campaign Playlists," *New York Times*, November 3, 2008, http://www.nytimes.com/2008/11/04/opinion/04wolfson.html.

31. Michael Kinsley, "White Men in Suits," *New York Times*, November 3, 2008, http://www.nytimes.com/2008/11/04/opinion/04kinsley.html.

32. This section is adapted from Vichot, "History of the Quiz." For the *New York Times*' quizzes, see http://learning.blogs.nytimes.com/category/news-quiz/. For an example of the *New Yorker*'s, see http://www.newyorker.com/magazine/bios/paul _slansky/search?contributorName=paul%20slansky.

33. Riann Smith, "Quiz: What Kind of Sexy Are You?" *Cosmopolitan*, http://www .cosmopolitan.com/quizzes-games/online-quiz/cosmo_quiz_what_kind_of_sexy _are_you. See http://www.cosmopolitan.com/quizzes-games/ for more.

34. Pace News Limited, *The Political Compass*, http://www.politicalcompass.org.

35. This section is adapted from Ray Vichot, "Novel Uses of the News Quiz: *Wonkette* and 'Which Emanuel Are You?'" *News Games*, January 16, 2009, http://jag.lcc .gatech.edu/blog/2009/01/novel-uses-of-the-news-quiz-wonkette-and-which-emanuel -are-you.html, and from Vichot, "History of the Quiz."

36. Juli Weiner, "Take Intern Juli's Advanced Emanuel Brothers Personality Test From Hell," *Wonkette*, November 10, 2008, http://wonkette.com/404277/ take-intern-julis-advanced-emanuel-brothers-personality-test-from-help.

37. Laura T. Ryan, "He Knows All the Answers (2 Words): Will Shortz," *Syracuse Post-Standard*, December 5, 2004, http://www.primate.wisc.edu/people/hamel/ heknows.

38. Meg Carter, "Why You Buy a Particular Paper," *Independent*, December 4, 2006, http://www.independent.co.uk/news/media/why-you-buy-a-particular-paper-9 -426912.html.

39. Dave Fisher, "Have You Ever Bought a Newspaper Just to Do the Crossword Puzzle?" About.com, http://puzzles.about.com/od/crosswords/qt/PuzzlePollNews .htm.

40. Archimedes' Laboratory, "Puzzles for Magazines & Newspapers," http://www .archimedes-lab.org/fornewspapers_puzzles.html.

41. Kristin Tillotson, "Across and Down: Invasion of the Irate Puzzle People," *Minneapolis Star Tribune*, February 4, 2001, http://www.crosswordtournament.com/ articles/art0201.htm.

42. Ibid.

43. Bill Archer, "Crossword a Hobby That Is Challenging, Addictive," *Bluefield Daily Telegraph*, January 12, 2004, http://www.crosswordtournament.com/articles/ bdt011204.htm.

44. Russell Beattie, "Crosswords Are the Prototypical Mobile Killer App," *Russell Beattie Notebook*, January 31, 2003, http://www.russellbeattie.com/ notebook/1001742.html.

45. Elizabeth Birge, "What's the Next Sudoku? Now There's a Puzzle," *Star-Ledger* (Newark, N.J.), June 10, 2007, http://seattletimes.nwsource.com/html/living/ 2003738042_puzzles10.html.

46. Here's one: http://sudokugenerator.com; but a quick Web search will reveal many hundreds more.

47. IGDA Casual Games Special Interest Group, *2008–2009 Casual Games White Paper*, The International Game Developers Association, http://www.igda.org/casual/ IGDA_Casual_Games_White_Paper_2008.pdf.

48. Peter Farago, "Apple iPhone and iPod touch Capture U.S. Video Game Market Share," Flurry Analytics, March 22, 2010, http://blog.flurry.com/bid/31566/ Apple-iPhone-and-iPod-touch-Capture-U-S-Video-Game-Market-Share.

49. Adam Satariano and Ari Levy, "Zynga May Be Valued at $1 Billion on Face _book Craze," Bloomberg, November 23, 2009, http://www.bloomberg.com/apps/ news?pid=newsarchive&sid=aK27lRYbSPqU.

50. Eric Krangel, "eBay Misses Q4 Revenue, Guidance Light (EBAY)," *Business Insider*, January 21, 2009, http://www.businessinsider.com/2009/1/ebay-misses-q4-revenue -guidance-light-ebay.

51. Elinor Mills, "Report Estimates Craigslist 2008 Revenue at $80 Million," *CNET News*, April 3, 2008, http://news.cnet.com/8301-10784_3-9911097-7.html.

52. Telegraph Media Group Limited, *CluedUp* (*The Daily Telegraph*), http://www .clueduppuzzles.telegraph.co.uk/site/index.php.

53. Print circulation was taken from the NMA facts and figures service, http://www .nmauk.co.uk/nma/do/live/factsAndFigures?newspaperID=11. As of October 2009, reported circulation for the *Daily Telegraph* was 814,087 during August 2009, the last available month during which data were available.

54. See http://www.parade.com/corporate/parade_facts.html.

6 Literacy

1. James Paul Gee, *What Video Games Have to Teach Us about Learning and Literacy* (New York: Palgrave Macmillan, 2003), 31.

2. Soenke Zehle, "Interventionist Media in Times of Crisis," *Sarai Reader 04: Crisis/ Media* (2004): 29–41.

3. Gee, *What Video Games Have to Teach Us*, 17–21.

4. See Shayne Bowman and Chris Willis, *We Media: How Audiences Are Shaping the Future of News and Information* (Reston: The American Press Institute, 2003).

5. Such as in Michael Anderson, "Four Crowdsourcing Lessons from the *Guardian's* (Spectacular) Expenses-Scandal Experiment," *Nieman Lab*, June 23, 2009, http:// www.niemanlab.org/2009/06/four-crowdsourcing-lessons-from-the-guardians -spectacular-expenses-scandal-experiment/.

6. Gee, *What Video Games Have to Teach Us*, 18–19.

7. Finley Peter Dunne, *Observations by Mr. Dooley* (New York: Harper & Brothers, 1906), 240.

8. Hannah Arendt, *The Origins of Totalitarianism* (New York: Harvest Books, 1973), 231.

9. French Amnesty Canada, *Pictures for Truth* (Amnesty International, 2008), http:// www.picturesfortruth.com/indexF.html.

10. Gee, *What Video Games Have to Teach Us*, 102.

11. First-person camera *was* proven to increase "presence" in the case of one game (*Morrowind*) featuring a choice between a default first-person and a faultily pro- grammed third-person camera in Kari Kallinen et al., "Presence and Emotion in Computer Game Players during 1 Person vs. 3 Person Playing View: Evidence from Self-report, Eye-tracking, and Facial Muscle Activity Data," *Presence* (2007): 187–190.

12. Evan Narcisse, "*Infamous* Review," *Crispy Gamer*, May 26, 2009, http://www .crispygamer.com/gamereviews/2009-05-26/infamous-ps3.aspx.

13. Nels Anderson, "*Fallout* and the Procedural Skald," *Above 49*, June 7, 2009, http://www.above49.ca/2009/06/fallout-and-procedural-skald.html.

14. Such as *WoW Radio*, "Azeroth's First & Only Talk Radio Station," http://wcradio.com/.

15. T. L. Taylor, *Play between Worlds* (Cambridge, Mass.: MIT Press, 2006), 155–162.

16. See Ian Bogost, *Persuasive Games* (Cambridge, Mass.: MIT Press, 2007), 275–282.

17. Sergio Goldenberg, "Newseum Invites You to Be a Journalist!" *News Games*, March 6, 2009, http://jag.lcc.gatech.edu/blog/2009/03/newseums-invites-you-to-be-a-journalist.html.

18. Gee, *What Video Games Have to Teach Us*, 50–51.

19. See http://www.newsu.org for more information.

20. Sergio Goldenberg, "Being a Reporter with NewsU's Online Course," *News Games*, March 28, 2009, http://jag.lcc.gatech.edu/blog/2009/03/being-a-reporter-with-newsus-online-course.html.

21. Bobby Schweizer and Sergio Goldenberg, "*Global Conflicts* Pt. 1: Teaching Journalism," *News Games*, February 20, 2009, http://jag.lcc.gatech.edu/blog/2009/02/global-conflicts-pt-1-teaching-journalism.html.

22. Gee, *What Video Games Have to Teach Us*, 59–62.

23. Johan Huizinga, "Nature and Significance of Play as a Cultural Phenomenon," in *The Game Design Reader*, ed. Katie Salen and Eric Zimmerman (Cambridge, Mass.: MIT Press, 2006), 105–119.

24. Such as in the Order of Voln "Symbol of Recovery" quest from Simutronics, *Gemstone III* (Simutronics, 1990), http://www.play.net/gs4/.

25. Bryan Murley, "Newspaper Tycoon," *J-Lab Knight-Batten Awards*, http://www.j-lab.org/knight_batten/entry_comment/newspaper_tycoon/.

26. Ian Bogost, "Games and Transparency," *News Games*, November 9, 2008, http://jag.lcc.gatech.edu/blog/2008/11/games-and-transparency.html.

27. Jason Rohrer, *Crude Oil* (The Escapist, 2008), http://www.escapistmagazine.com/articles/view/columns/gamedesignsketchbook/5215-Game-Design-Sketchbook-Crude-Oil.

28. Douglas Wilson, "*Crude Oil*," *News Games*, January 30, 2009, http://jag.lcc.gatech.edu/blog/2009/01/crude-oil.html.

29. Such as Paul M. Weyrich, "Drill ANWR: Reason over Emotion," *Accuracy in Media*, May 23, 2006, http://www.aim.org/guest-column/drill-anwr-realism-over-emotion/.

30. Cliff Harris, "Policy Effect Change Proposals, and Your Thoughts," *Positech Games forums*, December 11, 2007, http://positech.co.uk/forums/phpBB3/viewtopic .php?f=10&t=1345.

31. Douglas Wilson, "*Democracy 2* and Transparency," *News Games*, October 27, 2008, http://jag.lcc.gatech.edu/blog/2008/10/democracy-2-and-transparency.html.

32. A. J. Perlis, "The Computer in the University," in *Management and the Computer of the Future*, ed. Martin Greenberger (Cambridge, Mass.: MIT Press, 1962), 180–219.

33. See Michael Mateas, "Procedural Literacy: Educating the New Media Practitioner," *On the Horizon: Special Issue on Games in Education* 13, no. 2 (2005): 101–111.

34. See Ian Bogost, "Procedural Literacy: Problem Solving with Programming, Systems, and Play," *Telemedium* winter/spring 05 (2005): 32–36.

35. Daniel Trotta, "How One Family's Mortgage Is Linked to Meltdown," *Forbes .com*, December 29, 2008, http://www.forbes.com/feeds/afx/2008/12/29/afx5864497 .html.

36. Lyndsey Layton, "Peanut Executive Takes the Fifth," *Washington Post*, February 12, 2009, http://www.washingtonpost.com/wp-dyn/content/article/2009/02/11/ AR2009021104174_pf.html.

7 Community

1. Rainey, "Response to gerben Wulf from Netizen kevikens," *World Without Oil*: The Texts, May 21, 2007, http://wwotext.blogspot.com/2007/05/response-to-gerben -wulf-from-netizen.html.

2. See Kenneth S. Deffeyes, *Hubbert's Peak: The Impending World Oil Shortage* (Princeton: Princeton University Press, 2008).

3. Interview by the authors with Alexis Bonte, October 2008.

4. Bill Kovach and Tom Rosenstiel, *The Elements of Journalism* (New York: Three Rivers Press, 2007), 167.

5. Ibid., 12.

6. David Golumbia, "Put a Little Serotonin in Me," *in media res* (March 16, 2007), http://mediacommons.futureofthebook.org/imr/2007/03/16/put-a-little-serotonin -in-me.

7. Ian Bogost, *Persuasive Games* (Cambridge, Mass.: MIT Press, 2008), 63–64.

8. *eRepublik* Official Wiki, "Sweden: Newspapers," http://wiki.erepublik.com/index .php/Sweden#Newspapers.

9. Interview with Alexis Bonte.

10. The best-known example is Yochai Benkler, *The Wealth of Networks: How Social Production Transforms Markets and Freedom* (New Haven: Yale University Press, 2007). A more recent addition to the conversation about collective work is Clay Shirky, *Here Comes Everybody: The Power of Organizing without Organizations* (New York: Penguin, 2009).

11. Alex Pareene, "Top Ten Moments of Obama's Inauguration," *Gawker* (January 20, 2009), http://gawker.com/5135657/top-ten-moments-of-obamas-inauguration; Jake Tapper, "PEBO's Official Inauguration Swag," *ABC News* (January 15, 2009), http://blogs.abcnews.com/politicalpunch/2009/01/pebos-officia-1.html.

12. CNN, "The Moment," *CNNPolitics.com*, January 2009, http://www.cnn.com/SPECIALS/2009/44.president/inauguration/themoment/.

13. 42 Entertainment, *I Love Bees* (Microsoft, 2004), http://ilovebees.com/.

14. Scott Rettberg, "Avant-Gaming: An Interview with Jane McGonigal," *Iowa Review*, July 2006, http://www.uiowa.edu/~iareview/mainpages/new/july06/mcgonigal.html.

15. Jane McGonigal. "Why I Love Bees: A Case Study in Collective Intelligence Gaming," in *The Ecology of Games: Connecting Youth, Games, and Learning*, ed. Katie Salen (Cambridge, Mass.: MIT Press, 2008), 201.

16. For one example, see Judith Ann Maupin, *The Kentucky Lake Cemetery Relocation Project* (Winchester, Kentucky: Winchester Printing, 1975).

17. Jane McGonigal, "Alternate Reality Gaming: Experimental Social Structures for MMOs" (Presentation at Game Developers Conference, Austin, Texas), 2005, http://avantgame.com/McGonigal_ARG_Austin%20Game%20Conference_Oct2005.pdf.

18. A different version of this section appeared as Ian Bogost, "Persuasive Games on Mobile Devices," in *Mobile Persuasion: 20 Perspectives on the Future of Behavior Change*, ed. B.J. Fogg and Dean Eckles (Palo Alto: Stanford Captology Media, 2007).

19. Janet Murray, *Hamlet on the Holodeck: The Future of Narrative in Cyberspace* (Cambridge, Mass.: MIT Press, 1997), 71.

20. Andrés Duany, Elizabeth Plater-Zyberk, and Robert Alminana, *New Civic Art: Elements of Town Planning* (New York: Rizzoli International Publications, 2003).

21. Ian Bogost, *Unit Operations* (Cambridge, Mass.: MIT Press, 2006), 107.

22. Frank Lantz et al., *Pac Manhattan* (NYU Interactive Telecommunications Program, 2004), http://pacmanhattan.com/.

23. Institute for the Future, "Superstruct FAQ," http://www.superstructgame.org/s/superstruct_FAQ.

24. ABC has since taken down the *Earth 2100* Web site, http://www.earth2100.tv, but Archive.org provides a copy which contains the basic information: http://web.archive.org/web/20080822220029/http://earth2100.tv/.

25. Sharon Burke and Christine Parthemore, "Climate Change War Game: Major Findings and Background" (working paper), Center for a New American Security, June 2009, http://www.cnas.org/files/documents/publications/Climate_War_Game_Working%20Paper_0.pdf.

26. Espen Aarseth, *Cybertext: Perspectives on Ergodic Literature* (Baltimore: Johns Hopkins University Press: 1997), 1.

27. *Rochester Democrat & Chronicle* and Rochester Institute of Technology, *Picture the Impossible*, 2009, http://picturetheimpossible.com/.

28. Betsy Aoki, "picture the impossible (with rit, democrat and chronicle and bing)!" Bing Community, September 04, 2009, http://www.bing.com/community/blogs/search/archive/2009/09/04/picture-the-impossible-with-rit-and-bing.aspx.

29. Tazwalker, "Evolution of a PTI Gamer," *Picture the Impossible* Forum, http://picturetheimpossible.com/forums/general-discussion/7907.

30. See http://picturetheimpossible.com/about.

8   Platforms

1. The Knight Foundation's "News Challenge" grant program offers a rare example of a funding organization promoting the creation of systems and platforms over content. See http://www.newschallenge.org.

2. ImpactGames, *Play the News* (self-published, http://www.playthenewsgame.com). Updates to the game ceased in late 2008, and the state of the Web site as of fall 2009 reflects its status at that time.

3. See http://www.playthenewsgame.com/portal/game.action?gameTurnId=241.

4. Interview by the authors with Eric Brown and Asi Burak, February 2009.

5. Comments from screen names Laurens, Hex, and ND, respectively: http://www.playthenewsgame.com/portal/game.action?gameTurnId=241.

6. Interview by the authors with Eric Brown and Asi Burak.

7. Ibid.

8. Ibid.

9. Nick Montfort and Ian Bogost, *Racing the Beam: The Atari Video Computer System* (Cambridge, Mass.: MIT Press, 2009), 2.

10. Ray Vichot, "History of Fantasy Sports and Its Adoption by Sports Journalists," *News Games*, January 2, 2010, http://jag.lcc.gatech.edu/blog/2009/01/history-of -fantasy-sports-and-its-adoption-by-sports-journalists.html.

11. Bill Parsons, "Love Fantasy Football? Learn How It Started," *Articlesbase*, October 28, 2008, http://www.articlesbase.com/football-articles/love-fantasy-football-learn -how-it-started-608437.html.

12. Timothy Sexton, "The Origins of Rotisserie Baseball—The Earliest Form of Fantasy Baseball," Associated Content, August 26, 2008, http://www.associatedcontent.com/ article/952197/the_origins_of_rotisserie_baseball.html?cat=14.

13. Allan Kreda, "The Fantasy Football Frenzy," *Portfolio.com*, September 6, 2007, http://www.portfolio.com/culture-lifestyle/culture-inc/sports/2007/09/06/ Fantasy-Football-Booming/.

14. Jim McCormick, "From Cult to Culture: The History of Fantasy Football," *Blitz Magazine*, August 28, 2009, http://blitzmagonline.com/fantasy-football.cfm/Post/ 16/. The league followed the American Football League, since the Oakland Raiders were an AFL-affiliated city.

15. Daniel Okrent, "The Year George Foster Wasn't Worth $36," *Inside Sports*, May 1981.

16. Portions of this section are adapted from Ray Vichot, "History of Fantasy Sports and Its Adoption by Sports Journalists," *News Games*, January 2, 2009, http:// jag.lcc.gatech.edu/blog/2009/01/history-of-fantasy-sports-and-its-adoption-by -sports-journalists.html.

17. The paper evolved into *USA Today Sports Weekly*, which covers major- and minor-league baseball, NCAA baseball, and the NFL.

18. See http://games.espn.go.com/frontpage.

19. See http://www.fswa.org.

20. Joe Keenan, "Fantasy Sports: A Marketers Dream … Especially in 2009," *eMarketing and Commerce*, May 1, 2009, http://www.emarketingandcommerce.com/story/ marketwatch-fantasy-sports-marketers-dream-especially-2009. Most of this income derives from advertising and sponsorships, although some providers charge sub-scription fees for premium services.

21. See http://www.hsx.com.

22. Andrew Lee, *Fantasy Congress* (self-published, 2006). The service launched in 2006 at http://www.fantasycongress.com, and disbanded in late 2008. It is no longer online.

23. Joe Blancato, "Fantasy Congress," *Escapist*, October 30, 2007, http://www .escapistmagazine.com/articles/view/issues/issue_121/2572-Fantasy-Congress.

24. Nina Czegledy and Maia Engeli, *Medieval Unreality* (Cultural Center Lindart, 2003), http://maia.enge.li/gamezone/lindart/.

25. The Electronic Software Association, "Essential Facts about the Computer and Video Game Industry," http://www.theesa.com/facts/pdfs/ESA_EF_2007.pdf.

26. Arrogancy Games, *Angry Barry* (Microsoft, 2009), http://marketplace.xbox.com/ en-US/games/media/66acd000-77fe-1000-9115-d8025855021e/?bt=0&sb=1&mt=32 &gu=66acd000-77fe-1000-9115-d8025855021e&p=1&of=0.

27. Apple.com Press Release, July 14, 2009, http://www.apple.com/pr/library/2009/ 07/14apps.html. By the end of 2009, the number had reached 100,000. As we write this in March 2010, the number of apps exceeds 150,000.

28. IDG News Service, "Nintendo Launches Wii News Channel," *PC World*, January 31, 2007, http://www.pcworld.com/article/157647/nintendo_launches_wii_news _channel.html.

29. Bill Kovach and Tom Rosenstiel, *The Elements of Journalism* (New York: Three Rivers Press, 2001), 166.

30. Interview by the authors with Joellen Easton, November 2, 2009.

31. Ibid.

32. The discourse takes place within the same game, which distinguishes it from the counterargument games proposed by Bogost in *Persuasive Games: The Expressive Power of Videogames* (Cambridge, Mass.: MIT Press, 2007), 63–64.

33. See http://positech.co.uk/forums/phpBB3/viewtopic.php?f=10&t=1334&p =11200#p11200.

9 Journalism at Play

1. Louis Hau, "Web Video Takes Off, Ads Trail," *Forbes.com*, September 20, 2006, http://www.forbes.com/2006/09/19/video-youtube-ads-tech-media-cx_lh _0919video.html.

2. Erick Schonfeld, "BrightRoll: Video Ad Rates Dropped 12 Percent in First Quarter, and the Pre-Roll Is Still King," *TechCrunch.com*, April 27, 2009, http://www .techcrunch.com/2009/04/27/brightroll-video-ad-rates-dropped-12-percent-in -first-quarter-and-the-pre-roll-is-still-king/.

3. Joe Sharkey, "An Airport Security Game That Rivals the Real Thing," *New York Times*, January 16, 2007, http://www.nytimes.com/2007/01/16/business/16road. html?ex=1326603600&en=3f951d1402297de7&ei=5090&partner=rssuserland&emc =rss.

4. Adam Rogers, Game Reviews, *Wired Magazine*, 14.12 (December 2006).

5. Greg Bluestein, "Educators Put Politics into Video Games," *USA Today*, January 22, 2007, http://www.usatoday.com/tech/gaming/2007-01-22-opinion-games_x.htm.

6. ABC News, "Video Games to Save the World," February 5, 2007, http://abcnews .go.com/Video/playerIndex?id=2850798.

7. Brian Crecente, "Games: Trend Watch," *Playboy*, April 2007, 34.

8. Dennis McCauley, "Cultural Milestone: *New York Times* to Carry Newsgames," *GamePolitics.com*, May 25, 2007, http://www.gamepolitics.com/2007/05/25/ cultural-milestone-new-york-times-to-carry-newsgames.

9. At the time, the paper's subscription service, TimesSelect, was still in operation. The entire op-ed section, including these games, sat behind the subscription wall, and editors were reticent to include advertising in that context.

10. Andrew DeVigal, "Telling Data-rich, Interactive Stories," presentation at the 2008 Society for News Design Conference, September 7, 2008, Las Vegas, Nevada.

11. Josh Williams and Tyson Evans, "Las Vegas Sun: Site Redesign," presentation at the 2008 Online News Association Conference, September 12, 2008, Washington, D.C.

Bibliography

Written Material

Aarseth, Espen. *Cybertext: Perspectives on Ergodic Literature*. Baltimore, Maryland: Johns Hopkins University Press, 1997.

"About Visualization Lab." *NYTimes.com*. http://vizlab.nytimes.com/page/About .html.

American Public Media. "Behind the Numbers." http://budgethero.publicradio.org/ widget/numbers/#11.

Adams, Ernest. "Asymmetric Peacefare." *Gamasutra*. January 31, 2007. http://www. gamasutra.com/features/20070131/adams_01.shtml.

Anderson, Michael. "Four Crowdsourcing Lessons from the *Guardian*'s (Spectacular) Expenses-Scandal Experiment." *Nieman Lab*. June 23, 2009. http://www.niemanlab .org/2009/06/four-crowdsourcing-lessons-from-the-guardians-spectacular-expenses -scandal-experiment/.

Anderson, Nels. "*Fallout* and the Procedural Skald." *Above 49*. June 7, 2009. http:// www.above49.ca/2009/06/fallout-and-procedural-skald.html.

Aoki, Betsy. "Picture the Impossible (With Rit, Democrat and Chronicle and Bing)!" *Bing Community*. September 4, 2009. http://www.bing.com/community/blogs/ search/archive/2009/09/04/picture-the-impossible-with-rit-and-bing.aspx.

Archer, Bill. "Crossword a Hobby That Is Challenging, Addictive." *Bluefield Daily Telegraph*, January 12, 2004. http://www.crosswordtournament.com/articles/ bdt011204.htm.

Archimedes' Laboratory. "Puzzles for Magazines & Newspapers." *Archimedes Laboratory*. http://www.archimedes-lab.org/fornewspapers_puzzles.html.

Arendt, Hannah. *The Origins of Totalitarianism*. New York: Harvest Books, 1973.

Arnot, Michelle. *What's Gnu? A History of the Crossword Puzzle*. New York: Vintage, 1981.

Ashcraft, Brian. "Konami's Iraq War Game Brouhaha." *Kotaku*, April 8, 2009. http://kotaku.com/5204550/konamis-iraq-war-game-brouhaha.

Assyrian International News Agency. "Cartoons of Muhammed Published by the Danish Newspaper *Jyllands-Posten*." *AINA.org*, February 1, 2006. http://www.aina.org/releases/20060201143237.htm.

Bartle, Richard. *Designing Virtual Worlds*. New York: New Riders, 2003.

Bazin, André, and Hugh Gray. *What Is Cinema?* vol. 1. Berkeley: University of California Press, 2005.

B.B.C. News. "JFK Shooting Game Provokes Anger." *BBC News*, November 22, 2004. http://news.bbc.co.uk/2/hi/uk_news/scotland/4031571.stm.

Beattie, Russell. "Crosswords Are the Prototypical Mobile Killer App." *Russell Beattie Notebook*. January 31, 2003. http://www.russellbeattie.com/notebook/1001742.html.

Benkler, Yochai. *The Wealth of Networks: How Social Production Transforms Markets and Freedom*. New Haven, Conn.: Yale University Press, 2007.

Birge, Elizabeth. "What's the Next Sudoku? Now There's a Puzzle." *Star-Ledger*, June 10, 2007. http://seattletimes.nwsource.com/html/living/2003738042_puzzles10.html.

Blancato, Joe. "Fantasy Congress." *Escapist*. October 30, 2007. http://www.escapistmagazine.com/articles/view/issues/issue_121/2572-Fantasy-Congress.

Bluestein, Greg. "Educators Put Politics into Video Games." *USA Today*. January 22, 2007. http://www.usatoday.com/tech/gaming/2007-01-22-opinion-games_x.htm.

Bogost, Ian. *Persuasive Games: The Expressive Power of Videogames*. Cambridge, Mass: MIT Press, 2007.

Bogost, Ian. "Persuasive Games on Mobile Devices." In *Mobile Persuasion: 20 Perspectives of the Future of Behavior Change*, ed. BJ Fogg and Dean Eckles. Palo Alto: Stanford Captology Media, 2007.

Bogost, Ian. "Procedural Literacy: Problem Solving with Programming, Systems, and Play." *Telemedium* winter/spring 05 (2005): 32–36.

Bogost, Ian. "Roll Your Own Zidane Headbutt Game." *Water Cooler Games*, July 20, 2006. http://www.bogost.com/watercoolergames/archives/roll_your_own_z.shtml.

Bogost, Ian. *Unit Operations*. Cambridge, Mass: MIT Press, 2006.

Bogost, Ian, and Cindy Poremba. "Can Games Get Real? A Closer Look at 'Documentary' Digital Games." In *Computer Games as a Sociocultural Phenomenon: Games without Frontiers, War without Tears*, ed. Andreas Jahn-Sudmann and Ralf Stockmann. London: Palgrave Macmillan, 2008.

Barrionuevo, Alexei. "Food Imports Often Escape Scrutiny." *New York Times*, May 1, 2007. http://www.nytimes.com/2007/05/01/business/01food.html.

Bowman, Shayne, and Chris Willis. *We Media: How Audiences are Shaping the Future of News and Information*. Reston, Virginia: The American Press Institute, 2003.

Brightman, James. "Atomic Games at Death's Door?" *Industry Gamers*, August 7, 2009. http://www.industrygamers.com/news/rumor-atomic-games-at-deaths-door/.

Burke, Sharon, and Christine Parthemore. "Climate Change War Game: Major Findings and Background" (working paper). Center for a New American Security (June 2009). http://www.cnas.org/files/documents/publications/Climate_War _Game_Working%20Paper_0.pdf.

Caillois, Roger. *Man, Play, and Games*. Translated by Meyer Barash. Champaign, Ill.: University of Illinois Press, 2001.

Cairo, Alberto. *Sailing to the Future: Infographics in the Internet Era*. University of North Carolina: Produced for Multimedia Bootcamp, 2005. http://www.albertocairo.com/ index/index_english.html.

Cairo, Alberto. "The Ethics Issue: What Should You Show in a Graphic?" *Design Journal* 99 (2006): 30–33.

Card, Stuart K., Jock D. Mackinlay, and Ben Shneiderman. *Readings in Information Visualization*. San Diego: Academic Press, 1999.

Carey, Anne R., and Keith Simmons. "Radio rebounding with iPod generation." *USA Today*, November 24, 2008.

Carlson, Gretchen. *Fox and Friends*. June 11, 2009.

Carney, Scott, Siggi Eggertsson, and Michael Doret. "Cutthroat Capitalism: An Economic Analysis of the Somali Pirate Business Model." *Wired* 17.7, July 2009.

Carter, Meg. "Why You Buy a Particular Paper." *Independent*, December 4, 2006. http://www.independent.co.uk/news/media/why-you-buy-a-particular-paper-9 -426912.html.

Chittum, Ryan. "Newspaper Industry Ad Revenue at 1965 Levels." *Columbia Journalism Review* (August 2009): 19. http://www.cjr.org/the_audit/newspaper _industry_ad_revenue.php.

Cook, John. "Master of the Game." *Eastside Journal*. April 8, 1998.

Cox, Ana Marie. "Viva Viagra?" *New York Times*, November 3, 2008. http://www .nytimes.com/2008/11/04/opinion/04cox.html.

Crecente, Brian. "Games: Trend Watch." *Playboy*, April 2007.

Deffeyes, Kenneth. *Hubbert's Peak: The Impending World Oil Shortage*. Princeton, New Jersey: Princeton University Press, 2008.

DeVigal, Andrew. "Telling Data-Rich, Interactive Stories." Presentation at the 2008 Society for News Design Conference, Las Vegas, Nevada, September 7, 2008.

Dezsö, Zoltan, Eivind Almaas, A. Lukács, B. Rácz, I. Szakadát, and A.-L. Barabási. "Dynamics of Information Access on the Web." *Physical Review E: Statistical, Nonlinear, and Soft Matter Physics* 73 (066132) (2006): 1–6.

Duany, Andrés, Elizabeth Plater-Zyberk, and Robert Alminana. *New Civic Art: Elements of Town Planning.* New York: Rizzoli International Publications, 2003.

Dunne, Finley Peter. *Observations by Mr. Dooley.* New York: Harper & Brothers, 1906.

The Electronic Software Association. "Essential Facts about the Computer and Video Game Industry." http://www.theesa.com/facts/pdfs/ESA_EF_2007.pdf.

eRepublik. "eRepublik Offical Wiki: Sweden: Newspapers." *eRepublik.* http://wiki .erepublik.com/index.php/Sweden#Newspapers.

Fahey, Mike. "Making a Game Out of Today's War." *Kotaku,* April 14, 2009. http:// kotaku.com/5252157/making-a-game-out-of-todays-war.

Farago, Peter. "Apple iPhone and iPod touch Capture U.S. Video Game Market Share." *Flurry Analytics,* March 22, 2010. http://blog.flurry.com/bid/31566/ Apple-iPhone-and-iPod-touch-Capture-U-S-Video-Game-Market-Share.

Farhi, Paul. "CNN Hits the Wall for the Election." *Washington Post,* February 5, 2008.   http://www.washingtonpost.com/wp-dyn/content/article/2008/02/04/ AR2008020402796.html.

Fisher, Dave. "Have You Ever Bought a Newspaper Just to Do the Crossword Puzzle?" *About.com.* http://puzzles.about.com/od/crosswords/qt/PuzzlePollNews.htm.

Frasca, Gonzalo. "Croc Hunter Newsgame." *Water Cooler Games,* September 7, 2006. http://www.bogost.com/watercoolergames/archives/croc_hunter_new.shtml.

Frasca, Gonzalo. "This Just In: Playing the News." *Vodafone Receiver* 17 (2006): 3.

Frasca, Gonzalo. "Videogames of the Oppressed: Critical Thinking, Education, Tolerance, and Other Trivial Issues." In *First Person: New Media as Story, Performance, and Game,* ed. Noah Wardrip-Fruin and Pat Harrigan. Cambridge, Mass.: MIT Press, 2004.

Frons, Marc. "The New York Times Data Visualization Lab." *NYTimes.com,* October 27, 2008. http://open.blogs.nytimes.com/2008/10/27/the-new-york-times-data -visualization-lab/.

Fullerton, Tracy. "Documentary Games: Putting the Player in the Path of History." In *Playing the Past: History and Nostalgia in Video Games,* ed. Zach Whalen and Laurie N. Taylor. Nashville: Vanderbilt University Press, 2008.

Galloway, Alexander. *Gaming: Essays on Algorithmic Culture*. Minneapolis: University of Minnesota Press, 2006.

Galloway, Dayna, Kenneth B. McAlpine, and Paul Harris. "From Michael Moore to *JFK Reloaded*: Towards a Working Model of Interactive Documentary." *Journal of Media Practice* 8 (3) (2007): 325–339.

Gaudiosi, John. "A Virtual Farm Turns New Ground for Game Developers." *Reuters*, March 25, 2010. http://www.reuters.com/article/idUSTRE62O1NB20100325?type=technologyNews.

Gee, James Paul. *What Video Games Have to Teach Us about Learning and Literacy*. New York: Palgrave Macmillan, 2003.

Goldfin, Jessica. "Knight News Game Awards." *Knight Foundation*, May 29, 2009. http://www.knightblog.org/knight-news-game-awards/.

Goldenberg, Sergio. "Being a Reporter with NewsU's Online Course." *News Games*. March 28, 2009. http://jag.lcc.gatech.edu/blog/2009/03/being-a-reporter-with-newsus-online-course.html.

Goldenberg, Sergio, and Bobby Schweizer. "*Global Conflicts* Pt. 1: Teaching Journalism." *News Games*. February 20, 2009. http://jag.lcc.gatech.edu/blog/2009/02/global-conflicts-pt-1-teaching-journalism.html.

Goldenberg, Sergio, and Bobby Schweizer. "Less Magic in the CNN Wall." *News Games*. March 16, 2009. http://jag.lcc.gatech.edu/blog/2009/03/newseums-invites-you-to-be-a-journalist.html.

Goldenberg, Sergio, and Bobby Schweizer. "Newseum Invites You to Be a Journalist!" *News Games*. March 6, 2009. http://jag.lcc.gatech.edu/blog/2009/03/newseums-invites-you-to-be-a-journalist.html.

Goltz, Gene. "Personal Profits Gathered by Mayor and Other Notables." In *The Pulitzer Prize Archive*, ed. Heinz-Dietrich Fischer. Berlin: Walter de Gruyter, 1990.

Golumbia, David. "Put a Little Serotonin in Me." *in media res*. March 16, 2007. http://mediacommons.futureofthebook.org/imr/2007/03/16/put-a-little-serotonin-in-me.

Good Game Guides. "The History of the Game Show." http://www.ukgameshows.com/page/index.php?title=History_of_the_Game_Show.

Gorham, Joan. *Mass Media 98/99*. New York: McGraw Hill, 1998.

Halter, Ed. *From Sun Tzu to Xbox: War and Video Games*. New York: Thunder's Mouth Press, 2006.

Harris, Cliff. "Policy Effect Change Proposals, and Your Thoughts." *Positech Games Forums*. December 11, 2007. http://positech.co.uk/forums/phpBB3/viewtopic.php?f=10&t=1345.

Hartmann, Margaret. "Octuplets' Grandmother Adds to Criticism of Her Daughter." *Jezebel*, February 9, 2009. http://jezebel.com/5149489/octuplets-grandmother-adds -to-criticism-of-her-daughter.

Hatch, Joshua, and Juan Thomassie. "Delegate Tracker." *USA Today*, February 11, 2008. http://www.usatoday.com/news/politics/election2008/delegate-tracker.htm.

Hau, Louis. "Web Video Takes Off, Ads Trail." *Forbes.com*. September 20, 2006. http://www.forbes.com/2006/09/19/video-youtube-ads-tech-media-cx_lh _0919video.html.

Holmes, Nigel. *Designer's Guide to Creating Charts and Diagrams*. New York: Watson-Guptill Publications, 1984.

Huang, Jon, Baden Copeland, Lisa Iaboni, and Craig Allen. "Hurricane Gustav Sweeps across the Region." *New York Times*, September 2, 2008. http://www.nytimes .com/interactive/2008/09/01/us/20080901-gustav-map.html.

Huizinga, Johan. *Homo Ludens*. Boston: Beacon Press, 1955.

Huizinga, Johan. Nature and Significance of Play as a Cultural Phenomenon. In *The Game Design Reader*, ed. Katie Salen and Eric Zimmerman, 105–119. Cambridge, Mass: MIT Press, 2006.

IDG News Service. "Nintendo Launches Wii News Channel." *PC World*. January 31, 2007. http://www.pcworld.com/article/157647/nintendo_launches_wii_news _channel.html.

IGDA Casual Games Special Interest Group. "2008–2009 Casual Games White Paper." The International Game Developers Association. http://www.igda.org/ casual/IGDA_Casual_Games_White_Paper_2008.pdf.

IGDA Quality of Life Special Interest Group. *Quality of Life in the Game Industry: Challenges and Best Practices*. Mt. Royal, N.J.: International Game Developers Association, 2004.

infosthetics. "CNN Magic Wall versus SNL 'The MegaMap.'" *Infosthetics.com*, October 28, 2008. http://infosthetics.com/archives/2008/10/cnn_magic_wall_versus _the_megamap.html.

Institute for the Future. "Superstruct FAQ." *Superstruct.org*. http://www .superstructgame.org/s/superstruct_FAQ.

Itzenson, Jen, and Jacky Myint. "All Together Now." *Portfolio.com*. http://www .portfolio.com/interactive-features/2008/05/Boeing-Dreamliner/.

Jackson, Tom, and Archie Tse. "Is It Better to Buy or Rent?" *New York Times*, June 2, 2008. http://www.nytimes.com/2007/04/10/business/2007_BUYRENT_GRAPHIC .html.

Kallinen, Kari, Mikko Salminen, Niklas Ravaja, Ryszard Kedzior, and Maria Sääksjärvi. "Presence and Emotion in Computer Game Players during 1 Person vs. 3 Person Playing View: Evidence from Self-Report, Eye-Tracking, and Facial Muscle Activity Data." *Presence* (2007): 187–190.

Keenan, Joe. "Fantasy Sports: A Marketers Dream … Especially in 2009." *eMarketing and Commerce*. May 1, 2009. http://www.emarketingandcommerce.com/story/marketwatch-fantasy-sports-marketers-dream-especially-2009.

Kerris, Natalie, and Jennifer Bowcock. Apple's App Store Downloads Top 1.5 Billion in First Year." *Apple.com.* July 14, 2009. http://www.apple.com/pr/library/2009/07/14apps.html.

Kinsley, Michael. "White Men in Suits." *New York Times*, November 3, 2008. http://www.nytimes.com/2008/11/04/opinion/04kinsley.html.

Koster, Raph. *A Theory of Fun for Game Design.* Scottsdale: Paraglyph Press, 2005.

Koster, Raph. "(Un)dressing a Game." *Raph Koster's Website*, January 6, 2006. http://www.raphkoster.com/2006/01/06/undressing-a-game/.

Kovach, Bill, and Tom Rosenstiel. *The Elements of Journalism: What Newspeople Should Know and the Public Should Expect.* New York: Three Rivers Press, 2007.

Krangel, Eric. "eBay Misses Q4 Revenue, Guidance Light (EBAY)." *Business Insider.* January 21, 2009. http://www.businessinsider.com/2009/1/ebay-misses-q4-revenue-guidance-light-ebay.

Kreda, Allan. "The Fantasy Football Frenzy." *Portfolio.com.* September 6, 2007. http://www.portfolio.com/culture-lifestyle/culture-inc/sports/2007/09/06/Fantasy-Football-Booming/.

Lamb, Chris. *Drawn to Extremes: The Use and Abuse of Editorial Cartoons.* New York: Columbia University Press, 2004.

Lewi, Paul J. "Playfair and Lineal Arithmetics." *Speaking of Graphics*. Self-published, 2006. http://www.datascope.be/sog.htm.

Lupton, Ellen, and Abbott Miller. *Design Writing Research: Writing on Graphic Design.* New York: Phaidon, 1999.

"Many Eyes." IBM Research. http://manyeyes.alphaworks.ibm.com/manyeyes/page/About.html.

"Map Showing How the States Voted." *New York Times*, November 3, 1920.

Marcus, Robert H., Jay Melosh, and Gareth Collins. "Earth Impact Effects Program." 2005. http://www.lpl.arizona.edu/impacteffects/.

Maslin, Paul. "The Clincher." *New York Times*, November 3, 2008. http://www.nytimes.com/2008/11/04/opinion/04maslin.html.

Mateas, Michael. "Procedural Literacy: Educating the New Media Practitioner." *On the Horizon. Special Issue on Games in Education* 13 (2) (2005): 101–111.

Maupin, Judith Ann. *The Kentucky Lake Cemetery Relocation Project*. Winchester, Kentucky: Winchester Printing, 1975.

McCauley, Dennis. "Cultural Milestone: *New York Times* to Carry Newsgames." *Game Politics*, May 25, 2007. http://www.gamepolitics.com/2007/05/25/ cultural-milestone-new-york-times-to-carry-newsgames.

McCauley, Dennis. "Gamer War Vet Fears That Six Days in Fallujah Will Dishonor Those Who Served in Iraq." *Game Politics*, April 8, 2009. http://www.gamepolitics .com/2009/04/08/gamer-war-vet-fears-six-days-fallujah-will-dishonor-those-who -served-iraq

McCormick, Jim. "From Cult to Culture: The History of Fantasy Football." *Blitz Magazine*. August 28, 2009. http://blitzmagonline.com/fantasy-football.cfm/Post/ 16/.

McClellan, Jim. "The role of play." *Guardian*, May 13, 2004. http://www.guardian .co.uk/technology/2004/may/13/games.onlinesupplement.

McClelland, Edward. "All in the Game." *Chicago Magazine*, May 2009. http://www .chicagomag.com/Chicago-Magazine/May-2009/All-in-the-Game/.

McGonigal, Jane. "Alternate Reality Gaming: Experimental Social Structures for MMOs." Presentation at Game Developers Conference, Austin, Texas, 2005. http:// avantgame.com/McGonigal_ARG_Austin%20Game%20Conference_Oct2005.pdf.

McGonigal, Jane. "Why I Love Bees: A Case Study in Collective Intelligence Gaming." *In The Ecology of Games: Connecting Youth, Games, and Learning*, ed. Katie Salen, 201. Cambridge, Mass: MIT Press, 2008.

Meyer, Eric K. *Designing Infographics*. Indianapolis: Hayden Books, 1997.

Meyer, Eric K. "Labor Unions." *Fortune*, 1939.

Mills, Elinor. "Report Estimates Craigslist 2008 Revenue at $80 Million." *CNET News*. April 3, 2008. http://news.cnet.com/8301-10784_3-9911097-7.html.

Montfort, Nick, and Ian Bogost. *Racing the Beam: The Atari Video Computer System*. Cambridge, Mass: MIT Press, 2009.

Murley, Bryan. "Newspaper Tycoon." *J-Lab Knight-Batten Awards*. http://www.j-lab .org/knight_batten/entry_comment/newspaper_tycoon/.

Murray, Janet. *Hamlet on the Holodeck: The Future of Narrative in Cyberspace*. Cambridge, Mass: MIT Press, 1997.

Narcisse, Evan. "*Infamous* Review." *Crispy Gamer*. May 26, 2009. http://www .crispygamer.com/gamereviews/2009-05-26/infamous-ps3.aspx.

The National Security Archive. "Report by Soviet Deputy Interior Minister M. N. Holodkov to Interior Minister N. P. Dudorov." In *The 1956 Hungarian Revolution: A History in Documents*. Washington, D.C.: The National Security Archive.

The New York Times Staff. "Topics of the Times." *New York Times*, November 17, 1924.

Nichani, Maish, and Venkat Rajamanickam. "Interactive Visual Explainers—A Simple Classification." *eLearningPost*. September 1, 2003. http://www.elearningpost. com/articles/archives/interactive_visual_explainers_a_simple_classification/.

Orland, Kyle. "Columbine Game Blocked from Receiving Slamdance Special Jury Prize." *Joystiq*, January 31, 2007. http://www.joystiq.com/2007/01/31/ columbine-game-blocked-from-receiving-slamdance-special-jury-pri/.

Pareene, Alex. "Top Ten Moments of Obama's Inauguration." *Gawker*. January 20, 2009. http://gawker.com/5135657/top-ten-moments-of-obamas-inauguration.

Parsons, Bill. "Love Fantasy Football? Learn How It Started." *Articlesbase*. October 18, 2008. http://www.articlesbase.com/football-articles/love-fantasy-football-learn -how-it-started-608437.html.

Pear, Robert. "Point System for Immigrants Incites Passions." *New York Times*. June 5, 2007. http://query.nytimes.com/gst/fullpage.html?res =9503E4D91130F936A35755C0A9619C8B63.

Pedercini, Paolo. "Faith Fighter." La Molleindustria, 2009. http://www. molleindustria.org/faith-fighter-old.

Perlis, A. J. "The Computer in the University." In *Management and the Computer of the Future*, ed. Martin Greenberger, 180–219. Cambridge, Mass: MIT Press, 1962.

Pilger, John. *Tell Me No Lies: Investigative Journalism That Changed the World*. New York: Basic Books, 2005.

Playfair, William. In *Playfair's Commercial and Political Atlas and Statistical Breviary*, ed. Howard Wainer and Ian Spence. Cambridge: Cambridge University Press, 2005.

Plunkett, Luke. "Konami Pulls Controversial Iraqi War Game." *Kotaku*, April 27, 2009. http://kotaku.com/5229129/konami-pulls-controversial-iraqi-war-game.

Possley, Maurine. "Missteps Delayed Recall of Deadly Cribs." In *The Pulitzer Prizes* archive, http://www.pulitzer.org/archives/7767. Originally published in the *Chicago Tribune*, September 24, 2007.

Pousman, Zachary, John Stasko, and Michael Mateas. "Casual Information Visualization: Depictions of Data in Everyday Life." *Proceedings of IEEE InfoVis* 2007. http://www.cc.gatech.edu/gvu/ii/infovis/.

Prast, Rhonda, Jamie Hutt, Pam Louwagie, Jane Friedmann, James Shiffer, Dave Braunger, Jaime Chismar, et al. "13 Seconds in August." *Minneapolis–St. Paul Star Tribune*, December 5, 2007. http://www.startribune.com/local/12166286.html.

Raessens, Joost. "Reality Play: Documentary Computer Games beyond Fact and Fiction." *Popular Communication* 4 (3) (2006): 213–224.

Rettberg, Scott. "Avant-Gaming: An Interview with Jane McGonigal." *Iowa Review.* July 2006. http://www.uiowa.edu/~iareview/mainpages/new/july06/mcgonigal. html.

Rogers, Adam. "Game Reviews." *Wired* 14.12, December 2006.

Rohrer, Jason. "A Note about *Gravitation.*" http://hcsoftware.sourceforge.net/ gravitation/statement.html.

Ryan, Laura. "He Knows All the Answers (2 Words): Will Shortz." *Syracuse Post-Standard*, December 5, 2004. http://www.primate.wisc.edu/people/hamel/heknows.

Salen, Katie, and Eric Zimmerman. *Rules of Play: Game Design Fundamentals.* Cambridge, Mass: MIT Press, 2003.

Satriano, Adam and Ari Levy. "Zynga May Be Valued at $1 Billion on Facebook Craze." *Bloomberg*, November 23, 2009. http://www.bloomberg.com/apps/news?pid =newsarchive&sid=aK27lRYbSPqU.

Schlosser, Eric. *Fast Food Nation: What the All-American Meal Is Doing to the World.* New York: Harper, 2001.

Schonfeld, Erick. "BrightRoll: Video Ad Rates Dropped 12 Percent in First Quarter, and the Pre-Roll Is Still King." *TechCrunch.com.* April 27, 2009. http://www .techcrunch.com/2009/04/27/brightroll-video-ad-rates-dropped-12-percent-in-first -quarter-and-the-pre-roll-is-still-king/.

Schudson, Michael. *Discovering the News: A Social History of American Newspapers.* New York: Basic Books, 1978.

Sexton, Timothy. "The Origins of Rotisserie Baseball—The Earliest Form of Fantasy Baseball." *Associated Content.* August 26, 2008. http://www.associatedcontent.com/ article/952197/the_origins_of_rotisserie_baseball.html?cat=14.

Sinclair, Upton. *The Jungle.* New York: Bantam, 1981.

Sharkey, Joe. "An Airport Security Game That Rivals the Real Thing." *New York Times*, January 16, 2007. http://www.nytimes.com/2007/01/16/business/16road .html?ex=1326603600&en=3f951d1402297de7&ei=5090&partner=rssuserland&emc =rss.

Shirky, Clay. *Here Comes Everybody: The Power of Organizing Without Organizations.* New York: Penguin, 2009.

Shuman, Sid. "Six Days in Fallujah Preview." *GamePro*, April 8, 2009. http://www
.gamepro.com/article/previews/209611/six-days-in-fallujah-revealed/.

Shur, Emily. "The Puzzle Master." *Wired*, November 2003.

Sicart, Miguel. *The Ethics of Computer Games*. Cambridge, Mass: MIT Press, 2008.

Sicart, Miguel. "Newsgames: Theory and Design." Paper presented at the International
Conference on Entertainment Computing, Pittsburgh, 2008.

South Asia News. "Chronology Until 1400 GMT: Mumbai Terrorist Attack."
Deutsche Press-Argentur, November 27, 2008. http://www.monstersandcritics.com/
news/southasia/news/article_1445378.php/CHRONOLOGY_UNTIL_1400_GMT
_Mumbai_terrorist_attack_.

Spence, Robert. *Information Visualization*. New York: ACM Press, 2001.

Spiegel, Der. "At the Mercy of Somali Pirates." *Spiegel Online*, August 11, 2009. http://
www.spiegel.de/international/world/0,1518,641752,00.html.

Tapper, Jake. "PEBO's Official Inauguration Swag." *ABC News*, January 15, 2009.
http://blogs.abcnews.com/politicalpunch/2009/01/pebos-officia-1.html.

Taylor, T. L. *Play between Worlds*. Cambridge, Mass: MIT Press, 2006.

Tazwalker. "Evolution of a PTI Gamer." *Picture the Impossible Forum*. October 24,
2009. http://picturetheimpossible.com/forums/general-discussion/7907.

Thompson, Clive. "Saving the World, One Video Game at a Time." *New York Times*,
July 23, 2006. http://www.nytimes.com/2006/07/23/arts/23thom.html.

Tillotson, Kristin. "Across and Down: Invasion of the Irate Puzzle People." *Minneapolis
Star Tribune*, February 4, 2001. http://www.crosswordtournament.com/articles/
art0201.htm.

Totilo, Stephen. "Walden: The Game Is in Development." *Kotaku*, May 29, 2009.
http://kotaku.com/5272278/walden-the-game-is-in-development.

Townsend, Emru. "The 10 Worst Games of All Time." *PC World*, October 23, 2006.
http://www.pcworld.com/article/127579/the_10_worst_games_of_all_time.html.

Treanor, Mike, and Michael Mateas. "Newsgames: Procedural Rhetoric Meets Political
Cartoons." Breaking New Ground: Innovation in Games, Play, Practice and Theory
(Proceedings of the Digital Games Research Association Conference, Brunel
University, September 2009), http://www.digra.org/dl/display_html?chid=http://
www.digra.org/dl/db/09300.09505.pdf.

Trotta, Daniel. "How One Family's Mortgage Is Linked to Meltdown." *Forbes.com*.
December 29, 2008. http://www.forbes.com/feeds/afx/2008/12/29/afx5864497
.html.

Tufte, Edward. *The Visual Display of Quantitative Information*. Cheshire, Conn.: Graphic Press, 1983.

Tufte, Edward. *Visual and Statistical Thinking: Displays of Evidence for Making Decisions*. Cheshire, Conn.: Graphic Press, 1997.

Tuohey, Jason. "*JFK Reloaded* Game Causes Controversy." *PC World*, November 24, 2004. http://www.pcworld.com/article/118717/jfk_reloaded_game_causes _controversy.html.

Vichot, Ray. "The Crossword as a Platform for Journalism." *News Games*, November 10, 2008. http://jag.lcc.gatech.edu/blog/2008/11/the-crossword-as-platform-for -opinioneditorial-discourse.html.

Vichot, Ray. "History of Fantasy Sports and Its Adoption by Sports Journalists." *News Games*, January 2, 2009. http://jag.lcc.gatech.edu/blog/2009/01/history-of-fantasy -sports-and-its-adoption-by-sports-journalists.html.

Vichot, Ray. "History of the Quiz." *News Games*, December 15, 2008. http://jag.lcc .gatech.edu/blog/2008/12/history-of-the-quiz.html.

Vichot, Ray. "The News Quiz." *News Games*, November 17, 2008. http://jag.lcc .gatech.edu/blog/2008/11/the-news-quiz.html.

Vichot, Ray. "Novel Uses of the News Quiz: Wonkette and 'Which Emanuel Are You?'" *News Games*, January 16, 2009. http://jag.lcc.gatech.edu/blog/2009/01/ novel-uses-of-the-news-quiz-wonkette-and-which-emanuel-are-you.html.

Vichot, Ray. "Professionalism in the New York Times Op-Ed Puzzle." *News Games*, November 3, 2008. http://jag.lcc.gatech.edu/blog/2008/11/professionalism-in-the -new-york-times-op-ed-puzzle.html.

Wattenberg, Laura. *The Baby Name Wizard: A Magical Method for Finding the Perfect Name for Your Baby*. New York: Broadway Press, 2005.

Wattenberg, Martin. "Baby Names, Visualization, and Social Data Analysis." In *Proceedings of the 2005 IEEE Symposium on Information Visualization*. Washington, D.C.: IEEE Computer Society, 2005.

Weiner, Juli. "Take Intern Juli's Advanced Emanuel Brothers Personality Test from Hell." *Wonkette*, November 10, 2008. http://wonkette.com/404277/ take-intern-julis-advanced-emanuel-brothers-personality-test-from-help.

Weyrich, Paul. "Drill ANWR: Reason Over Emotion." *Accuracy in Media*. May 23, 2006. http://www.aim.org/guest-column/drill-anwr-realism-over-emotion/.

Williams, Josh, and Tyson Evans. "Las Vegas Sun: Site Redesign." Presentation at the 2008 Online News Association Conference, Washington, D.C., September 12, 2008.

Wilson, Douglas. "Crude Oil." *News Games*, January 30, 2009. http://jag.lcc.gatech .edu/blog/2009/01/crude-oil.html.

Wilson, Douglas. "*Democracy 2* and Transparency." *News Games*, October 27, 2008. http://jag.lcc.gatech.edu/blog/2008/10/democracy-2-and-transparency.html.

Wilson, Douglas. "Digital Media and Unfinish." *News Games*, December 8, 2008. http://jag.lcc.gatech.edu/blog/2008/12/digital-media-and-unfinish-part-2.html.

Wilson, Douglas. "Game-Like Infovis: Hurricane vs. Asteroid." *News Games*, January 15, 2009. http://jag.lcc.gatech.edu/blog/2009/01/game-like-infovis-hurricane-vs -asteroid.html.

Wolfson, Howard. "Campaign Playlists." *New York Times*, November 3, 2008. http:// www.nytimes.com/2008/11/04/opinion/04wolfson.html.

Yau, Nathan. "5 Best Data Visualization Projects of the Year." *Flowing Data*, December 19, 2008. http://flowingdata.com/2008/12/19/5-best-data-visualization-projects-of -the-year/.

Zehle, Soenke. "Interventionist Media in Times of Crisis." *Sarai Reader 04: Crisis/ Media* (2004): 29–41.

Zilber, Jon. "Living on the Grid: Merl Reagle on His New Role as Movie Subject and the Ultimate Test of Wordplay." *San Francisco Chronicle*, June 25, 2006.

Games

_altr_KMA and Psycho_Goldfish. *Terri Irwin's Revenge*. Self-published, 2006. http:// 13gb.com/media.php?media_id=1939.

Activision. *Kaboom!* Activision, 1981.

American Public Media. *Budget Hero*. St. Paul, Minn.: American Public Media, 2008. http://marketplace.publicradio.org/features/budget_hero/.

Arrogancy Games. *Angry Barry*. Redmond, Wash.: Microsoft, 2009.

Atomic Games. *Six Days in Fallujah* (project suspended). http://www.atomic.com/.

Anonymous Collaborators. *Raid Gaza!* Newgrounds, 2009. http://www.newgrounds. com/portal/view/476393.

Bethesda Game Studios. *Fallout 3*. Rockville, Maryland: Bethesda Softworks, 2008.

Bioware. *Neverwinter Nights*. New York: Atari, 2002.

Blue Fang Games. *Zoo Tycoon*. Redmond, Wash.: Microsoft, 2001.

Callhamer, Allan B. *Diplomacy*. Self-published, 1959.

Capcom Production Studio 1. *Dead Rising*. Osaka, Japan: Capcom, 2006.

Cole, Jeff, Mike Caloud, and John Brennon. *9-11 Survivor.* Self-published, 2003. http://www.selectparks.net/911survivor/.

Crawford, Chris. *Balance of Power.* Mindscape, 1985; TRANS Fiction Systems, *Hidden Agenda.* Springboard, 1988.

Crick, Michael and Barbara Crick. *Crickler.* Bellevue, Wash.: Michael and Barbara Crick, 2004–present.

Czegledy, Nina, and Maia Engeli. *Medieval Unreality.* Tiranë, Albania: Cultural Center Lindart, 2003.

Davidson. *Math Blaster.* Torrance, California: Davidson & Associates, 1987.

Demirbas, Kerem. *Huys/Hope.* Self-published, 2009. KafaAyari.wordpress.com.

DMA Design. *Grand Theft Auto.* New York: BMG Interactive, 1997.

Double Fine Productions. *Psychonauts.* Edison, N.J.: Majesco Entertainment, 2005.

EA Digital Illusions CE. *Battlefield: Bad Company.* Stockholm: Electronic Arts, 2008.

Eklund, Ken. *World Without Oil.* San Jose, California: Writerguy, 2007.

eRepublik Labs. *eRepublik.* Madrid, Spain: eRepublik Labs, 2009.

Firaxis Games. *Sid Meier's Civilization IV.* New York: 2K Games, 2007.

Flanagan, Mary. *[domestic].* Self-published, 2003.

42 Entertainment. *I Love Bees.* Redmond, Washington: Microsoft, 2004.

Frasca, Gonzalo. *Kabul Kaboom.* Self-published, 2003. http://ludology.typepad.com/ games/kabulkaboom.html.

French Amnesty Canada. *Pictures for Truth.* London, U.K.: Amnesty International, 2008.

Gamelab. *Diner Dash.* San Francisco, Calif.: PlayFirst, 2004.

Game Show Network. *So You Think You Can Drive, Mel?* GSN.com, 2006. http://www .gsn.com/games/game_lobby.php?link_id=G402.

Gotham Gazette. *Voting Arcade/Dig Dug Kellner/Donkey Con.* Self-published, 2004.

ImpactGames. *PeaceMaker.* Pittsburgh, Penn.: ImpactGames, 2006.

ImpactGames. *Play the News.* Pittsburgh, Penn.: ImpactGames, 2008.

Infinity Ward. *Call of Duty 4: Modern Warfware.* Encino, Calif.: Activision, 2007.

Institute for the Future. *Superstruct.* Palo Alto, Calif.: Institute for the Future, 2008.

Jellyvision. *You Don't Know Jack.* Los Angeles, Calif.: Sierra On-Line, 1995.

Jellyvision. *You Don't Know Jack DisOrDat.* Chicago, Ill.: Jellyvision, 2006–present.

Jiggman and Greg Wohlwend. *Effing Hail.* Self-published, 2009. http://www.intuitiongames.com/effing-hail/.

Kuma Games. *John Kerry's Silver Star.* Self-published, 2005. http://www.kumawar.com/Kerry/description.php.

L'Agence Torich. *The Octuplet's Game.* Torich, 2009. http://octupletsgame.lagencetorich.com/.

La Molleindustria. *McDonald's Videogame.* Self-published, 2006. http://www.mcvideogame.com/.

Laminar Research. *X-Plane Mobile.* Laminar Research, 2008. http://www.x-plane.com/.

Laminar Research. *Sully's Flight.* Laminar Research, 2009. http://www.x-plane.com/index_mobile.html.

Lantz, Frank, Amos Bloomberg, Kate Boelhauf, Dennis Crowley, Christopher Hall, Will Lee, Morekwe Molefe, Mike Olson, Megan Phalines, Mattia Romeo, Oli Stephensen, Pakorn Thienthong, Peter Vigeant. *Pac Manhattan.* New York: NYU Interactive Telecommunications Program, 2004.

LeDonne, Danny. *Super Columbine Massacre RPG!* Washington, D.C.: Danny LeDonne, 2005.

Lee, Andrew. *Fantasy Congress.* Self-published, 2006. http://www.fantasycongress.com. (Defunct.)

Leighton, Robert, Amy Goldstein, and Mike Shenk. "Patriot Games." *New York Times,* July 5, 2003. http://www.nytimes.com/2003/07/05/opinion/05PUZZ.html.

Leighton, Robert, Amy Goldstein, and Mike Shenk. "Puzzles: Country Club." *New York Times,* October 22, 2007. http://www.nytimes.com/2007/10/22/opinion/22puzzle.html.

Loodo. *Calabouço Tétrico.* Self-published, 2009. http://loodo.com.br.

Majewski, Krystian. *Trauma.* Self-published, 2010. http://www.gamedesignreviews.com/trauma/.

Maxis. *SimCity.* Brøderbund, 1989.

Maxis. *The Sims.* Electronic Arts, 2000.

MicroProse. *Sid Meier's Railroad Tycoon.* Hunt Valley, Maryland: MicroProse, 1990.

Mindware Studios. *Dreamkiller.* Austin, Texas: Aspyr, 2009.

Minnesota Educational Computing Corporation. *The Oregon Trail.* Eugene, Oregon: Broderbund, 1974.

Molleindustria. *Faith Fighter*. La Molleindustria, 2008. http://www.molleindustria
.org/faith-fighter.

Molleindustria. *Faith Fighter 2*. La Molleindustria, 2009. http://www.molleindustria
.org/faith-fighter-2,

Neversoft Entertainmnet. *Gun*. Santa Monica, Calif.: Activision, 2005.

Nintendo EAD, *Super Mario World*. Nintendo Corporation, 1990.

Number None. *Braid*. Redmond, Wash.: Microsoft, 2008.

O Estadao de Saõ Paolo. *Jogos de sustentabilidade*. Self-published, 2009. http://www
.estadao.com.br/especiais/jogos-da-sustentabilidade,54937.htm.

Pajitnov, Alexey, and Vadim Gerasimov. *Tetris*. Honolulu, Hawaii: The Tetris
Company, 1984–present.

Paul, Nora, and Matt Taylor. *Disaster at Harperville*. Minneapolis, Minn.: Institute
for New Media Studies, 2008.

Persuasive Games. *Airport Insecurity*. Atlanta, Georgia: Persuasive Games, 2005.

Persuasive Games. *Cold Stone Creamery: Stone City*. Scottsdale, Ariz.: Cold Stone
Creamery, 2005.

Persuasive Games. *Food Import Folly*. New York: The New York Times Company,
2007.

Persuasive Games. *Points of Entry*. New York: The New York Times Company, 2007.

Persuasive Games. *The Arcade Wire: Airport Security*. Mountain View, Calif.:
Shockwave, 2006.

Persuasive Games. *The Arcade Wire: Bacteria Salad*. Mountain View, Calif.: Shockwave,
2006.

Persuasive Games. *The Arcade Wire: Oil God*. Mountain View, Calif.: Shockwave,
2006.

Persuasive Games. *The Arcade Wire: Xtreme Xmas Shopping*. Mountain View, Calif.:
Shockwave, 2006.

Persuasive Games, and Traffic Games. *Killer Flu*. UK Clinical Virology Network, 2009.
http://www.clinical-virology.org/killerflu/killerflu.html.

PopCap Games. *Bejeweled*. PopCap Games, 2001.

Positech Games. *Democracy 2*. Devizes, U.K.: Positech Computing, 2007.

Powerful Robot Games. *Madrid*. Powerful Robot, 2004. http://www.newsgaming
.com/games/madrid/.

Powerful Robot Games. *September 12th*. Newsgaming.com, 2003. http://www .newsgaming.com/games/index12.htm.

Red Mercury. *Scoop!* Glenview, Ill.: Red Mercury, LLC, 2007.

Rochester Democrat & Chronicle. Picture the Impossible. Rochester, N.Y.: Rochester Institute of Technology, 2009.

Rockstar North. *Grand Theft Auto III*. New York: Rockstar Games, 2001.

Rockstar North. *Grand Theft Auto IV*. New York: Rockstar Games, 2008.

Rockstar North. *Grand Theft Auto IV: The Lost and Damned*. New York: Rockstar Games, 2009.

Rohrer, Jason. *Crude Oil*. Durham, N.C.: Themis Group, 2008.

Rohrer, Jason. *Gravitation*. Self-published, 2008. http://hcsoftware.sourceforge.net/ gravitation.

Serious Games Interactive. *Global Conflicts: Latin America*. Copenhagen: Serious Games Interactive, 2008.

Serious Games Interactive. *Global Conflicts: Palestine*. Copenhagen: Serious Games Interactive, 2007.

Sierra On-Line. *King's Quest*. Los Angeles: Sierra On-Line, 1994.

Simutronics. *Gemstone III*. Saint Charles, Missouri: Simultronics, 1990.

Slapp-me-do. *The Impossible Quiz*. New York: AddictingGames, 2009.

Smallbore Webworks, and Dennis Crowther. *Cutthroat Capitalism, Wired* 17.7, online addendum, July 20, 2009. http://www.wired.com/special_multimedia/2009/ cutthroatCapitalismTheGame.

Stene. *Berlin Wall*. Team Garry, 2008. http://www.garrysmod.org/downloads/ ?a=view&id=49861.

Sucker Punch Productions. *Infamous*. Tokyo, Japan: Sony Computer Entertainment, 2009.

Taito. *Elevator Action*. Taito, 1983.

Tiltfactor Labratory. *Layoff!* Tiltfactor, 2009. http://www.tiltfactor.org/layoff/.

Traffic Games. *JFK: Reloaded*. Self-published, 2004. http://www.jfkreloaded.com.

2D Boy. *World of Goo*. Kyoto, Japan: Nintendo, 2008.

2DPlay. *Rooney on the Rampage*. Addicting Games, 2009. http://www.addictinggames. com/rooneyontherampage.html.

Ubisoft Montpellier. *Beyond Good and Evil*. Montreuil-sous-Bois: Ubisoft, 2003.

USC Game Innovation Lab. *The ReDistricting Game*. Self-published, 2007. http://www.redistrictinggame.org/.

ValuSoft. *Tabloid Tycoon*. Minneapolis, Minn.: ValuSoft, 2005.

Virtual Playground. *Prison Tycoon*. Minneapolis, Minn.: ValuSoft, 2005.

VIS Entertainment. *State of Emergency*. Scotland: Rockstar Games, 2002.

Zensoft. *Super Obama World*. Zensoft, 2009. http://superobamaworld.com/.

Film/Multimedia

ABC News. *Earth 2100* (Web, video, and television). http://web.archive.org/web/20080822220029/http://earth2100.tv/.

ABC News. "Video Games to Save the World" (television). February 5, 2007.

CNN Politics. "The Moment" (Web). January 2009. http://www.cnn.com/SPECIALS/2009/44.president/inauguration/themoment/.

Cox, Amanda, Shan Carter, Kevin Quealy, and Amy Schoenfeld. "For the Unemployed, the Day Stacks Up Differently." *New York Times*, July 31, 2009. http://www.nytimes.com/2009/08/02/business/02metrics.html.

Cox, Amanda, Shan Carter, Kevin Quealy, and Amy Schoenfeld. "How Different Groups Spend Their Day." *New York Times*, July 31, 2009. http://www.nytimes.com/interactive/2009/07/31/business/20080801-metrics-graphic.html.

Don Wittekind, and R. Scott Horner, "2000 Butterfly Ballot: See How the Palm Beach County Ballot Confused Voters." SunSentinel.com, November 10, 2000. http://www.sun-sentinel.com/broadband/theedge/sfl-edge-n-butterflyballot,0,4467323.flash.

deeplocal. "Pittsburgh Bike Map" (Web). 2007. http://www.bike-pgh.org/onlinemap2/.

Eisenstein, Sergei. *The Strike*. Boris Mikhin, 1951.

Elephant, DVD. Directed by Gus Van Sant. New York: HBO Films, 2003.

Fast Food Nation. DVD. Directed by Richard Linklater. Los Angeles: Fox Searchlight Pictures, 2006.

Microsoft Photosynth. "The Moment" (Web). January 22, 2009. http://photosynth.net/inauguration.aspx.

National Public Radio. *Wait Wait, Don't Tell Me* (radio). National Public Radio, 1998–present. http://www.npr.org/templates/story/story.php?storyId=111028646.

Night and Fog. DVD. Directed by Alain Resnais. New York: The Criterion Collection, 2003.

Original Media for Gamers. *WoW Radio* (Internet radio). http://wcradio.com/.

Pace News Limited. *The Political Compass* (Web). http://www.politicalcompass.org.

Playing Columbine. DVD. Directed by Danny Ledonne. Alamosa, Colo.: Emberwilde Productions, 2007.

Schindler's List. DVD. Directed by Steven Spielberg. Los Angeles: Universal Pictures, 2003.

South Florida Sun Sentinel. "Make Your Own Hurricane" (infographic). *SunSentinel.com.* http://www.sun-sentinel.com/broadband/theedge/sfl-edge-t-canemaker,0,4142989. flash.

The Lumière Brothers' First Films. DVD. Narrated by Bertrand Tavernier. New York: Kino Video, 1996.

This American Life: Second Season, DVD. Narrated by Ira Glass. New York: Killer Films, 2009.

Telegraph Media Group Limited. *CluedUp* (Web). *Daily Telegraph.* http://www .clueduppuzzles.telegraph.co.uk/site/index.php.

Wattenberg, Martin. NameVoyager. Generation Grownup, LLC: 2005. http://www .babynamewizard.com/voyager.

Window Water Baby Moving (film). Directed by Stan Brakhage (1959).

Index